Vegetarian
Christian Saints

Mystics,
Ascetics
& Monks

Dr. Holly Roberts

नमस्

PUBLISHED BY
ANJELI PRESS

Vegetarian Christian Saints: Mystics, Ascetics & Monks
by Dr. Holly Roberts

Published by
Anjeli Press
www.anjelipress.com

ISBN 0-9754844-0-0

Book design and production by Ruth Marcus, Sequim, WA.
Printed in the United States of America.
Printing by Lightning Source.

This book is not only for those of Catholic faith,
nor is it only for Christians.

It is for people of all religions
and all faiths
who wish to learn how beliefs in non-violence,
merciful living, and the sanctity of all life
have manifested themselves
within the depths
and foundations of ancient Christianity.

This is a book to inform, enlighten,
and inspire each of us
as to how we might live,
treading gently upon our earth
sharing mercy with all beings,
and peace with all creation.

Finally, this book seeks to rekindle passion
that each of us
has the ability
to journey through life
sharing
values of peace, non-violence and unconditional compassion
with all beings
upon our beloved planet.

Table of Contents

PREFACE   xi

ACKNOWLEDGMENTS   xiii

INTRODUCTION   1

PART I: BACKGROUND

Chapter 1: EVOLUTION OF VEGETARIAN VALUES   5
Early Humans, Early Judean Communities, Early Western
Philosophers, Early Christians, Vegetarian Religious Orders,
Recent Christian Vegetarians.

Chapter 2: THE MEANING OF SAINTHOOD   13
Evolution of Criteria for Canonization
Present Criteria for Canonization
Spiritual Legacies of the Saints

PART II: THE VEGETARIAN CHRISTIAN SAINTS

Chapter 3: EASTERN MONASTIC & HERMITIC SAINTS   20
Saint Anthony of Egypt, Saint Hilarion, Saint Macarius the Elder,
Saint Palaemon, Saint Pachomius, Saint Paul the Hermit,
Saint Marcian, Saint Macarius the Younger, Saint Aphraates,
Saint James of Nisibis, Saint Ammon, Saint Julian Sabas, Saint Apollo,
Saint John of Egypt, Saint Thais, Saint Jonas the Gardener,
Saint Euphrasia, Saint Porphyry of Gaza, Saint Dorotheus the Theban,
Saint Theodosius the Cenobiarch, Saint Sabas, Saint Fulgentius of
Ruspe, Saint Gerasimus, Saint Mary of Egypt, Saint Dositheus, Saint
Abraham Kidunaja, Saint John the Silent, Saint Theodore of Sykeon

Chapter 4: WESTERN MONASTIC & HERMITIC SAINTS 59
Saint Lupus of Troyes, Saint Lupicinus, Saint Romanus, Saint Gundelinis,
Saint Liphardus, Saint Maurus of Glanfeuil, Saint Urbicius, Saint Senoch,
Saint Hospitius, Saint Winwaloe, Saint Kertigan, Saint Fintan, Saint Molua,
Saint Amatus, Saint Guthlac, Saint Joannicus, Saint Theodore the Studite,
Saint Lioba, Saint Euthymius the Younger, Saint Luke the Younger, Saint Paul
of Latros, Saint Antony of the Caves of Kiev, Saint Theodosius Pechersky,
Saint Fantinus, Saint Wulfstan, Saint Gregory of Makar, Saint Elphege, Saint
Theobald of Provins, Saint Stephen of Grandmont, Saint Henry of Coquet,
Saint William of Malavalle, Saint Godric, Saint Stephen of Obazine, Saint
William of Bourges, Saint Humility of Florence, Saint Simon Stock, Saint
Agnes of Montepulciano, Saint Laurence Justinian, Saint Herculanus of
Piegaro

Chapter 5: MYSTIC SAINTS 100
Saint Francis of Assisi, Saint Clare of Assisi, Saint Aventine of Troyes,
Saint Felix of Cantalice, Saint Joseph of Cupertino

Chapter 6: FOUNDERS OF MONASTIC ORDERS 110
Saint Benedict, Saint Bruno, Saint Alberic, Saint Robert of Molesme,
Saint Stephen Harding, Saint Gilbert of Sempringham, Saint Dominic,
Saint John of Matha, Saint Albert of Jerusalem, Saint Angela Merici

Chapter 7: PATRON SAINTS 127
Saint Paula, Saint Genevieve, Saint David, Saint Leonard of Noblac,
Saint Kevin, Saint Anskar, Saint Ulrich, Saint Yvo, Saint Laurence
O'Toole, Saint Hedwig, Saint Mary of Onigines, Saint Elizabeth of
Hungary, Saint Ivo Helory, Saint Philip Benizi, Saint Albert of Trapani,
Saint Nicholas of Tolentino, Saint Rita of Cascia, Saint Francis of Paola,
Saint John of Capistrano, Saint John of Kanti, Saint Peter of Alcantara,
 Saint Francis Xavier, Saint Philip Neri, Saint Mary Magdalen of Pazzi,
Saint John Francis Regis, Saint Leonard of Porto-Maurizio,
Saint Jean-Marie Vianney

Chapter 8: DOCTORS OF THE CHURCH *158*
   Saint Basil the Great, Saint Jerome, Saint Ephraem, Saint Peter Damian, Saint Bernard, Saint Catherine of Siena, Saint Robert Bellarmine

Chapter 9: THE VEGETARIAN POPE *171*
   Saint Peter Celestine

Chapter 10: ASCETIC SAINTS 174
   Saint Olympias, Saint Publius, Saint Malchus, Saint Asella, Saint Sulpicius Severus, Saint Maxentius, Saint Monegundis, Saint Paul Aurelian, Saint Coleman of Kilmacduagh, Saint Bavo, Saint Amandus, Saint Giles, Saint Silvin, Saint Benedict of Aniane, Saint Aybert, Saint Dominic Loricatus, Saint Richard of Wyche, Saint Margaret of Cortona, Saint Clare of Rimini, Saint Frances of Rome, Saint James de la Marca, Saint Michael of Giedroyc, Saint Mariana of Quito, Saint John de Britto

Chapter 11: SAINTS KNOWN FOR ANIMAL MERCY *199*
    Saint Callistratus, Saint Marianus, Saint Brendon of Clonfert, Saint Kieran (Carian), Saint Stephen of Mar Saba, Saint Anselm, Saint Martin de Porres

Chapter 12: MARTYR SAINTS *207*
   Saint Procopius, Saint Boniface of Tarsus, Saint Serenus

Chapter 13: LEGACIES OF THE VEGETARIAN CHRISTIAN SAINTS *211*

APPENDIX I: Vegetarian Saints by Saint Days *214*

APPENDIX II: Vegetarian Saints in Alphabetic Order *217*

APPENDIX III: End Notes *220*

GLOSSARY *241*

BIBLIOGRAPHY *245*

INDEX OF SAINTS 254

PEACE FOR ALL BEINGS

And then it came to pass,
that the people of our lands
began to recognize the value of one's living with
understanding,
compassion,
and total non-violence
toward all beings.

So they began to study the lives of ancient sages
whose lives exemplified
models of merciful concern
for all.

Initially,
our people combed the literature
of distant cultures,
in search of such role models.

They thought they must search far away
to find individuals
whose lives embodied those peaceful ideals
they so desperately sought to honor.

Then, quite by chance,
they stumbled upon the fact
that people embodying such lives
of merciful compassion
and universal non-violence
had actually existed
right within their own heritage!

And the lives of these peace-loving individuals
of bygone eras
had not only been recognized,
but had been recorded
within the sacred writings
of the Christian Church.

These peace-loving sages of antiquity
whose lives epitomized
examples of universal non-violence,
were, in fact,
the mystic, ascetic, and monastic
Vegetarian Christian Saints.

And at last,
our people
felt the quiet peace
of knowing
that people possessing such merciful wisdom,
had truly existed
right within their heritage.

Even more fulfilling
was the knowledge
that these people had followed such lifestyles
in the name of Christianity.

As you, too, are on a quest
searching for those
whose lives embody
unconditional love, compassion, and mercy
for all beings
I wish to share the life stories
of these
deeply spiritual and peaceful
mystic, ascetic and monastic
vegetarian Christian saints
with you.

May you find your journey through these pages of their lives
enriching, enlightening, and inspiring.
And may their commitments
strengthen your own –

That you are not alone
in your love, concern, and compassion
for all people, all beings,
and all creation.

Preface

While studying for my master's in Theology, I felt drawn to learn of ancient peoples within the history of the Western world who had lived embracing non-violence toward all beings. I knew that such people had existed within Eastern cultures and felt that similar individuals must have existed within Christianity. I just did not know who or where they were. So I began combing the literature and what I found was amazing to me. People who had lived showing non-violence towards the entirety of creation had not only existed within Christianity but had actually been canonized by the Church!

These people had been so sincere. Many of them felt such love for other beings that they not only sacrificed themselves for other humans, but also for animals, birds, insects, and even worms. Fortunately, the early Christian Church had begun canonizing holy individuals, and this process immortalized their lives. I recognized that the sort of people for whom I was searching would have lived as vegetarians. That was because, similar to the paths of Eastern sages, they could not have taken the life from an animal just for food. But what I had never envisioned was how most of these individuals would have lived as mystics, ascetics, and monks.

The information about the lives of these individuals was difficult to retrieve. Much of it was buried in huge treatises along with the life stories of three thousand other saints. Unless one was prepared to spend months reading through the lives of each and every saint, the messages of these few would have remain buried in these forgotten pages. I knew my mission!

I began reading of their lives, often feeling drawn to their humble personalities seeking nothing for themselves, fleeing from glory, spending years in isolated meditation, and acting with compassion, even towards the wildest of beasts and the slimiest of worms. It did not take me long to realize why their messages had not been disseminated—these people were just so different. While some lived in meditation, others lived in mystical union with all creation. With time, I began to feel for these saints. I began to realize that the oddity of their lives contained precious fragments of spiritual wisdom: wisdom I believe our planet so dearly needs.

These individuals seemed to possess a peace that came with the recognition of a unity of all life. They recognized that the longings of one's own heart were the same longings within the hearts of all in existence. They also recognized that each being has his or her own quiet ability to share God's peace with all other beings.

I began a methodical study of each and every person canonized by the Church over these two thousand years. Then I pulled out those saints whom I believed had lived in total non-violence. Finally, I tried to understand each saint's motivations. I searched for those few words that might lead me to understand how each treated weaker beings, and then, why. Many of the phrases I was seeking lay within descriptions of their dietary habits, yet many of these were described in such ancient terminology that they became almost cryptic. One major challenge I faced was that the term vegetarian had not even existed throughout most of Christian history. In many instances, I was left to interpret such phrases as, 'never would he bring the flesh of animals to his lips.'

I also realized I would never be able to identify each and every saint who had lived a life of total non-violence. That was because much of the information concerning lesser-known saints was often so scant that it did not mention how they treated weaker life forms, no less what they ate.

It is a privilege to share the life stories of these one hundred and fifty vegetarian Christian saints with you. May their stories and their lives and values give you strength to continue your own life-path sharing God's compassion, concern, and mercy with all beings.

Acknowledgements

It is with sincere gratitude that I thank Dr. Judith Schubert, RSM, Chair of Georgian Court University's Graduate School of Theology for inspiring me in my quest, as well as all my other professors at Georgian Court College - Dr. Johann Vento, Dr. Jim Bridges, Sister Janet D'Arcy, Father Norman Demeck, Professor Dan Jackson, Sister Joyce Jacobs, Father Richard LaVarghetta, Father Michael Manning, Dr. Lou McNeil, Dr. Joseph M. Springer, Father Robert Terentieff, and Father Richard Viladesau of Fordham University.

Additionally, I would like to thank Sister Allison Lee for her insightful editing, Dr. Cindy Shearer for encouraging me to illustrate this book myself, Sister Maureen Conroy for her guidance, Nancy Warner for her skillful photography, Aleksander Carendi for sharing his soul in his photos, Paul Daligan for his computer expertise, Rose Hightower for her literary advice, and Ruth Marcus for creatively blending all together.

Dedicated to

all who seek mercy

for all beings.

Introduction

Compassion toward all humans, all creatures, and indeed all creation has been a foundational belief within the Christian Church. Yet the concept of compassion toward all creatures and all creation is rarely discussed in present day Christian literature. Many have been left to think that such beliefs are simply confined to yogis of Eastern faiths. In reality, however, principles of compassionate and unconditional non-violence toward all creation—Gandhi's concept of *ahimsa*—had been as important to many early Christians, as they have to Hindus and Buddhists. In fact, the Catholic Church has canonized just those individuals whose lives exemplified loving kindness toward all of creation.

More than one hundred and fifty Christian saints lived lives of non-violence toward all humans, all animals, and the entirety of creation. They would never inflict even the slightest harm upon any innocent being, nor would they consume the flesh of any mammal, fish, or fowl. Most strove to live lives of anonymity, personal sacrifice, unconditional non-violence, universal compassion, and loving kindness. Interestingly, the majority lived as peaceful and meditative mystics, ascetics and monks.

While following such dedicated life paths, some chose to live as cenobitic monks while others as wandering ascetics, solitary hermits, or mystics. When viewed from present day perspectives, these saints definitely appear to have been quite focused, self-motivated, and intriguing. Their lives were filled with meaningful missions, personal passions, spiritual quests, and what might appear as combinations of ambiguities. Although some lived conforming to mainstream Christianity, most lived conforming quite closely to the lives lived by Eastern sages.

These saints represented a somewhat varied group, each following his or her life's calling for diverse reasons. Some were deeply religious, others shunned personal gain, and still others wanted to experience the suffering of Jesus. Some chose to immerse themselves in physical, mental, and spiritual practices of meditation, contemplation, and personal austerity.

When I began writing this book, I was focused upon discovering that compassionate vegetarians had existed within early Christian history. I soon recognized, however, that I had opened a door leading to the study of deeply spiritual, fascinating, and mystical individuals. While reading of their sacrifices, I was able to sense each saint's longing to grasp the meaning of life, as well as his or her hope of attaining knowledge of an ultimate truth.

Many of these saints saw God in all creation and sought to avoid causing even the slightest misuse of the environment. They strove to sacrifice themselves for the welfare of all other beings— human and non-human. Others quested for spiritual enlightenment through isolation, elimination of desire, self-sacrifice, meditation, and emptying their souls of all ego. As a group, their biographies offer deep and meaningful insight

into the lives of wise sages of yore who, while striving to unite themselves with God, helped to direct the course of Christianity.

The marked similarity in lifestyles between early Christian saints and early Eastern sages is not a mere coincidence. Both Christian and Eastern religious traditions emerged within the isolated deserts and mountainous regions of Eastern lands. During these ancient eras, diverse groups of spiritually dedicated seekers from numerous faiths left society in search of wisdom. These seekers were of such numbers, that they filled the once isolated deserts, plains, and mountains of Eastern lands by the thousands. Whether of Eastern faiths or the Christian religion, these holy sages shared information and traditions with one another. Although traveling on different paths and calling God by different names, all were on spiritual quests of the same essence.

Gradually other people, in addition to the saints and sages, began to inhabit these same desert lands. Some were wanderers seeking their fortunes through trade, while others were refugees fleeing war, famine, or slavery. All contributed to the further dissemination of spiritual wisdom and the growth of ideologies. Hence, these seekers influenced the spiritual and religious growth of one another, and their accumulated wisdom flourished.

The lifestyles of most vegetarian saints fall into several distinct patterns. These include those of contemplative, world-renouncing monks and ascetics, and of spiritual mystics. In general, they were not charismatic church leaders, religious champions, or renowned orators. Nor did they wish to be. Rather, they were self-effacing, self-sacrificing, and peace loving individuals living as wandering sages, cloistered monks, silent hermits, and spiritual mystics. Yet as eclectic a group of individuals as these saints may appear from a modern perspective, to early Church leaders, they possessed exactly those characteristics valued as representative of Christian holiness.

Knowledge that the early Church held tremendous respect for such values is quite significant. It demonstrates that among the wide variety of expressions of holiness and virtue the Church recognized were those of compassion for all creation. The fact that the Church historians respected each of these saints' beliefs in unconditional mercy for all beings enough to write about them, adds insight concerning the Church's honoring such beliefs.

For one who appreciates the value of compassionate vegetarianism, this book will reinforce one's faith that vegetarianism has been engraved within the heritage of the Church. For one who believes in silent meditation, contemplation, and prayer as aids to one's attainment of inner peace and enlightenment, this book will demonstrate that such practices were similarly respected by sages of early Christianity. And for one who feels humble love toward all creation and is saddened by environmental abuse and other acts of violence toward any being—human or non-human, this book will reveal that vegetarian Christian saints shared these same feelings.

This book reviews the lives of one hundred and fifty vegetarian saints. Its pages narrate the lives of both well-known and lesser-known saints, even such well-known saints as Saint Jean-Marie Vianney, Saint Clare, Saint Benedict, Saint Catherine of Siena, Saint David, Saint Dominic, Saint Francis of Paola, Saint Jerome, and Saint Francis of Assisi. The information was obtained from numerous sources including initial writings of early Jesuit historians, the Bollandists, and secondary accounts by hagiographers such as Reverend Alban Butler, Herbert Thurston, and Reverend S. Baring-Gould. I sincerely hope you will find these readings informative, enlightening, and inspiring.

✠

Chapter 1

Evolution of Vegetarian Values

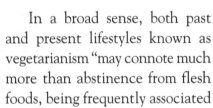

Many of the ancient treatises about saints did not often express the reasons why the vegetarian saints chose their specific flesh-free diet. If one reflects upon similar life paths of other vegetarians over the past two thousand years, however, one might gain insight into the motivations behind each saint's actions. This chapter will delve into the patterns those on flesh-free diets have taken in the past. Although the reasons specific individuals may have chosen such lifestyles are often as varied and divergent as their ethnic heritages and their community mores, some basic values seem to stand out. These include their seeing God's presence in all creation, belief that animals have souls, love and concern for all creation, seeking mercy for all beings, empathy and compassion for another being's suffering and death, and a strong desire to live a life of total non-violence.

In a broad sense, both past and present lifestyles known as vegetarianism "may connote much more than abstinence from flesh foods, being frequently associated with asceticism, philosophy, or other specific benefits."[1] Many vegetarians have sought not only to avoid dietary consumption of flesh, but also to avoid practices that somehow, down a chain of cascading events, might cause pain, suffering, or death of innocent creatures.

While studying the history of vegetarian saints, one may assume that those ancients who followed vegetarian diets probably knew little of nutrition and even less of the relationship between a meat-based diet and the incidence of cancer or cholesterol related heart disease. That is why one may sense most vegetarian saints chose their diets purely for reasons other than health. These reasons include their concern for other beings as well as their desire to live merciful, compassionate, ascetic, and self-sacrificial lives. "Vegetarianism pursued for reasons of physical health is a relatively recent event historically. Before the 19th century, avoidance of animal food was supported by moral and metaphysical arguments."[2] In general, during both past and present times, most vegetarians have been deeply spiritual, concerned, compassionate believers in total non-violence toward all beings.

This chapter will lay a foundation for understanding that vegetarian values are not new or trendy. They have persisted as philosophical and humanitarian beliefs for centuries. It will also lay a foundation for understanding those values that led to the Christian Church's honoring non-violent, namely pacific, vegetarians with sainthood.

Evolution of the Human Diet

Contrary to several common misconceptions, most prehistoric humans did not consume the flesh of other animals. Approximately five to seven million years ago, when the human species evolved from apes, humans were actually herbivorous, with only a small percentage living as omnivores. When archeological searches in Ethiopia discovered one of the oldest remains of a human who had lived approximately three million years ago, they found that she would more likely have been preyed upon than have been a predator herself. It is believed that such early humans lived in social groups of twenty-five to thirty so that their group might create a common defense against attacking carnivores. A study of the teeth of early human ancestors indicates that theirs were not the teeth of meat-ripping carnivores; rather, they contained grooves indicating they ate rough vegetation and often bit into shells. Such humans "evolved out of a vegetarian past, and although they might have occasionally eaten termites, lizards, or other small creatures, they relied primarily on vegetation."[3]

Why then do so many Westerners believe that humans were innately destined to eat meat? Archaeologist Glynn Isaac states that, "The notion that in times before civilization, men were mighty meat-eating hunters is deeply embedded in the folklore, sacred myths and philosophy of West European cultures."[4] It was actually during a much later evolutionary stage that humans began to eat any meat at all. Cambridge anthropologist Robert Foley believes that two million years ago, early humans on the African Savanna became minimally reliant on the meat of large herbivores, and did so only as an adaptation to the seasonal lack of plant foods. [5]

An American anthropologist and archaeologist, Lewis Binford, found that even 40,000 years ago, humans were far from mighty hunters, rather, they appeared to have been the most marginal of scavengers.[6] It was not until 10,000 years ago that humans actually became "hunters-gatherers" and regularly consumed animal flesh. "This adaptation occurred, not in the remote past, but quite recently from an evolutionary perspective."[7]

Although animals were consumed for sustenance during the ice age, researchers present evidence that ancient humans had great respect for animals. During the Ice Ages, man's primitive cave artwork showed a fascination with animal forms, as animals were thought to embody the spirits and powers of nature. Ancient astronomers, in their attempts to explain miracles of the universe, envisioned creation and life in terms of animals, and expressed this belief in their celestial reverence for other creatures in the zodiac, which they literally termed "circle of animals."[8] Animals were respected for their own self-worth, not merely for a role they might have played as an entity to be consumed by humans.

Early Judean Communities

The Hebrew Scriptures lent insight into the evolution of the human diet four to five thousand years ago. The culture of ancient Jews living in Eastern lands laid the foundation for many religious and cultural beliefs that subsequently became the norm within the Western world today,

such as the tradition of eating flesh of only those animals which have not been of a predatory species themselves.[9] According to Scripture, the initial human diet was to consist of fruits, nuts, and seeds (Genesis 1:29). Only later was the original diet modified to include the herb, meaning the plant itself, (Genesis 2:18) thus adding vegetables to the diet. Following the flood, when vegetation was either destroyed or scarce, and human life was struggling for survival, God granted permission for humans to use animal flesh as food (Genesis 9:3).[10] One only needs sense the anguished plight of these indigent tribal people wandering through the arid Middle-Eastern desert to understand why their society would have eaten anything, plant or animal, to survive:

> The Earth dries up and withers,
> the world languishes and withers,
> the exalted of the earth languish.
> Isaiah 24:4 [11]

During the time of Jesus, Judaism was an extraordinarily diverse religion.[12] The historian Josephus wrote that as far back as a century before Jesus, there were at least three sects among the Jews: Pharisees, Sadducees, and Essenes.[13] The Essenes, living at Qumran, Palestine and in Damascus between 150 and 100 BCE, were predominantly a vegetarian sect. Porphyry, Philo, Josephus, and Pliny the Elder all reported that the Essenes were primarily vegetarian.[14] Josephus revealed that the Essenes did not offer sacrifice of other beings, but offered themselves as sacrifices. The Essenes devoted their lives entirely to agricultural husbandry.[15]

Early Western Philosophers

Among the ancient Western Philosophers, one of the earliest to recognize that the consumption of animal flesh involved unnecessary violence was Pythagoras, c.570-490 BCE, the mathematician-philosopher responsible for the Pythagorean theorem. Pythagoras was a Greek known to have been a brilliant scientist, mathematician, and astronomer, who is often considered the Father of Western Vegetarianism. His moral objections to the eating of flesh evolved from his religious beliefs in the immortality of the soul. He believed that the soul migrates from one being, human or non-human, to another after death.[16]

Pythagoras' beliefs were influenced by Egyptian knowledge. While still a youth, Pythagoras was sent to Egypt, 560 to 520 BCE, to study under wise sages, learning astronomy, number symbolism, comparative religion, philosophy and other arcane subjects.[17] Evidence suggests that he may have met members of the Egyptian priestly class who never consumed animal flesh because of their philosophical beliefs in transmigration of souls between terrestrial, marine, avian, and human souls.[18] These Egyptian priests felt such great concern for all forms of life that they even refused to wear clothes made of animal skins.

Pythagoras held great respect for their teachings and in his later years did not permit his disciples to wear wool, rather replacing these with cloth of plant origin, such as linen. Pythagoras believed in an ethical kinship of all living creatures. Diogenes Laertius, a Greek philosopher of the third century BCE, transcribed the many teachings of Pythagoras in his book, 15 of Ovid's Metamorphosis. The following passage is a poetic extract in which Diogenes restated some of Pythagoras' beliefs in vegetarianism:

> Oh, what a wicked thing it is for flesh
> To be the tomb of flesh,
> For the body's craving
> To fatten on the body of another,
> For one creature to continue living
> Through one live creature's death.[19]

Pythagoras was not the only Greek philosopher who believed it wrong to kill animals for food. Centuries after Pythagoras, Porphyry (223–304 CE) wrote a treatise, De abstinentia ab esu animalium, which represented a series of books largely concerned with asceticism and the unjust act of consuming animal flesh.[20] Another philosopher, Plutarch of Chaironeia, (56-120 CE) appealed to his colleagues pleading that animals deserved moral consideration. He questioned what state of mind humans were in when they first brought their lips to the flesh of a dead creature.[21] Other prominent Greek philosophers who practiced and professed vegetarianism because of deep spiritual and philosophical beliefs in non-violence toward all beings included Empedocles, Theophrastus, Plotinus, and Plato.[22]

A series of Western philosophers, humanitarians, and religious persons have upheld the belief that it is unnecessary, unhealthy, or inhumane to take the lives of their fellow beings for consumption. Such individuals include Socrates, Plato, Seneca, Voltaire, Diogenes, Henry David Thoreau, John Milton, Ralph Waldo Emerson, Leo Tolstoy, George Bernard Shaw, Leonardo da Vinci, Thomas Edison, Mark Twain, Sir Isaac Newton, William Wordsworth, Dr. Albert Schweitzer, Isaac Bashevis Singer, Dr. Benjamin Spock, Ellen G. White, Percy Shelley, Henry Heimlich, M.D., John Wesley, Upton Sinclair, Steven Jobs, Louisa May Alcott, Charlotte Bronte, Dr. John Harvey Kellogg, Susan B. Anthony, Clara Barton, Henry Ford, and Shelton Walden.

The 18th century Enlightenment Period elevated science to a process of investigation and proof. By applying scientific method, a London physician, William Lambe, was able to prove that ingestion of animal flesh was not necessary for human health or for human survival. Prior to that time, it was generally assumed that ingestion of animal flesh, because of its similarity to human muscle, was needed to provide humans with greater strength and endurance. Dr. Lambe was the first to scientifically disprove this simplistic concept when he demonstrated that all nutrients needed for the creation of human muscle were present and abundant in vegetation.[23]

Early Christians

Reflecting back to the days of Jesus brings us to John the Baptist. Questions still remain unanswered as to what influence, if any, John the Baptist and the Essenes (a vegetarian Jewish sect) might have had upon one another.[24] John had been baptizing followers just a few miles down the Jordan River from the site where the Essenes were baptizing their followers. According to the scriptures, John lived on locusts and wild honey (Matthew 3:4), and his disciples often fasted (Luke 5:38). Although we presently know that locust are members of the animal kingdom, the ancient Hebrews may not have considered them as such because they did not belong to categories of mammals, fish, or fowl. There must have been some spiritual or ethical significance to John's diet of locust or ancient historians would not have chosen to narrate this tiny aspect of his personal life. We will never know if they were trying to express John's avoidance of other foods, such as fish, fowl, or mammals.

The traditional Western belief that human life possesses greater value than other animal life is termed anthropocentrism. An interpretation of such a belief system implies that only humans have a soul and that all other things, living and non-living, have been placed here for humankind's interests, needs, and desires.[25] Traditional anthropocentrism has recently been redefined to include three broad conceptual relationships between humans and the rest of creation: dominion, stewardship, and evolutionary perspectivism.

Beliefs in dominion are rooted in the Hebrew Scriptures as well as in the ancient Greek philosophies that all of nature exists to serve the needs and interests of humans. Stewardship is a modified version of the dominion belief system with its roots concerning human dominance tracing back to Judeo-Christian tradition. This concept states that the human species matters more than other species yet recognizes that other species possess inherent value. It implies that although humans possess the facilities to conquer other species, they should remain humane caretakers of them. The third concept, evolutionary perspectivism, recognizes that it is natural for each of the

species to look out for its own survival, yet stresses that humans must look to the common-good and the common-end of all creation, or there will be no sustainable life, as we know it, on this planet.[26]

Over the centuries, mainstream Christianity viewed other animals from a dominion perspective, rather than from perspectives of stewardship or evolutionary perspectivism. This lack of recognition of the plight and suffering of animals may have evolved as an inevitable consequence of Christianity's birth from a desert community at a time when food was scarce. At that time Christianity traditionally taught, "Compassion and reverence for all life, but at the same time allows the slaughter...of animals for food."[27]

Within the early Church, however, several influential Christians, including vegetarians such as Tertullian, Clement of Alexandria, and Origen, pleaded with others that humans and animals should live together in peace. Tertullian, an ancient Father of the Church who was born in Carthage in the middle of the second century wrote strongly concerning such beliefs.[28] He was a man with a great knowledge of history, anthropology, medicine, and archaeology and was also considered a pillar of moral integrity by other Christians.[29] He spoke against the eating of meat, claiming that people maintained better intellect and possessed greater sensitivity and depth of emotions when they did not consume meats and wines. He also felt that the eating of flesh blocked spiritual awareness.[30]

Just prior to the fall of the Roman Empire, Clement of Alexandria, another Father of the Church, appealed to people to refrain from consumption of animal flesh, "Let us refrain from such food. Have we not sufficient great variety in fruit and milk and all sorts of dry aliments?"[31] Clement, born in Athens, 150 CE, wrote extensively of the values he thought worthwhile for the new Christian Church.[32] He wrote, "Matthew the apostle used to make his meal on seeds and nuts and herbs, without flesh meat."[33]

Other ancient Christian philosophers, including Hegesippus and Saint Augustine wrote that Saint James never ate animal flesh, but lived on seeds and vegetables.[34] Pliny the Younger wrote that the apostle Peter lived on grain and fruit, and his followers strictly adhered to a harmless, innocent diet.[35] Clement of Alexandria denounced meat eaters as "gluttons" and reminded his hearers, "the apostle Matthew partook of seeds and nuts and vegetables without flesh."[36]

Several early Church mystics maintained flesh-free diets, including Basilius the Great, Elisabeth Von Thuringen, Saint Hedwig of Schliesien, Simeon Stylites, and Saint Anthony the Great. Prior to the Middle Ages, several very important monastic orders that helped to sustain the values of the Church adhered to vegetarian principles, including the Augustinian, Franciscan, and Cistercian Orders.[37]

Vegetarian Religious Orders

After the fall of the Greek and Roman empires, the ideals of vegetarianism were all but lost from recorded Western literature and might have virtually disappeared were it not for the organized monastic movements within the Christian Church. The Rule of Saint Benedict, in the days of Charles the Great, also known as Charlemagne, (768-814 CE) required that all monks, except the weak and the sick, abstain from the flesh of four-footed animals and of birds. Another monastic order, the Cistercians, did much to preserve the concept of vegetarianism. "Most faithful to the original Rule were the Cistercian monks, from which the reformed Trappist Order [Order of the Cistercians of the Strict Observance] evolved in the seventeenth century. Their manner of life went far beyond the original Rule of St. Benedict and the Cistercian practice." Even today, most Cistercians maintain vegetarian values.[38]

Recent Christian Vegetarians

Before the nineteenth century, the only founder of a major Christian denomination to have been a staunch vegetarian was John Wesley, founder of the Methodist denomination.[39] However, founders of several smaller Christian denominations were vegetarian. One such founder was Reverend William Cowherd who started the first vegetarian church of recent times, the Bible Christian Church, 1809, in Salford, England. A principle of his church concerned the religious significance of vegetarianism and of one's living without causing harm to any being. By 1817, Reverend Cowherd's nephew, Reverend William Metcalfe, carried a branch of this church to Philadelphia, creating the first vegetarian church on American soil.[40]

Reverend Sylvester Graham, a Presbyterian minister, was a staunch vegetarian. He launched modern food reform by ensuring that essential nutrients were not removed from vegetarian foods. Focusing on breads, Graham strived to ensure their vitamins were not removed during processing.[41] Through his teachings and his ability to manufacture and deliver healthy plant-based foods to the masses, he was able to help people obtain complete nutrition from vegetarian sources, hence 'Graham Crackers.'

During the same time period, the first official vegetarian Christian denomination was formed, the Seventh-day Adventists. Ellen G. White, one of the founders of the Seventh-Day Adventist Church, was considered a prophetess by many because of her visions of God's intent for humans to be vegetarian. She felt that part of God's promise was a merciful existence for all beings. Even today, half of all Seventh-day Adventists are still totally vegetarian.[42]

Chapter 2

The Meaning of Sainthood

Evolution of Criteria for Canonization

An understanding of the meaning of sainthood and the evolving criteria that have been used to declare sanctity will be helpful in understanding why saints who were vegetarian were more likely to have been chosen for canonization during certain time periods than during others. Basically, the criteria have centered on three main beliefs: That such individuals have achieved the blessings of Jesus, that grace flows through when their names are invoked during prayer, and that they are examples of holiness for their fellow human beings to follow.

In declaring people saints, the Church did not necessarily recommend that others imitate each and every aspect of the saints' lives, but rather that they imitate the essence of their sanctity.[1] Some might feel that popes have been anxious to make saints. Actually it has been the people who have sought to honor holy individuals as saints. Often the clergy have had to restrain the masses from declaring sainthood too easily.[2]

The manner in which the Catholic Church determines who is named a saint has evolved gradually through a series of processes. Centuries before the process of canonization was organized and centralized in Rome, local churches maintained lists of regional saints, usually martyrs, who died for the faith. Numerous calendars were created listing days on which followers might venerate specific saints. It wasn't until the seventh century, however, that these local calendars were merged together to form a universal Calendar of Saints for the entire Catholic Church.[3]

The word canonization is a religious term that came into being only during the twelfth century. The standards for holiness and lifestyles that the Church was seeking to find in candidates for sainthood, however, have remained unchanged since the time of the Apostles. The earliest Christian saints were martyrs, and they patterned their lives after Jesus.[4] The word martyr actually means primary witness. The apostles were primary witnesses to the resurrection of Jesus. The first martyrs mentioned in the New Testament were Stephen and the apostle James. Later, others who confessed the name of Jesus and because of this lost their lives were also honored as martyr saints.

During the early years of Christianity, numerous Christians lost their lives through martyrdom, either in battle or by being thrown to wild beasts. One well-known example was Saint Ignatius of Antioch, who was thrown to the lions at the Coliseum in Rome in 107 CE.[5] The essence, however, behind the determination of which individuals would be canonized was their love of God.[6]

Actually, the process of honoring saintly people is almost as old as the Church itself. In earlier years, no appointed judges or formal judicial system was needed to pronounce sainthood. A Bishop had the right to authorize canonization of an individual within his diocese. In those days, the Church consisted merely of a small flock of followers, and those individuals honored as saints were often the martyrs who had been publicly sentenced to death when they refused to renounce their faith.[7]

Saint Cyprian was one of the first to recommend that diligence was needed while investigating claims concerning those who were said to have died for their faith. He stated that all aspects of each individual's life needed to be investigated, including an inquiry into his or her faith and into the specific motivation that led each on a sacrificial path. By using these criteria, Saint Cyprian hoped to instill caution and ensure that canonization did not honor an undeserving individual.[8]

The fourth century saw a marked change in the concept of sainthood. Now the title of saint was extended to a variety of other Christians, not only to those who had died a martyr's death.[9] By this time, peace began to prevail in the Roman Empire commencing an era in which ascetic, monastic and contemplative followers of Jesus were considered outstanding examples of discipleship. Their dedication was considered an example of the holiness of one on a path toward canonization.[10] When canonization was being formalized, the names of candidates were written on tablets and read at Mass.[11] The local churches or councils acted independent of one another honoring holy people with sainthood and selecting specific days as Saint's Feast Days.

By the fifth through the tenth centuries, bishops assumed a direct role in supervising the process of canonization. Before petitioners were able to give the name of an individual as a potential candidate to their bishop, they were required to submit a written account of the candidate's life, virtues, and death, as well as his or her miracles and, where applicable, his or her martyrdom. By initiating such a formal process, the declaration of sanctity became a sophisticated religious function.[12]

By the twelfth century, the process of investigating the lives and miracles of those selected for sainthood underwent standardization.[13] By then it became understood that the pope would be the one to publicly and solemnly declare people saints.[14] In 1234, Pope Gregory IX published specific laws called the Decretals. These were a collection of official Church laws, in which he asserted that he possessed absolute jurisdiction over all cases of canonization. Thus, Pope Gregory made this rule binding upon the entire Church.[15]

By the thirteenth century, the canonization process had become a closely scrutinized procedure. The pope declared that only individuals designated by him could be called saints and those venerated by their local religious leader or by a religious order would only be called *beati* (blessed).[16] Prior to 1270, sainthood was bestowed upon a large and diverse group of candidates, including bishops who exemplified correct use of authority, laity

who labored on behalf of social justice, penitents who converted from lives of sin, those who facilitated monastic reforms, and founders of new religious Orders. By the thirteenth century, the variety of individuals accepted for canonization narrowed chiefly to those within religious Orders favored by the papacy. During this time, martyrs fell from Rome's favor.[17]

Many of those favored for sainthood during this era were those who embraced radical forms of poverty, chastity and obedience, paths that distinguished those in religious life from those of the laity. By the twelfth century, a paradigm for canonization had shifted toward a new category of saint, the mystic. Mystics were highly spiritual individuals who saw God in every being, as well as in every object, animate or inanimate. Saint Francis of Assisi was just such a mystic who was revered as a visionary, and also because he was the first person known to have received the stigmata, or crucified wounds, of Jesus. His spiritual sister, Saint Clare of Assisi, was canonized for her contemplative nature.[18] Clerics such as Saint Dominic (canonized in 1234) and Saint Thomas Aquinas (canonized in 1323) were revered for their spiritual writings. The major trend in canonization was toward self-effacing ascetics and intellectual defenders of the faith, several of whom were graced with mystical experiences.[19]

By the thirteenth century, an increasing emphasis was placed upon one's inner spirituality. This led to respect being bestowed upon one following a contemplative life over one maintaining an active life. One living a life detached from material gains was respected even more than one living a contemplative life. Sanctity was effectively redefined as control of one's inner life rather than control of the outer world. It was believed that once one reached a state of inner tranquility (lacking desires), one's soul had elevated to a higher level. Inner control, along with a rejection of marriage and domestic life, was believed to strengthen one's intensity and quality of spirituality.[20] Such spiritually advanced individuals were perceived as those whom God had predestined for lives far beyond the capabilities of most humans.

The procedure for canonization became formalized by the use of lengthy investigations and legislation. The entire life of the individual was subjected to precise and thorough enquiry, including a meticulous analysis of his or her writings, virtues, and alleged miracles. Witnesses were sworn in, interrogated, re-interrogated, and obliged to give oaths on their affirmations concerning the candidate for sainthood.[21] No steps were taken toward declaring sainthood unless the candidate had been deceased for some time, as the papacy was concerned that the enthusiasm of the moment might sway public opinion.[22]

Persons nominated for canonization must have commanded a wide reputation for holiness and miraculous power. If the individual had written books or other teachings, these were examined specifically to confirm they did not contain beliefs contrary to Christian faith or morals.[23] The final and most arduous trial for the candidate began with enquiry into the very nature and genuineness of their individual miracles and virtues.[24]

By the seventeenth century, the entire process of canonization was firmly in control of the papacy. The popes demanded greater proof of miracles and virtue from reliable sources.[25] This control was fully formalized during the reign of Pope Urban VIII (1623-1644), who declared that the papacy would maintain total control over determinations of sainthood.[26]

During the reign of Pope Benedict XIV (1740-1758), procedures tightened further. Investigation involving miracles became more scientific and it became clear that heroic virtue had now reached greater significance in the declaration of sainthood than had the experience of visions, ecstasies, and paranormal phenomena.[27] Strict guidelines were established, witnesses were essential, and investigators were employed to determine that all visions and other phenomena proceeded from God.[28]

Present Criteria for Canonization

Until this century, saints were identified according to categorizes developed during the initial four centuries of the Church's existence. Basically saints were classified as either martyrs or confessors. Confessors were further categorized as bishops, priests or monks if they were men, and widows or virgins if they were women. All other categories were not defined and fell into the group "none of the above."[29]

By the 1900's the entire subject of canonization opened up an entirely new field of questioning. These included: What was it that constituted sanctity? What degree of virtue and proof of virtue were to be required by the Church? How did the sanctity of martyrs differ from that of confessors?[30] Through this inquiry, it was decided that two characteristics were essential in the theological determination of sanctity: First, that there was conformity and union between the saint's life and the values of Jesus, and second, that the saint lived a life of significance both to the Church and to society.[31]

By 1983, Pope John Paul II enacted changes that reformed the entire canonization process to make it simpler, faster, more productive, and better aligned with modern day values. Inevitably, these changes affected the choices of candidates as well as the process involved. Essentially, the process verified the accuracy of the saint's history and that the saint's achievements represented models of holiness for modern day Christians.[32]

Under these new guidelines, the process of canonization was sped up remarkably. Over the prior seven hundred years, from 1234 CE until John Paul II became pope; fewer than three hundred Saints had been canonized.[33] By following these new criteria, Pope John Paul II was able to beatify and canonize more individuals than all of his twentieth century predecessors combined. Some believe that Pope John Paul II's unprecedented determination to proclaim saints from every corner of the globe will remain one of his most enduring legacies and represent a powerful mechanism for conveying to Christians all over the world what it means to be a disciple of Jesus.[34] By enacting this new policy, Pope John Paul II has become a powerful evangelist. His actions reveal great understanding concerning the value of examples, as well as recognition of the ability of those declared as saints to exist immortally through the process of canonization.[35]

Concerning the value of declaring individuals saints, this is what the Carmelite sisters said during the canonization of Saint Edith Stein,

Jesus is never merely alone, rather He is always found in the company of His friends in spirit, both living and dead...Keeping company with the saints in the spirit of Jesus encourages faith, and bonds each individual with the millions of other people throughout the world and throughout history who feel this same bond. All who follow are members of the body of Jesus and in some way are all connected.[36]

Spiritual Legacies of the Saints

To fully appreciate the value that the honor of sanctification has had, and will continue to have, for the millions of followers of the Christian faith, one must appreciate the spiritual meaning of canonization. The canonized saint is an individual whom the Roman Catholic Church has chosen as embodying the values and teachings of Jesus. Because such an individual has lived an extraordinarily spiritual and meaningful life, and because others have been recipients of miracles after having called upon the spirit of that holy individual, the Church stands by its beliefs that such individuals have lived lives embodying the image of God.[37]

There comes a time
in the life of each individual
when each must choose those values
by which to venture forth
in his or her life path.

Each has been given the opportunity
to choose a path
sharing blessings of peace and kindness
with each and every being.

Each has the ability to look beyond his or her own form
so as to feel empathy
with those beings
whose essence each may never understand.

And each has the wisdom to look past variations
in form, intelligence, and species,
so as not to pass judgment
upon which beings should live
and which should die.

As you embark upon your journey
learning the values and passions
of the mystic, ascetic and monastic vegetarian saints,
you will learn of each saint's concern for all creation
and each saint's compassion for other beings.

Those saints whose messages are contained
within the pages you are about to read
truly sought to share God's blessings of peace and mercy
with all God's creatures and
all God's creation.

Chapter 3
Eastern Monastic and Hermitic Saints

The deeply spiritual religious sages within this category of saints are frequently referred to as the Desert Fathers. They are a fascinating group of individuals who evolved as an ecclesiastically significant entity within the vast desert regions of Egypt, Palestine, Arabia, and Persia, during the fourth century. Though these spiritually motivated Christian sages inhabited the isolated deserts in large numbers, they were certainly not the only holy individuals to have done so. There were numerous meditative and contemplative thinkers of various faiths and traditions who sought refuge and enlightenment within the silence of the desert.

As the numbers of these sages grew, so too did the depth of their theological and philosophical understanding. Their ranks included not only men of all ages and all callings, but also women. Although some might consider it odd that these enlight-

ened desert sages were considered so representative of Christian holiness that they were canonized, one must remember that many of the seeds of emerging Christianity first blossomed within the barren deserts of Palestine. It is important to keep in mind that a good number of the major religions of the world were conceived, and found life, within deserts, plains, and mountaintops of similarly isolated regions.

During those times, numerous barren deserts and mountains of the Middle East were considered spiritually sacred sites. Numerous wandering sages with one quest, to find spiritual enlightenment and peace, inhabited them. As most of these individuals lived lives of extreme austerity, non-violence, personal sacrifice, and self-motivated holiness, their disciplined minds led them from a world of materialism into deeper worlds of spiritual understanding.

These desert inhabitants lived in a variety of settings. Some lived as Christian cenobitic monks, congregating together by the thousands in enormous monasteries. Others lived as isolated hermits in small cells on the sides of cliffs or in thatched huts, tending the sparsest of gardens. Yet all were motivated to abandon the chaotic cities of the pagan masses in hopes of attaining personal salvation in the solitude of the desert.

An extraordinarily large number of the desert saints and sages lived without ever taking the life of any creature; hence, they lived as vegetarians. Their values conformed to those that modern society might expect to find in contemplative spiritual philosophers. Thomas Merton stated that these desert monks were not seeking to be different or to act superior toward others; rather, they just wanted to live the simplest of lives possible in an environment where all beings lived in equality.[1]

In describing the desert saints, Thomas Merton wrote, "In the fourth century A.D., the deserts of Egypt, Palestine, Arabia and Persia were peopled by a race of men and women who have left behind them a strange reputation. They were the first Christian hermits who left behind the pagan world to live in solitude."[2] Thomas Merton recognized them as men and women of principle who felt that to drift along with the waves of a society whose values they could not condone, was purely and simply spiritual disaster.[3]

These desert saints did not believe in letting themselves be passively guided and ruled by a society devoid of the ethical and spiritual principles they valued. What they sought was deeper understanding and patterning of their own true selves, in the light of the values of Jesus.[4] According to Merton, these desert inhabitants did not seek approval from their contemporaries, nor did they value the tangibles of society. In general, they were quiet, sensible, and sensitive people, seeking merely a deeper understanding of human nature, of creation, and of God.

There were several interrelated reasons why the monastic saints felt committed to living on diets devoid of animal flesh. These included their striving to lead lives of simplicity and austerity, to live taking no more from nature than was essential, to achieve inner control of all worldly temptations, to live in harmony with the entirety of creation, to live with compassion toward all beings, and to protect the essence of God's soul within each and every creature. The following biographies contain summaries of the lives and goals of those Eastern desert and monastic saints who chose to live as vegetarians.

Saint Anthony of Egypt

c. 251 - 356 CE
January 17

Recognizing the uncontrollable forces of the Nile River, Saint Anthony realized that all power rested in the hands of God.

Saint Anthony lived just several generations after the time Jesus had walked upon the lands of the Middle East. Born to devout Christian parents in a small village on the banks of the Nile River in Upper Egypt, Anthony's values were deeply rooted in the teachings of Jesus. He personally forged such a spiritually deep path in the formation of early Christianity that he has often been regarded as the first monk, as well as the first hermit, within the Christian Church. His life was one of simplicity. He was a man who sought to live in harmony with all of creation. From the time of his youth, the erratic nature of the Nile River taught him that all man's labors were minor compared to the will of God. He realized that what man needs, his daily sustenance and his safety, are actually given to him only through the grace of God.[5]

His parents, wealthy landowners, died when he was only twenty years of age, leaving him with many fields and pastures. Over the years, he began to long for greater meaning within his own life and often recalled Jesus' words, "If you wish to be perfect, go sell your possessions and give the money to the poor...then come, follow me." (Matthew 19:21). He finally resolved to follow this gospel literally, giving his fields and money to the poor, and leaving the materialistic world to become a disciple of a local spiritual sage.[6]

Anthony remained a student with this wise hermit for thirteen years, during which time the aged sage taught him how to conquer worldly temptations, how to appreciate prayer and work, and how to bring his soul closer to God. Young Anthony achieved the ability to calm his sensual appetites through regular fasting. Yet he also learned the value of moderation, and of not depriving his body of too much, lest it might lose its will to go on. He also gained an appreciation of the gifts of the earth, and strove not to deplete it of more than his bare sustenance required. It was based upon such values that Anthony chose to live, sustaining himself merely on bread, water, and a few dates—never swaying from these meager choices.[7]

After gaining much wisdom from other desert sages, Anthony journeyed to an abandoned hilltop fort in the Arabian Desert[8] where he remained in contemplation for twenty years. He lived in great asceticism and solitude, strengthening his mind by fervent prayer, as well as by hard work. He cultivated a small garden on the mountainside and wove simple mats.[9] When a wandering philosopher asked him if he missed the consolation of books, Anthony replied, "My book, O Philosopher, is the nature of created things, and any time I want to read the words of God, the book is before me."[10]

Saint Anthony's life exemplified just that life path followed by the Christian desert saints of the fourth century C.E. He sought, and found, the meaning of salvation, particularly salvation from those values of a society he found spiritually unacceptable.[11] Anthony believed in a life of poverty, tribulation, and discretion —a life in which one might free oneself from material possessions. His feeling was that if monks were to dwell with men of the world, they would lose their determination to sustain solitary prayer, and would be then drawn to outside goals rather than adhere to internal growth.[12]

After many years, Anthony recognized that he must share his wisdom with others, so he began to share his teachings of compassionate values with all those who might benefit from them. He never refused a concerned student, believing that, "Life and death depend on our neighbor. If we gain our brother, we gain Jesus; but if we harm our neighbor, we sin against Jesus."[13] Although his teachings were strict, his actions toward others were gentle. When a visitor admitted he was unable to follow the gospel and to turn the other cheek, Saint Anthony did not reprimand him. Rather, he advised his disciples to prepare a meal for this visitor, and pray for him as he was weak and needed their assistance.

Much of his wisdom was drawn from the simple teachings of nature. Once Saint Anthony advised an abbot to insult a stone and beat it unceasingly. After the abbot did this, Anthony asked him if the stone answered back. When the abbot replied it had not, Saint Anthony said that he, too, must reach the state of total acceptance—the state in which he no longer took offense at anything.[14] As the years passed, although Anthony grew to a man of great age, he remained a simple desert farmer—body erect, eyes clear, and character filled with values.

After his passing, stories of healing miracles occurring with intercession of his name abounded, particularly during the epidemics of the twelfth and thirteenth centuries. Saint Anthony believed that all existence emanated through God's grace,[15] and conducted his humble life harming no human and no weaker being. He became a man full of spiritual fulfillment as well as a man at peace with his fellow beings and with God.

Saint Hilarion

c. 291-371 CE
October 21

Saint Hilarion felt humbled
by the mystery of creation.
By tilling the soil, he sought
to unite his soul with the rest
of God's creation.

While still in his youth, Saint Hilarion already showed signs of possessing a deeply spiritual nature. Recognizing this, his family decided to send him to Alexandria, Egypt to pursue higher studies. Hilarion had been born the son of idol worshipers in a small village south of the Gaza region[16] of Palestine.[17] It was during his studies in Egypt that he became a Christian. After completing these studies, he felt a calling to travel to the Egyptian desert to live with a wise sage about whom he had heard much—that sage being Saint Anthony. While living with Saint Anthony, Hilarion imitated Anthony's asceticism and his vegetarian practices. Several years later, Hilarion returned to Palestine hoping to lead a life of quiet, isolated contemplation. It was on his return home at the age of fifteen that Hilarion learned of his parents' deaths. Although they left him an inheritance, he chose not to keep it, but rather renounced it all, dividing it between his brothers and the poor.[18]

Hilarion returned to the desert, making his home in a barren region between a sea and a swamp where he lived a life of extreme austerity in a tiny cell. He sustained himself by tilling the soil and weaving baskets, believing that strong, hard work was essential to elevate the spirit. Hilarion stated that, "He that will not work, neither let him eat."[19] He resolved to sustain his existence on vegetation, consuming only figs, bread, vegetables, and only the minimum amount of these foods required to sustain his health.[20] In his later years, he ate grain steeped in water, dry bread with salt, the juice of herbs, and eventually when he sensed his vision weakening, on the oil of vegetation.[21]

Hilarion lived in the desert for the greater part of his years, journeying but once to Jerusalem. He fulfilled this journey so as to remain reverent to the Church that he honored. He held true to his belief that the worship of God was not confined to any particular place.[22] After having lived and meditated in the desert twenty years, his depth of wisdom had become so profound that many felt drawn to him. Masses of the sick among the pagans came seeking health through Hilarion's ability to cure chronic illnesses, and his skill in healing those stung by serpents and insects. He also possessed the ability to cure many by blessing oil and then anointing their wounds with it. Over the years, he repeatedly helped the blind to see, the barren to conceive, the young with fever to be relieved, and the weak to gain strength.

As the saint grew in age, he felt the need for greater peace and solitude, yet masses continued to flock to him. He felt the need to find a place where he might live unknown, so he began an almost endless quest that took up the remainder of his life. He journeyed to Egypt, Sicily, Greece, and Cyprus.[23] Yet news of his arrival as a holy man preceded him in every country and every city, and crowds clamored around seeking from him wisdom and healing.[24] Because of the multitude seeking his abilities, he was never fully able to remain in solitude, yet he found a measure of peace in Cyprus, where he remained until his eightieth year.[25] He spent the remainder of his life healing the sick, praying for the downtrodden, and adhering to a totally non-violent diet, never taking more of God's gifts than his humble existence required.

Saint Macarius the Elder

c. 300-390 CE
January 19

When a young woman accused Saint Macarius of assaulting her, rather than see the woman suffer, he chose to suffer himself.

Saint Macarius the Elder is often referred to as Macarius the Egyptian or Macarius the Great, so as to distinguish him from Macarius of Alexandria. He was born in Upper Egypt and although he spent his youth driving camels, he felt a compelling pull to devote himself to prayer and to live the life of a contemplative, meditative hermit. He spent his days alternating his time between physical work and passionate prayer. Finally, he made the decision that he must live in contemplative solitude in the desert. He created a shelter within a small cell on the side of several rocks and sustained himself on the most austere of diets—consuming only foods derived from the vegetation of the soil and the fruits of the trees.

One day, a young woman who had chosen a wayward path found herself pregnant. When her parents asked who was responsible, she falsely accused Macarius of having violently attacked her. Because the town's people believed the woman, they dragged Macarius through the streets, beat and insulted him, and accused him of being a base hypocrite under the garb of a monk. Through it all, he suffered with patience and sent the woman what he earned from his work, saying to himself, "Well, Macarius, having now another to provide for, you must work all the harder."[26]

It was during the anguish of the young woman's labor that she confessed Macarius' innocence, and named the individual who had seduced her. Then the town's people regarded Macarius as a saint for having silently accepted the prior shame, as well as the responsibility it entailed. Macarius, however, wanted neither the people's insults nor their praises. He sought only a life of humility - so he fled to the desert, lest he might become proud from all the praises of these townspeople. While in the desert, he lived a life of silence, humility, self-denial, and continual prayer.[27]

Although Macarius remained hard on himself, seeking to live without praise or possessions, he practiced charity toward all other monks and all passing travelers in need. He longed to live a life of personal sacrifice, humility, and austerity, and to sustain himself on vegetation. Thus he lived neither harming nor abusing any weaker being.[28]

Saint Palaemon

Fourth Century
January 11

Saint Palaemon was a man of peace and compassion. He sought to teach his disciples the blessing of patience.

A great deal of that which is known concerning Saint Palaemon had been obtained from the accountings of his faithful and respectful pupil, Saint Pachomius, who later became the founder of Egyptian monasticism. After having lived sparse years in the deserts of Upper Egypt, Palaemon had become an aged hermit. The younger student, Pachomius, came to learn from his spiritual wisdom. When Palaemon met the young aspiring pupil, he informed him that, "I eat nothing but bread and salt" and "I never touch wine, and I watch half the night." The aspiring pupil replied, "I believe in Jesus my Lord, who will give me strength and patience to assist thee in thy prayers to follow thy holy conversion."[29]

The old hermit then looked at this young aspiring pupil with a sense of spiritual warmth and agreed to teach his ways of patience, austerity, and holiness. Over the many years that followed, the two men grew in wisdom through prayer and contemplation. Eventually, however, the young Pachomius felt the need to start a monastery so as to aid in the spiritual education of many faithful followers. Though his heart remained rooted in his life of solitary enlightenment, simplicity, and contemplation, Palaemon acquiesced to his pupil's wishes. As a man dedicated to peace and wisdom, Palaemon continued to guide Pachomius, as well as other pupils, in the ways of austerity, reverence for all life, and the spiritual values of a life devoid of passion, pride, or violence. Having lived a life of purity and simplicity, the aged Palaemon survived to see his values gain appreciation in the hearts of many, and died shortly after witnessing the start of the monastery.

Saint Pachomius

c. 292 - 346 CE
May 9

Sharing his vision with others, Saint Pachomius gathered other Christian ascetics in the desert to form the first community of Christian monks.

Saint Pachomius was a pupil who, in his youth, journeyed to the Egyptian desert to live as a disciple of Saint Palaemon. It is believed to have been because of his ability to touch the souls of others that he had become the first individual capable of gathering Christian ascetics together into larger communities as monks and to have attained the insight needed to draw written rules for their guidance. His humble origins began with his birth into a family in Upper Egypt—a family of no religious faith whatsoever. At the age of twenty, Pachomius had to leave his family as he was conscripted into the emperor's army. He and other recruits were conveyed down the Nile River under wretched conditions, yet the Christians there received them with great kindness. He never forgot their kindness. When the army disbanded, he made his way back up the Nile River and began to work with these Christians.[31]

After receiving baptism, Pachomius sought out the elder Christian hermit, Palaemon, who had been recognized as a man of great wisdom. Pachomius built a cell in the desert and with the older sage, lived a life of great austerity, consuming only bread and salt, and occupying himself in manual labor and inner prayer. Over the ensuing years, other monks arrived in such great numbers to learn from their wisdom, that they eventually built twelve monasteries to accommodate these disciples, nine monasteries for men and three for women. Often, they would spend the entire night in prayer vigils and would meditate upon Psalms and other passages from the Bible.

Pachomius seemed to possess the ability to read the thoughts of others and to feel the essence of their souls. His natural ability to relate to others was an essential factor in his attracting an enormous following of holy individuals and in sustaining the functional unity of all the monasteries.[32] Pachomius met his untimely death from the plague. Yet the example he set as an understanding, wise, and sacrificing individual able to read the needs of others, and of a man resolved to live on a diet obtained without violence, left a lasting impression on the path of the monastic Christian tradition for generations to come.

Saint Paul the Hermit

The First Hermit of Egypt
c. 229 - 342 CE
January 15

Following Jesus' words, "If you wish to be perfect, leave everything and follow me" Saint Paul lived as a desert hermit, His closest companion was a raven.

Even as a young man, Saint Paul possessed a distinctly gentle and compassionate soul. A native of Egypt, Paul lost both his parents when he was fifteen years of age and inherited their entire estate. He had been well educated and was proficient in both Greek and Egyptian scholarship. But what he valued most were those times that he devoted to contemplative prayer. During this time period, violent Emperors Decius and Valerius had invoked sweeping, cruel dictums over all the Churches of Egypt. Paul was twenty-two years of age when a storm of persecution had erupted throughout the country, and he was forced to seek refuge elsewhere.

Saint Paul fled in fear of his life and embarked upon a journey into the desert. Once there, he set up a peaceful, meager dwelling in a small cave on the edge of a cliff. The spreading leaves of an ancient date palm tree shielded the cave, and a nearby stream provided him with much needed water. He chose to live as a total vegetarian, sustaining himself solely on the fruit of the palm tree, until reaching his forty-third year. Legend has it that a raven supplied him with morsels of bread during his remaining years.[33]

His beloved dwelling offered him shelter for prayer and solitude, and he felt such a lifestyle embodied the literal answer to follow Jesus' command, "If you wish to be perfect, leave everything and follow me." Matthew 19.21. After years of solitude, another monk, Saint Anthony, heard of Paul's wisdom and went to see him. When they met, the two kindred spirits embraced one another. Saint Paul said to Anthony, "Behold him whom thou has sought with such labor; with limbs decayed by age, and covered with unkempt white hair. Behold, thou seest but a mortal, soon to become dust."[35] Paul died at the age of one hundred and thirteen, in the ninetieth year of his solitude. He was a contemplative man who recognized that one must find God within oneself.

After his death, his body was found on bent knees with his frame erect and his arms held high as though in prayer. Saint Paul lived a contemplative life, adoring and praising God. He lived his years as a vegetarian so as to exist in a state of humble non-violence, simplicity, and peace.

Saint Marcian

c. 320 - 387 CE
November 2

Saint Marcian felt compassion for all beings, believing that one hears God's voice through the callings of His innocent creatures.

Saint Marcian was born into a well-established family in Syria and actually held a position in the imperial court. A career in politics seemed to be unfolding for him. But while still young, handsome, and at the peak of his career, he felt a calling to search for a higher meaning for life. He decided to leave his friends and family and secretly set off into the desert between Antioch and the Euphrates River. Once there, he renounced the tangible world and built a small enclosure for himself in the most remote part of the desert.

His life became one of simplicity and sincerity. His diet consisted of only one food—bread, and his life was filled with reading, praying, working, and reciting psalms. He ate only in the evening, and even then only the smallest of portions. He thought it better that he consume small quantities of food every day, rather than eat sporadically, as that led to his craving food in excess.[36] He lived in constant contemplation and perceived that through such a lifestyle he had become enlightened to the wonderful knowledge of many truths, as well as to the mysteries of faith.[37] After some time, a considerable number of disciples sought to gain from Marcian's spiritual guidance, and took up meager residence along with him in the desert.

When famous individuals sought his advice, Saint Marcian felt humbled. He replied to them with statements such as, "God speaks to us every day through his fellow creatures, and through the world around us. God speaks to us through the Gospel, from which we learn what to do both for ourselves and for others. What more can Marcian say that can be of use?"[38] His fame as a worker of miracles spread far and wide. Yet he longed to live without fame and glory, so when people would visit him to request his performance of miracles to help them, he would pretend to refuse them. But when they would return home, and could no longer praise him, they would find their request for miracles answered.

Once when an aged hermit came to visit Marcian, the older man appeared frail and faint, so Marcian offered him cooked herbs and vegetables. When the visitor stated that he never ate before evening, Marcian reassured him that fasting was what one does to oneself, yet charity was what God commanded us to do for others. Through such compassionate reassurance, Marcian encouraged the aged visitor to sit down, and both partook of their humble meal together.

Marcian lived to an old age, and died a man filled with inner grace, rather than a man of worldly possessions. He did not reject society because he felt above others, but because he sought to live in God's world rather than in man's world. Marcian saw God in all nature, all life, and all the animals of the earth, and, hence, did not wish to take life from any of God's creatures. His words express his belief that

"God speaks to us from all Creation, through his fellow creatures."[39]

Saint Macarius
the Younger

c. 320 - 394 CE
January 2

When Saints Macarius the
Younger and Elder were
exiled down the Nile River,
they radiated such peace that
the transporting soldiers left
their jobs to join them.

Saint Macarius the Younger was born in
Alexandria, Egypt, into a poor family.
Although his parents were confectioners
by trade, as a young man, Macarius longed
desperately with all his heart to serve
God. He forsook the pleasures of the
world to retreat to a contemplative life
within the vast deserts of Egypt. He spent
sixty years in fervent penance and prayer,
initially in the upper deserts of Egypt, and
then in the lower, desolate regions, where
the mountains were filled with numerous
natural cells.[40]

Under the heat of the glaring, red,
desert sun, Macarius and the other solitary monks spent their days in manual
labor, weaving baskets, praying, and in
contemplation. They consumed no more
than raw herbs, grain, and, occasionally,
bread. They sought to leave the civilized
world that they felt had been misguided
into selfish luxury, abundance, and indifference.[41] These hermits felt the civilized
world was no longer a nurturing environ-

ment for honest individuals, as
the majority of people were
consumed with desires of the
flesh, cravings for personal
gain, and self-oriented pride.

After several years had
passed, Macarius was con-
vinced to leave his cell and
journey to Rome so that he might serve
the sick in hospitals. After having done
this for some time, he felt his actions had
grown into acts of vanity, in which he
attracted the eyes of others praising him.
He felt he was succumbing to the glory of
the esteem to which he was held.
Wanting no praise from humankind, as
he felt this would rob him of true humility, he returned to his life of prayer and
penance —silently beseeching God's
mercy for others.[42]

In 375 CE, a series of political events
led to the capture and exile of the two
humble sages—Saint Macarius the
Younger and the older Saint Macarius of
Egypt. As the two monks sat together in a
corner of a ferry transporting them down
the Nile River, the officers looked at these
aged monks in their tattered garbs and
questioned them as to the source of their
happiness. When they expressed their
simple peace of mind, the guards returned
home, renounced their wealth and rank,

and joined the monks to seek happiness in solitude.[43]

A great many of Saint Macarius' actions were considered holy, and the miraculous cure of a cancerous lesion on another priest has been related to his prayers.[44] His most enduring legacy, however, remains in the example he set by his sacrificial lifestyle, his vegetarian austerity, his finding total peace and fulfillment in a life devoid of materialism, and his unfaltering devotion to God.

Saint Aphraates

c. 280 - 345 CE
January 29

After meeting Saint Aphraates, the emperor underwent a spiritual conversion and, thenceforth, ruled with kindness and mercy.

Saint Aphraates was a sincere and serious individual who at a very young age felt that one must find God within one's self. He was born into a Persian family and while still a youth was converted to Christianity. He eventually settled at Edessa[45] in Mesopotamia,[46] which at that time was the stronghold of a religious community. Aphraates had been searching for the most perfect manner in which to serve God. He decided to live in an isolated tiny cave just outside the city limits where he spent his days in prayer and contemplation. The only foods he felt justified in consuming were breads, eaten after sunset. Subsequently in old age, he also consumed a small quantity of vegetables.[47]

After many years, Aphraates moved to a hermitage near Antioch,[48] enjoyed a reputation for sanctity and miracles, and was sought out by many for his advice. At first, all was peaceful. However, great havoc was beginning to spread throughout the lands—with Arians[49] taking over the churches and the emperor inflicting great harm upon the people. Aphraates left his cell and traveled far and wide providing consolation to the masses. During one of those missions, the emperor saw him on the road and enquired as to why a holy man, such as he, was so far from his cell. Aphraates replied, "It is not I who am to blame, but rather you who have kindled the flames that I am striving to extinguish." The emperor was greatly impressed by the wisdom and peaceful ambiance of the saint, and completely changed his violent course of actions as a direct result of the words of the aged saint.[50]

Saint Aphraates was a contemplative prayerful sage, and a man who sought to spread peace amongst all he met. Unceasingly, he shared his wisdom with others during their times of need. His decision to live the humble life of a desert hermit, to spread peace and consolation among all he encountered, and to consume only those foods obtained through compassionate means, were but examples of the depth of compassion of this peace loving man.

Saint James of Nisibis

c. 284 - 350 CE
July 11

Saint James raised his arms in prayer and a cloud of gnats swarmed down filling the nostrils of the enemy's horses. They were forced to retreat without any blood being shed.

Saint James was a Syrian monk who became the first Christian bishop within the region of Mesopotamia.[51] His religious commitment led him to build a basilica to educate future theologians, and to work passionately to uphold the early Christian principles of the Ecumenical Councils[52] of Nicea[53] and Athanasius.[54, 55] Possibly, his greatest achievement lay in his ability to write prolific and profound theological works, and it is because of this, that many refer to him by the title 'Doctor of the Syrian Church.'[56] Because the documents attributed to him were written at such an early date, however, authorities have lost the ability to confirm the authenticity of their authorship.

Initially, Saint James studied the sciences, but subsequently, cultivated an interest in sacred studies. He felt that ambition and vanity led people away from life's true meanings, and that it was only possible for one to find truth within one-self. This led him to recognize that the greatest step to one's understanding of life remained within each individual's ability to subdue his own self. James sought out and found the highest mountain abode within which he might live, and resided in a tiny cave there. He survived on raw wild roots and berries never taking the life of any animal. He spent his days in contemplation and prayer.

With time and patience, James developed the gift of prophecy and miracles—gifts that he subsequently shared with the masses. Then war broke out between his people and the Persians. Seeing a prodigious multitude of men and beasts cover the entire countryside, James beseeched God for help, pleading: "Lord, thou art able by the weakest means to humble thy enemies; defeat these multitudes by an army of gnats." The Saint had scarcely uttered these words when a cloud of gnats and flies came down and entered the trunks of the elephants, as well as the ears and nostrils of the horses. This forced the animals to throw off their riders leading to a series of military retreats that saved the city of Nisibis.[57] It was thenceforth believed that by his prayers for peace,

James was able to save his own people without a drop of blood having been shed on either side.

Saint James lived a humble and observant life. Although he was offered a position as abbot, he declined it so that he might remain in a hermitage amidst other devout monks who similarly sought disengagement from worldly possessions. His sense of charity was abundant. He would allow no poor person to be sent from his door without alms, and would empty the monastery granaries and stores to feed all who were in hunger. His life was that of a humble pacifist and a vegetarian. He had conquered the temptations of vanity and self-gratification, and found meaning in simplicity and a life of peace.[58]

Saint Ammon

c. 288 - 350 CE
October 4

Both Saint Ammon and his wife felt a calling to serve God. They joined separate religious communities and spent the remainder of their lives serving others.

While Saint Ammon was still a young and impressionable man in Egypt, he suffered the loss of both his parents. By the age of twenty-two, he was forced by rich relatives into a planned marriage. His instinctive calling, however, was to live the life of a contemplative religious individual, and fortunately, his young wife shared his same religious calling. Ammon and his wife lived together in humility and austerity for eighteen years. They possessed no more than they needed and their only foods were vegetation—fruits and vegetables. They would spend their evenings together in prayer and when they finally freed themselves of family pressures, they retreated to the desert. Ammon joined a desert hermitic community of monks and his wife organized a house of religious women. [59]

The community of monks that Ammon joined consisted of five thousand men, each living according to his own calling, so as to allow each time alone for prayer and time to serve others. Theirs was a great church, and contained quarters for guests, as well as for the indigent. Each man performed manual labor so that the community would not be a burden upon others and would remain self-sufficient. Saint Ammon lived in marked austerity and, over the years, a number of disciples followed him. He chose to live consuming only sparse quantities of bread and water, so as not to harm or waste any of God's creations. He spent a great deal of time in contemplation and prayer, and his holiness evolved into a spiritual gift enabling him to perform miracles aiding the needy and the infirm. [60]

Saint Julian Sabas

c. 288 - 378 CE
January 17

Upon seeing a young boy fall into a well, Saint Julian Sabas risked his own life to save the child.

Saint Julian was a man of humble origin and received the most rudimentary of education. Yet in spite of his limited personal resources, he felt a need to help others and to serve God. He left his village to live a simple life in the desert of Mesopotamia[61]—a life filled with prayer and contemplation. He limited his sustenance to the most frugal of meals—bread made of millet, vegetables, salt, and water. During this same time period, the emperor had launched a march against the Persians[62] throughout Syria and Mesopotamia. Saint Julian feared that the emperor, if victorious, would subsequently redirect his compulsive need for conquest to persecution of the Church. He spent ten days in incessant prayer that the outcome of the war would prevent such an event. Such an outcome occurred. For the emperor, failing in his attempted conquest, did not overthrow the Church.[63]

It was also believed that Julian's prayers contributed to the removal of a leader from Cyprus whose actions would have been detrimental to the development of Christianity.[64] During another time, when Saint Julian was traveling to Antioch[65] to motivate and encourage the faithful in their conflicts with the Arians, a pious woman went out of her way to serve Julian dinner. That evening, the woman's son who had been fetching water, suddenly fell into a well. Julian ran out, prayed, and hauled the child from this pit.

Saint Julian was known for his extraordinary asceticism and for the fact that he spent over fifty years in the desert near Edessa striving to encourage the faithful. Just the presence of this holy man, as well as observation of his ability to perform miracles through prayer, had a most encouraging effect upon the faithful.[66] Julian always worked for the good of others. He lived a life in union with God through simplicity and prayer. He preferred to live as a simple, humble vegetarian—without causing loss of life or harm to any being who, he felt, had been given life by God.

Saint Apollo

c. 310 - 395 CE
January 25

Saint Apollo felt such concern for others that he would throw himself in the middle of fights, rather than see others suffer.

At the age of fifteen, Saint Apollo embarked upon a spiritual journey. It was at this young age that he left home to live the life of a solitary, contemplative, prayerful hermit in the desert. His years passed within the desert, and after spending forty years sequestered in deeply religious prayer and thought, he felt ready to share the wisdom he had obtained with others. When he began to share his teachings, many felt so drawn by the wisdom that lay hidden within his teachings that a large group of followers joined him. Subsequently, he became head of a community of monks in Upper Egypt.

Some years later, Apollo heard that his brother had been imprisoned for his religious teachings and beliefs. So he went to the prison and by performing a miracle was able to open the prison gates and free his brother and others who had been imprisoned for similar pious actions.

Apollo felt such deep concern for the welfare of all others that once, when witnessing townspeople fighting, he threw himself into the middle of their conflict so as to convince them not to shed one another's blood.

On a different occasion, when his community lamented their lack of sustenance, Apollo began praying incessantly. Through his prayers, the community was delivered loaves of bread, fruit, honey, nuts and milk. His followers and he chose to live on such foods for the remainder of their years— as they considered such vegetarian food heavenly. Apollo's peaceful character was expressed in his sharing of advice with his monks:

> It behooves us to be ever joyous, for we ought not to be sad about our salvation. All those whose affections are fixed on earthly things have cause to be agitated in mind, but not we. [67]

Saint Apollo was a man who sought the minimal in worldly possessions and was willing to sacrifice himself for all he met. He believed that it was a heavenly privilege afforded him to live his life as a vegetarian—a life lived without taking life.

Saint John of Egypt

c.304 - 394 CE
March 27

Saint John desired nothing for himself. He lived in a tiny cave and received others who sought his spiritual guidance.

Saint John possessed the soul of a man with deep spiritual calling. He chose a life of contemplation and austerity as a desert hermit. A deep sense of inner peace and wisdom seemed to radiate from his presence. Because he was able to share this gift and help others gain inner peace in a life devoid of material possessions, many revered him as the Father of all Ascetics. John was born in the lower region of Egypt and was raised to be a carpenter. By the age of twenty-five, however, he recognized that his was a deeper, spiritual calling. He abandoned the materialistic world to study under a wise, religious sage who methodically trained him in the ways of obedience and self-surrender. John continued learning the sage's ways of peaceful obedience and humility until the death of this aged teacher, after which time John spent four to five years wandering and seeking understanding at various monasteries.[68]

When he felt his search for inner peace had been fulfilled, he retreated to an isolated site on the top of a steep hill. Once there, he carved out a cluster of three tiny cells within the rocks: one as a bedroom, the second as a workroom, and the third as a receiving room for others seeking his guidance. This third cell contained a tiny window through which he communicated with visitors seeking to grasp even a fragment of the essence of his spiritual wisdom. For five days each week, Saint John remained in seclusion, conversing only with God. It was on Saturdays and Sundays, however, when he spoke from his tiny cell to advise the many individuals hoping to gain from his wisdom and guidance.

His diet was one of extreme simplicity and one intended to fulfill a life of nonviolence. He consumed only dried fruits and vegetables, and those only in small quantities. In addition, he would not eat any foods that required cooking, and even avoided bread. Initially, John found this diet somewhat taxing upon his body. Yet once he had become accustomed to it, he acquired the ability to maintain his health on his plant-based diet—a diet upon which he lived from age forty until his death at ninety.[69]

Although he was not the founder of a religious community, those visitors seeking his wisdom had become so numerous that they formed large groups of dedicated disciples. These disciples, building upon the values they learned from Saint John, built a hospice to accommodate all who sought consolation. John became known as the Father of all Ascetics and was famous for his prophecies, miracles, and his ability to read the inner thoughts of his visitors.

The Emperor of Rome, Theodosius,[70] (364-395 C.E.), often visited John for spiritual consultation, and eventually had grown so impressed by the wisdom of this aged sage that he prohibited the practice of all pagan (non-Christian) activities within the Roman Empire. It was due to such actions that the Emperor became known as 'Theodosius the Great'. Saint John advised the Emperor on when to enter battle and when to avoid it, as well as when he might achieve victory and in which battles victory would be fraught with too much bloodshed for all involved. John even advised the Emperor as to when he would meet his death. The saint actually predicted the time of his own death and requested all to leave him alone so that he might be left to die on his knees at prayer.[71]

John was a man of great wisdom, compassion, and simplicity. He spent his life advising others and sharing his great gift of prophecy, yet never did he seek to achieve personal wealth or glory from these gifts. He chose to consume only the simplest of natural vegetation, recognizing that such a diet fulfilled all his physical needs and believing that this was the peaceful diet God intended for humankind.

Saint Thais

Fourth Century
October 8

After realizing her life of promiscuity had harmed others, Saint Thais discarded all her possessions and found peace within a monastery.

Saint Thais was a beautiful woman who lived in Alexandria,[72] Egypt. Although she was educated as a Christian, she worked as a woman of ill repute. Her beauty was considered exceptional. She became the cause of many furious contests between various rivals whose blood was lost as they lay at her door. During this time, an aged hermit, Paphnitus, who had been living in the desert, heard of this sad course of events. He decided to go to town to speak with Thais about the trail of deaths that followed her course of actions. When the old hermit first saw Thais' beauty, he trembled. Then he continued through with his mission and begged her to follow a path of living that would not endanger the lives of others.

Thais became filled with confusion concerning her previous actions and felt bitter sorrow that she had harmed others.

She threw herself at the sage's feet and asked what she might do to live correctly in the eyes of God. In remorse, she collected together all of her jewels, furniture, clothes, and gifts, and burnt them publicly in the street.[73] She decided to live in a monastery for women where she lived in a small cell eating only bread and water. While there, she spent her days in prayer. She asked God to grant her understanding and pleaded for His mercy.

One day, some monks living within the city witnessed a vision. In the vision, a place had been granted in heaven for a holy individual. At first, they thought the vision was of Saint Anthony, but then, realized it was of the humble penitent, Thais. As Thais had chosen a life of humble austerity, a life that was devoid of foods from animal flesh, free of material possessions, and filled with mercy toward others—her soul had become filled with grace. Thais' life was taken from her while she was still a young woman. She had attained the wisdom of one at peace with God and with all His creation, when her soul returned to the Lord.[74]

Saint Jonas the Gardener

Fourth Century
February 11

Saint Jonas realized that his fruit tree led students toward gluttony. He accepted loss of his tree to bring his students back to spiritual paths.

Saint Jonas lived and worked for eighty-five years as the simple and humble gardener of a small plot of fruit trees and shrubs in a monastery garden in Egypt. Although he grew and gathered fruits, including dates, figs, and grapes, he gave all of these to the monks and other guests. Never did he consume such rich foods himself. He existed on the most meager of diets—consuming only raw herbs and vinegar, and vowed that never would he consume the flesh of animals.

As time passed, an abundantly fruitful fig tree grew in the middle of the monastery garden. The young boys within the monastery often climbed the tree to partake of its fruits. When the senior monk came by to inspect the monastery, he felt that the tree was a source of gluttony and that it had become a temptation leading the youth astray from an ascetic life. So he asked Jonas to cut it down. Jonas felt greatly saddened to do so and did not follow his superior's orders. Within a few days, however, he found the tree withered and lifeless.

By this time, Jonas recognized that he had been given a holy message of the destruction that would follow one's living a life of excess and abundance. He learned that when one is led astray so as to no longer appreciate a life of simplicity and austerity, one will have lost more spiritually than one can ever gain materially.

Jonas was a peaceful, humble monk, who wanted nothing from the world but to serve others, to live in austerity, and to live a life of non-violence and peace.[75]

Saint Euphrasia

c. 380 - 410 CE
March 13

Saint Euphrasia possessed a spiritual soul. She joined the monastery at age seven as she felt a longing to live in communion with God.

Saint Euphrasia was born into a well-established Egyptian family. When she was barely one year of age, her father passed away. Her mother no longer wished to remain within the turmoil of the fast-paced city life. So taking Euphrasia she journeyed to live in a country estate owned by her family within the Egyptian desert. The estate was near a holy monastery in which one hundred and thirty nuns lived. These nuns never consumed any foods other than those grown in the soil—grains and herbs.

Euphrasia's mother followed the example of these holy women and decided to live according to their standards of religious dedication, sacrifice, and charity. By the time she had reached seven years of age, Euphrasia requested permission to serve God and to join the monastery. Her mother was overjoyed when she recognized the sense of religious serenity her daughter had attained and, with blessings, sent her to follow her calling and live in the monastery. Some time thereafter, Euphrasia's mother became seriously ill. Prior to her passing on, her last instructions to her daughter were: "Never think of what you have been, nor say to yourself that you are of royal extraction. Be humble and poor on earth, that you may be rich in heaven."[76]

After her mother's death, Euphrasia was petitioned to the emperor so that he might give her in marriage to a member of his royal court. Euphrasia wrote back that this was no longer possible as she had promised to dedicate her life to serving God. She also requested that the emperor distribute her family's estate among the poor, the orphans, and the church. Euphrasia lived the remainder of her years in humility, meekness, and charity. She resolved to live on a diet of grain and herbs as she felt that such a diet exemplified her vision of a life sharing God's mercy with all.

Saint Porphyry of Gaza

c. 353 - 420 CE
February 26

Saint Porphyry always helped others. Once when doing so, he received a vision of Jesus healing him. His own crippling deformities disappeared.

Saint Porphyry was born into a very wealthy family in Macedonia,[77] and at an early age showed signs of a spiritual yet compassionate character. By the time he was twenty-five years of age, he decided to leave the world and journey to a desert monastery to dedicate his life to the service of God. After five years in the monastery, he traveled to Jerusalem and commenced living in a small cave near the Jordan River. He had spent five years living in this desert cave when he suddenly became stricken with a crippling illness and was forced to leave the cave and return to Jerusalem. While there, with the use of a walking cane, he made daily visits to the holy places.[78]

Porphyry began to feel troubled that he had not yet disposed of his estate and that proceeds had not been distributed to the poor. He commissioned a close friend to complete these transactions, a job his friend fulfilled faithfully, subsequently returning with the proceeds. Porphyry distributed all these proceeds amongst the poor of Egypt and Palestine. After distributing them, he sensed a vision of Jesus healing him, and then his medical ailments totally resolved. Porphyry was able then to live a life of strenuous labor and to fully sustain himself on a diet of roots and coarse bread, adding small quantities of cheese and oil on holidays.[79]

When he reached forty years of age, the bishop of Jerusalem ordained him as a priest, and within three years, appointed him bishop of Gaza.[80] This appointment was conferred upon him against his will - as he did not desire to hold a position of such dignity. This appointment, however, was met with backlash. Later that year, a devastating drought swept the country, and the pagans ascribed it to Porphyry's arrival as the new Christian bishop.

The pagans accused Porphyry of causing the drought, so they captured him and locked him up. Another two months passed and still no rain fell. Then the Christians organized a procession to the church and, suddenly, the heavens opened up and rain poured down. The pagans freed the Christians and many converted to Christianity, destroying their prior pagan temples and idols during this conversion.[81] At the site upon which a pagan temple had previously stood, Porphyry began construction of a church—laying stones and mortar by himself. He lived to see many of the town's people baptized, to see the completion of the church, to spend his days serving the poor and giving them alms, and to spend the rest of his years as a man of peace—in labor, prayer, and personal sacrifice.

Saint Dorotheus the Theban

Fourth Century
June 5

Saint Dorotheus possessed such faith that even when seeing a snake in the well, he merely made a sign of the cross over his cup and kept drinking.

Saint Dorotheus was an exceptionally holy individual who joined a monastery to live and pray amongst the other monks of the Egyptian desert. He remained for several years in the religious community until he had acquired the skills necessary for one to live a hermitic life. Eventually, he felt the time was right to leave the monastery and live a contemplative, meditative life alone in the desert nine miles from Alexandria, Egypt. By this time, he recognized the value of hard, physical labor and chose to spend a good part of his life carrying stones to build hermitages for other hermits. His income was meager, only that earned by weaving baskets, and he used this to buy his daily rations of six ounces of bread and a few herbs—his sole nourishment.

Even when Dorotheus reached old age, he continued a life of strenuous work. He was dedicated to the welfare of the needy. He prayed for the infirm, and was a deeply religious man who contemplated God. Once when he saw a snake in a well from which he was about to take drinking water, he hesitated only slightly prior to dipping his cup. Then, making the sign of the cross over his cup, he swallowed the contents saying; "In the presence of the cross of Jesus, the devil loses his power."[82] Saint Dorotheus possessed complete faith in the love of God. He sought to live as a vegetarian so as to share God's compassionate, gentle mercy with all beings.

Saint Theodosius
the Cenobiarch

c. 423 - 529 CE
January 11

When the Emperor gave money to Saint Theodosius for safe keeping, Theoodosius answered a Higher calling. He distributed all the funds to the poor.

Saint Theodosius was born to religious parents in Cappadocia[83] and followed in their pious ways. Upon reaching adulthood, he sought to follow the examples of other holy individuals. He decided to leave his family to visit the Holy Lands and set out for Jerusalem. As he loved solitude, once there, he built a small cave in which to live amidst the rocks of a mountain range. This was the site where the three wise men were believed to have stopped on their way to Bethlehem. He spent the next thirty years there laboring with his hands, praying, fasting, and maintaining a plant-based diet of coarse grains and herbs. Many disciples were drawn to him and sought to serve God under his guidance. Never did he refuse to teach any sincere follower.[84]

Theodosius never ceased working for the welfare of others. He facilitated the building of a monastery that became a city of saints in the desert wilderness. Within the monastery, there were four churches annexed to the main one. Three accommodated individuals who spoke three different languages prevalent among those members of the Eastern, faith-seeking community at that time. The fourth was for those healing and recovering from illnesses they had inflicted upon themselves. The monastery also annexed several infirmaries, one for sick monks, two for sick lay people of neighboring villages, one for aged and feeble monks, and one for mentally ill persons. There were also several buildings to receive strangers.[85]

Emperor Anastasius[86] began to make frequent visits to Theodosius to seek advice concerning his personal goals. He sent Theodosius a considerable sum of money, ostensibly for charitable use, but in reality, seeking only to benefit from the monk's wisdom for personal gains. Theodosius accepted the money, but then distributed it to the poor. When the Emperor requested Theodosius' assistance in certain less then honorable matters, Theodosius refused. In retaliation, the Emperor, though stating he admired Theodosius' courage and strength of reasoning still sent troops over all of Egypt to capture the aged holy man and have him executed.

Theodosius traveled widely over the deserts of Egypt and Palestine to elude the troops, but was eventually captured and imprisoned. Fortunately, the Emperor met his final days, and was succeeded by an honorable common soldier named Justin. Justin was a Catholic. After Theodosius had been forced into eleven years of wandering to escape death, as well as years of imprisonment, Justin lifted the edict against him.[87]

In spite of all of these challenges, Theodosius never wavered from his compassion for all beings, man or beast, or from his love of simplicity and austerity. He found solace in living among the simple beauty of nature and his humble, peaceful life in the desert.

Saint Sabas

c. 439-532 CE
December 8

After falling upon an abandoned ancient cave-temple, Saint Sabas converted it into a church. From there, he shared spiritual teachings with a multitude of seekers.

Saint Sabas was born near Caesarea,[88] Palestine the son of an army officer. When his father was sent to war in Alexandria, he took his wife with him, leaving Sabas with relatives. These relatives treated him very harshly. He also became quite disillusioned when his two uncles became involved in a lawsuit over his family's property. By the time Sabas was eight years of age, he ran away to live in a monastery. Several years passed and his uncles eventually agreed to take him out of the monastery and restore his property to him. Having felt the harshness of the world, however, and preferring the peace of the monastery, Sabas felt his heart had grown united with God and he chose to remain in the monastery.[89]

Sabas spent his monastery days in prayer and manual labor, his free time helping the less fortunate, and his favorite time in silent prayer within the chapel. By the age of thirty, the monks granted him leave to live in contemplation in a cavern. Sabas left his isolated cave only on the Sabbath, joining the others at the monastery. Upon reaching forty years of age, he retired totally to remain in the cavern. He chose to live on a purely vegetarian diet of wild herbs and water from a brook.

Eventually, the local people began to bring him simple offerings of bread, cheese and dates.[90] As he grew in wisdom and sensitivity, his followers increased in great number, reaching one hundred and fifty men. He came upon an ancient sculptured cave-temple and converted it into a church. In the towns adjacent to his monastery, Sabas built hospitals for the infirm of Jerusalem and Jericho.

Sabas was a man devoid of personal vanity. With the passage of time, forty of his disciples decided to leave him to start a new community. Although they left him, word had gotten back to him that they were in very poor financial straights. So he immediately rushed to their aid. He did not rebuke them but helped them build a church. After he obtained funds for them to purchase the land, he also gave them food and money to sustain their new community.[91]

Towards the end of his life, the Emperor Justinian received Sabas with honors and offered to endow his monasteries. Saint Sabas replied, however, that he had no need for endowments and his followers had all they needed as long as they served God. Shortly after that trip, he became ill and asked to be brought back to his cave. It was at the age of ninety-three that he departed this world.[92] Rather than living a life of excess consumption or one of worldly possessions, Saint Sabas preferred a life of simplicity and unity with God. He shared his energy with all—building hospitals, developing churches, and spreading his spiritual wisdom. His choice to live a life devoid of animal flesh was consistent with that of a man who sought to live sharing God's mercy with all.

Saint Fulgentius of Ruspe

c. 468-533 CE
January 1

Although others felt Saint Fulgentius could not endure the difficult life of a monk in Africa, he did so with strength that he said came from God.

Saint Fabius Fulgentius was born to a noble family in Carthage, Africa[93] in a region that had been separated from the Roman Empire by the Barbarians[94] for thirty years. Although his mother, Marina, had become widowed at a young age, she taught him Greek and Latin, as well as how to run the family business. At a very young age, however, he tired of worldly possessions. When he was only twenty-two, he applied to enter a monastery. The Arian king[95] had driven most of the orthodox bishops from the monasteries. Fulgentius felt a calling to fill one of these roles. When others felt he was too frail to manage the harsh life within the monastery, he said: "He who hath inspired me with the will to serve him, can also furnish me with courage and strength."[96]

He lived in the monastery until fresh persecutions forced him to leave. So he returned to the life of a hermit to live in a small cave on the side of a mountain. There he lived a simple non-assuming life, sometimes going barefoot, and always eating only vegetarian foods of grains and herbs, sometimes mixed with oil. His modesty, meekness, and humility won him the affections of all. When the sick for whom he prayed had recovered, he ascribed the results totally to divine mercy stating: "We ought to receive all things as from the hand of God, with resignation and gratitude."[97]

Fulgentius wrote entire treatises for the instruction of the faithful in Africa, and was finally granted permission to return there. His preaching was so filled with compassion and love that many were brought to tears in recognizing that they had met such a dedicated man. The example he set by his austere, non-violent, and holy life, was a model of humility and compassion of one steeped in the holiness of God.[98]

Saint Gerasimus

c. 405 - 475 CE
March 5

Saint Gerasimus felt love for all beings. After he removed a thorn from the paw of a lion, the lion became his life long companion.

Saint Gerasimus was a native of Asia Minor,[99] where he had chosen a sparse, spiritual life before beginning a journey to Palestine. He traveled through the desert and while on this journey, met many other monks with whom he shared wisdom and knowledge. Then he set the destination for his journey as Jericho.[100] After hearing his spiritual teachings, numerous others sought to remain with him to learn from his teachings. To accommodate the many who followed him, he created small rock cells in caves for seventy contemplative holy individuals aspiring to learn from his eremitic life. His needs were of the simplest in nature, his possessions naught, and his food merely bread, dates, and water. He rarely even partook of cooked foods.[101]

Legend exists that Saint Gerasimus removed a thorn from the paw of an injured and suffering lion, then cleansed and bandaged its injured paw. The lion became a faithful friend to the elderly monk, and when the monk died, the lion's grief was inconsolable. The animal stretched himself over Saint Gerasimus' tombstone and was found dead upon the old man's grave several days later. Whether or not the story is literally true is secondary to the fact that the saint was known for his compassionate nature to all creatures, and for the fact that he never treated any human or beast unkindly.[102] Saint Gerasimus' choice to live as a vegetarian was consistent with his love for all God's creatures and for his passion to share God's message of mercy with all.

Saint Mary of Egypt

Fifth Century
April 2

Saint Mary traveled to an isolated region on the banks of the Jordan River to live a life of prayer and meditation.

Saint Mary was a saint of great popularity in both the East and the West. Legend has it that she was Egyptian by birth and ran away at the age of twelve for a life of pleasure and freedom in Alexandria. She survived as a woman of the streets engaged in prostitution for several years until one day she joined a party of travelers on a journey to Jerusalem for a religious pilgrimage. When she reached Jerusalem and attempted to enter the Church, an invisible force held her back from worshiping with the others. She realized this had occurred as a spiritual message concerning her prior poor life choices, and she was overcome with a sense of remorse.

She fell before an icon of the Holy Virgin Mother, vowed to renounce her prior life, and began a new path living in the image of God. After seeing the cross of Jesus, a distant voice advised her to, "Pass over the Jordan,[103] and thou wilt find rest."[104]

That night, she slept on the ground, took a few loaves of bread, and prepared to take a ferry to the desert on the far side of the Jordan River. She spent her next forty-seven years in the wilderness, in contemplative solitude away from other humans. During these years, she did not harm any other creatures and lived solely on herbs and wild dates.[105]

After Mary had spent many years in solitude, a priest wandering in the broad forest caught a glimpse of her unclothed body, blackened and burned by the fiery sun. He covered her with his cloak and prostrated himself on the ground before her. She communicated the story of inner conversion to him and asked him to return the next year. He did return with communion so she might receive the Body of the Lord. She received It and returned to the desert to continue her life of solitude, peace, and austerity. The following year, the priest returned again, only to find that Mary had passed away. He found her writings in the sand asking him to offer prayers for her to the Lord.[106]

Saint Mary, though led astray early in her life, found God in a life of peace and simplicity. She preferred to live the simplest of lives and to exist on the most humble of vegetarian diets—sharing God's abundance and forgiveness with all.

Saint Dositheus

c. 455 - 530 CE
February 23

Saint Dositheus was of such
gentle nature that others
teased him that he would
follow the way of the monks.
And he did.

Saint Dositheus was raised among soldiers as the ward of an officer. He grew up without any concept of religion until one day, upon hearing a conversation about Jerusalem, he felt a calling to go there. He was granted permission to journey to the Holy Lands and went to Gethsemane where he saw a painting of souls lost in the flames of hell. He listened to others talk about spiritual values and felt his interests suddenly aroused—particularly after he learned the values of right and wrong, and of truths he had never before contemplated. This awakening created such a deep impression upon him that he began to pray for wisdom. He decided to live the rest of his life refraining from taking the life from any being, as well as from consumption of animal flesh.

Others teased him that he would follow in the ways of the monks. Rather than shrinking from such criticism, Dositheus decided to seek out a community of monks and learn from their wisdom. He set out on his mission to find such a monastery. Once there, the monks observed his earnestness, and took him in as a disciple. He learned to live in simplicity and modesty. His superiors taught him: "Learn to eat sufficiently to satisfy thy need, but never devour food in excess of what is necessary." He learned to serve those infirm in the hospital, to diligently study the Holy Scriptures, and to accept with grace all God had chosen to offer him.

When his health began to fail and he began to exhibit signs of tuberculosis, he prayed for his health with unswerving faith. Because he felt such inner peace at having found God, Saint Dositheus lived his remaining few years on a humble non-violent diet, resolving to avoid causing harm to any living creature. His remaining years were filled with peace and tranquility, but the disease took its course and overcame his frail body. After his passing, others saw visions of him resting in peace and sanctity.[107]

Saint Abraham Kidunaja

Sixth Century
March 16

Saint Abraham built a Church in the middle of a hostile desert settlement. He was stoned and left for dead, yet managed to survive to continue his work

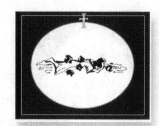

Saint Abraham was born near Edessa in Mesopotamia to a wealthy family. Though he felt called to join the Church, his parents insisted that he marry. After marrying, he felt an even stronger calling to lead a life of prayer and contemplation, and left all his earthly possessions to live as a recluse in the desert. For twelve years, Abraham lived in a tiny cell on a mountainside consuming only bread and water, and living without material possessions. After the death of his parents, he entrusted their property to be used to relieve the suffering of the poor.[108]

With some of the inheritance, Abraham built a Christian church in the midst of a desert settlement. He tried to turn people from pagan ways, and because of this was actually stoned in the streets and left for dead. Upon recovering consciousness, he returned to the town, and although sometimes attacked with sticks and stones, he continued to preach and teach for three years.

Finally, the tide turned, and the saint's meekness and patience convinced the people that he was indeed a holy man. He baptized one thousand individuals! Feeling fulfilled, yet frightened, that he was becoming too involved in the material world, he left the workings of the church to others, returning silently to live in the desert once again.[109] He was not destined to remain solitary for long, however, as others sought out his counsel and wisdom, and found him.

While in the desert, his seven-year-old niece, Mary, was brought to him after the death of her parents. At the age of twenty, Mary was seduced by a false monk who came in the pretense of studying under Abraham. She left with the man and was brought down to the level of a common prostitute in the city. For two years, Abraham cried and prayed daily. Finally he found her and brought her back to the holy life in the desert where God bestowed upon her the gift of healing and the ability to work miracles.[110]

Abraham's life was one of quiet contemplation and prayer, of healing words, and of adhering to a non-violent and possession-free lifestyle. He felt compassion for all and remained unceasingly reverent to God.

Saint John
the Silent

c. 454 - 558 CE
May 13

Saint John spent his years in silence. He felt at peace with God and no longer felt the need to communicate with man.

Saint John earned the name, Saint John the Silent, because of his love of silence and contemplation. He was born in Armenia[111] into a famous and respected family. After the death of his parents, he used his inheritance to build a monastery and a church in honor of Mary. He was personally devoted to prayer and asceticism. John's brother-in-law was the governor of Armenia and while in this position, he oppressed the church so cruelly that John decided to journey to Constantinople to seek support to reconcile the situation. He was successful in his discussions and, when this chore was completed, he felt peace and fulfillment. Thereafter, he longed to return again to a secluded life. Hence, he began a journey to Jerusalem.

He was thirty-eight years old at the time, and worked for Saint Sabas carrying stones and fetching water to help build a new hospital. He appreciated the opportunity to perform difficult, yet silent, work and always remained smiling and cheerful. His superiors felt that he was on a path to attain perfect contemplation and allowed him to occupy a separate hermitage. He spent six years conversing only with God, and sustaining his health on a diet of vegetation, consuming only wild roots and herbs.

His experience had taught him that "a soul accustomed to speak to God alone finds only bitterness and emptiness in all worldly intercourse."[112] When he reached old age, fame of his sanctity spread and many sought his advice. He was known to possess the ability to exorcize negative spirits from people and to lead others to God. He was a humble contemplative man of simple needs who sought to share peace with all beings—human and animal. He fulfilled his life's mission of living in God's service.

Saint Theodore of Sykeon

c. 545 - 613 CE
April 22

Saint Theodore was blessed with the ability to heal others. He healed the emperor's son of a skin disease believed to have been leprosy.

Saint Theodore was born in Asia Minor, the son of a prostitute. His mother, along with her aunt, ran an inn and a house of prostitution. By chance, a very devout holy man came to work at the inn as a cook. He took young Theodore under his wing and began to bring him to church and taught him how to pray and fast. This fortuitous situation imbued Theodore with a sense of spirituality and a desire to retreat and live alone to gain higher levels of inner wisdom. He decided to leave home to become a hermit, living in a cave attached to a chapel. While there, he was able to live in austerity and contemplation. Vegetables were his only sustenance and he would not partake of any foods if taking such meals involved the harming of animals or the consumption of animal flesh.[113]

Numerous visitors were attracted to him because of his reputation for holiness, and for his reputed ability of prophecy, of performing miracles, and of exorcising evil spirits. He journeyed to visit the Holy Lands after a long drought and, because abundant rainfall suddenly began to fall following his prayers, he was praised for his holiness. Theodore was also reputed to have foretold the ruler of Tiberius[114] of his victories in battle with the Persians and to have cured Emperor Constantine's[115] son of a skin disease, believed to have been leprosy.[116]

Although Theodore founded several monasteries and served as head of an abbey, his heart longed for the simplicity of life amidst the monks of the desert. In his old age, he was permitted to return to this humble, vegetarian, peaceful life in the desert and immerse himself totally in a life of prayer and praise of God.[117]

Chapter 4
Western Monastic and Hermitic Saints

Thurston and Attwater, well-respected and knowledgeable hagiographers, described the qualities of those religious people who lived as Christian hermits or monks as those who shunned superfluous amusements, frivolous praise from others, and idleness. They describe the benefits one gained from living such a life thus:

> Solitude and silence settle and compose
> the thoughts; the mind
> augments its strength and vigor by rest,
> and in this state of serenity
> is more fit to reflect upon itself and its
> needs and to contemplate
> the mysteries of divine grace and love,
> the joys of heaven and the
> grounds of our hope.

Those living in monasteries, or as religious hermits, devoted a great deal of their time to public and private prayer, self-reflection, self-criticism, meditation, and spiritual growth. These holy monks recognized that people do not find God in any special place, but rather right within the silence of their own heart.

> This solitude must be chiefly interior,
> that of the mind still more than
> the place, by disengaging ourselves from
> care and from business and
> from all those things and thoughts
> that disturb us, or which breed self-
> importance and vexation. If we do not
> cut off these things when in
> retirement we shall be more persecuted
> with distractions and the noise
> and cravings of our passions than in the
> midst of an active and busy life.[1]

During those bygone eras, an enormous number of holy monastic and hermitic individuals populated vast regions of the dry lands, swamps, forests, and mountain peaks of the entire continent of Europe. These individuals could not be included under the umbrella term Desert Fathers principally because the topography of Europe did not conform to that of a desert. Yet their lifestyles were extremely similar to those of the Desert Fathers in terms of their religious orientations. They spent their years renouncing the materialism of the world, and in replacing such worldly pursuits with dedicated prayer and contemplative meditation. They found fulfill- ment in lives of solitude, austerity, self-sacrifice, meditation, love of humanity, concern for all beings, and continual prayer for God's blessings. Excerpts from the lives of the European monastic and hermitic vegetarian saints described in the following passages will shed understanding concerning the wisdom embodied within their holy lives.

Saint Lupus of Troyes

c. 393-479 CE
July 29

Saint Lupus, as a man of peace, was able to appease the aggressive nature of Attila the Hun. He taught Attila that one is nothing but what God gifts one to be.

Saint Lupus was born into a well-established French family in Gaul.[2] He was educated in the finest schools and was trained to be eloquent in speech. Having attained such skills, he became an attorney. He married a sister of Saint Hilary of Arles,[3] but after six or seven years of marriage, the couple parted as mutual friends, with his joining a monastery and her becoming a nun.

Lupus renounced possession of all his goods and sold the greater part of his estate to benefit the poor.[4] He joined the priesthood and chose to live in the simplest of monasteries. During his later years, he was appointed as bishop of Troyes.[5] Over the entire fifty years during which he held this position, he continued to live an austere life dressing simply, fasting often, and spending untold hours in prayer. Although he fasted frequently, it was particularly during times of prayer that he lived on no more than barley and bread. Never did he swerve from his decision to avoid consumption of animal flesh.

When Attila the Hun[6] overran the country causing massive calamities, Lupus prayed fervently to God, even lying prostrate on the ground, for many days. Finally, he went to meet Attila himself, followed by a procession of his fellow clergy carrying a cross. Lupus said to Attila: "Let us respect whatever comes to us from God...remember you are to do nothing but what that almighty hand which governs and moves you permits."[7] Attila was struck with these words and promised to spare the city of Troyes, so long as Lupus accompanied him on some of his invasions. This was because he wanted the holy man present at his side.

Upon Lupus' return, although it had been his actions that saved the city of Troyes, the government forced him to spend two years in exile for accompanying Attila. Eventually, he was permitted to return to his beloved hermitage and live his remaining years in peaceful prayer.[8]

Saint Lupicinus

c. 415 - 480 CE
February 28

Saint Lupicinus lived, worked, and prayed in the solitude of the forest with his brother. They modeled their lives after the Christian Desert Fathers.

Saint Lupicinus longed to join his brother, Saint Romanus, in the solitude of the forest as a prayerful religious hermit. The two brothers found companionship with one another and thenceforth lived many years in the forests of the Jura Mountains between Switzerland and France. While there, Lupicinus spent his days studying, praying, analyzing the mysteries of life, and continually growing closer to God.

Both brothers believed it essential that they perform strenuous manual labor, so they worked diligently to till and cultivate the soil. With time, other spiritually oriented individuals came to join them and together they built a monastery.

They sought to imitate the austerities of the Desert Fathers so as to gain wisdom through contemplation and meditation, and to achieve communion with God. They adapted to the difficulties of harsh environmental conditions in the mountains of Europe with both enthusiasm and determination. Of critical importance to them, however, was their commitment never to consume the flesh of any animal, and that they only acquiesce to consumption of eggs and milk when very ill.

They lived in this solitary peaceful setting for the remainder of their lives, with Lupicinus outliving his brother by twenty years. He was revered for his dedication to his faith, his compassion toward his fellow man, and his concern for the life in all beings.[9]

Saint Romanus

c. 420 - 460 CE
February 28

After Saint Romanus healed
two lepers, multitudes flocked
to him to gain from his gifts
of healing and wisdom.

When Saint Romanus reached thirty-five years of age, he sensed the need to withdraw from society to the forest of the Jura Mountains—a region between Switzerland and France. He journeyed to live there as a hermit, bringing writings on the lives of the Desert Fathers with him to accomplish this goal. He discovered the perfect site—an uninhabited stretch between a steep overhang and a complicated, difficult access.

Carrying some seeds and a few tools, he proceeded to build the community that would later be known as the monastery at Condat. While in this isolated region, he followed a life of hard work, prayer, and contemplation, and maintained a diet that was devoid of all animal flesh. A growing number of individuals came to join him, including his brother Saint Lupicinus.[10]

There were also women who wished to live similar lives, so Romanus started a convent in a nearby city to accommodate these faithful female followers. After he successfully healed many inflicted with diseases, including two lepers on the road to Saint-Maurice, news of his healing capabilities spread far and wide. Actually, news spread all the way to Geneva and masses flocked to gain from his wisdom and his miracles of healing. Romanus died twenty years before his brother and was buried, as he had wished, in the cemetery of his sister's convent.[11] His belief in living an austere, humble, non-violent and religious life was continued after his passing by his numerous faithful followers.

Saint Gundelinis

c. 480 - 530 CE
March 28

After hearing the Lord,
Saint Gundelinis and his wife
left the materialistic world
to follow lives of service.

Saint Gundelinis, otherwise known as Saint Gwynllyw, has been honored as a saint throughout Wales. He was the eldest son of a royal chieftain. After his father's death, Saint Gundelinis divided the inheritance among his six brothers. It was said that while he was young, he lived a reckless life, kidnapping his wife and becoming enamored with trivial worldly possessions.

This changed when his wife, Gladusa, and he witnessed the presence of a spiritual voice stating: "I will show you the way you must walk to obtain God's inheritance. Lift up your hearts and do not imperil your souls by what is perishable."[12] Both Gundelinis and his wife left their home, built separate small hermitage cells in caves on the side of a river, and gave their lives over to prayer, mortification, and labor.[13]

They lived eating only those foods that could be obtained without aggression, predominantly barley-bread and water, and wore only sackcloth. Their lives were filled with prayer and contemplation, as well as with reverence for all creation. After their deaths, many miracles of healing were said to have occurred at the site of their tombs.[14] Both Gundelinis and Gladusa remain examples of dedicated holy individuals who sought to live in simplicity and in harmony with all of nature, and who believed strongly that one must live without inflicting harm upon other beings.

Saint Liphardus

Saint Liphardus
c. 477 - 550 CE
June 3

Although Saint Liphardus
had become the highest-
ranking judge in the country,
he gave up all
to become a monk.

Saint Liphardus had been a lawyer with an impeccable reputation for honesty and integrity.[15] He had risen to one of the highest judicial posts when he decided to leave secular life, as well as all of his worldly possessions, to live the hermitic life of a holy sage. He retired to live as a hermit in the ruins of an old castle and built himself a hut amidst the ruins. He lived an extraordinarily simple, austere, and contemplative life, and consumed only foods obtained from the soil and streams—barley bread and water.[16]

Soon others came to join him and as this group grew in numbers, they formed a small community of prayerful contemplative monks. Eventually, a flourishing religious community developed at this site. Liphardus organized the building of a monastery to accommodate the large numbers of individuals seeking to learn from his ways.

Through all his years of guiding others, he never wavered from living a humble contemplative life, and never held back sharing his knowledge with all who sought his wisdom. He died at the age of seventy-three and after his passing, his community built a church in the town of Meung-sur-Loire.[17, 18] Saint Liphardus is remembered for his simplicity, honesty, and love for all beings. His humble lifestyle and diet attest to the merciful nature of his soul.

Saint Maurus
of Glanfeuil

c. 519 - 584 CE
January 15

Saint Maurus was a man of such faith, that when he rushed to save a boy drowning in a well, witnesses saw him walk on the water.

When Saint Maurus was just a young boy of twelve, he was given to the holy patriarch, Saint Benedict, to be raised and educated. While there, he proved to be a particularly spiritual and devout youth. When Benedict was entrusted with the responsibility of directing the formation of a new colony of pious monks to live in the tradition of the cenobites, he felt Maurus was the person to head such a mission.

Maurus accepted this challenge and began to form and spread the traditions of his ascetic and devout religious sect. He followed the holy rules with reverence and respect, and led his followers on paths of simplicity and austerity. He consumed only foods of vegetarian origin, predominantly bread, and dedicated himself to the devotion of God and all His creation.[19]

His religious pursuits had reached such high levels of spirituality and devotion that he thought nothing of losing his own life to save a boy who had fallen into a well. Witnesses said that when Saint Maurus saved the child, he actually walked on the water, thus permitting him to preserve the lives of both the drowning boy and himself. Although this tale may have grown from an act into a legend, its message reflects the high level of compassion and sacrifice of this devout monk.[20] Maurus' striving to live in total austerity, to sustain his life without causing harm to any other being, and to sacrifice his own life for the life of another attests to the holy nature of this humble vegetarian saint.

Saint Urbicius

Sixth Century
June 3

Feeling a religious calling, Saint Urbicius joined an aged Christian sage, Saint Liphardus, in an abandoned castle to learn from his wisdom.

A paucity of information exists concerning the humble, austere, and vegetarian life of Saint Urbicius. What is known is that he set out on a journey to become a companion and disciple of Saint Liphardus in barren, forsaken lands outside an old castle near the Loire River[21] in France. Together, they lived within the ruins, eventually building the most meager of huts so they might safely live as far away from the temptations of the materialistic world as possible. They believed that to attain higher levels of contemplative and spiritual thoughts, one must remove oneself, physically and mentally, from the material pulls of the world.[22]

Upon recognizing their dedication and holiness, such a large group of dedicated followers gravitated toward them, that they filled an entire monastery. This newly formed community began to thrive. Initially, Liphardus was appointed abbot. But as he approached the time of his death, he appointed Urbicius as his successor.

The monks lived both physically strenuous and austere lives, yet were blessed with spiritual fulfillment. Never would they consume the flesh of animals, existing, rather, on bread and water. Never would they withhold mercy and kindness from anyone they met, even those who were initially antagonistic toward them. Their community flourished, filled with the belief that a life spent sharing compassion and mercy with all beings was a life embodying the holiness of God.[23]

Saint Senoch

c. 520 - 579 CE
October 24

Saint Senoch was so touched
by the needs of society that
when he received payments
for guiding others, he used
all to free slaves.

Saint Senoch was born to pagan parents in Tours, France.[24] During his younger years, he had been converted to Christianity and had decided to leave his home with the intention of becoming a religious hermit. He journeyed to a small village and settled in some old ruins that were said to have been the remains of a monastery. Using some of the dismantled stones, he built two small cells—one for his quarters and another for a chapel.

Eventually, others came to join Senoch as disciples. He preferred, however, to spend most of his time as a recluse within his own cell. He existed on the most meager of vegetarian diets including barley-bread and water, always went barefoot, and performed manual labor daily to earn his keep.

When people from the surrounding villages heard of this wise contemplative saint, they came seeking his advice and guidance. He helped all in need. When villagers offered him reimbursement for his services, he accepted these so he could pay for the release of slaves and to aid other needy people. Often when Senoch was traveling, large masses would gather around to hear his teachings. His friend and contemporary, Saint Gregory, advised him that such accolades would lead him on a path of vanity and would detract from his spiritual growth. Senoch heeded Gregory's words and humbly recognized that although his gifts may have come through him, they were not of him. He took great solace in accepting the blessings of simplicity, including the peace of a life of poverty and compassion.[25]

Saint Hospitius

c. 530 - 581 CE
May 21

When invaders attacked the city, Saint Hospitius prayed for peace. As an invader lifted his sword to strike him, the attacker's arms froze in the air.

Only tiny fragments of information have been gathered and recorded concerning the life of Saint Hospitius (also known as Saint Hospice). These have it that he resided in an old tower during the latter part of the sixth century. The Tower was located on a narrow strip of land jutting out from a peninsula between Villefranche[26] and Beaulieu. He chose to live a physically strenuous life. He bore heavy burdens in his daily workload, yet subsisted on a small pittance of bread and dates. For all of his physical poverty, however, he was exceedingly rich in spirit. He was endowed with the gifts of both prophecy and miracles.

Because he was able to predict that people called the Lombards were going to attack the city, the citizens of his region were able to flee prior to the invasion. Hence the lives of many were saved. During the war, other monks at a nearby monastery were only concerned about saving themselves and left Hospitius alone to incur the wrath of invading forces. Hospitius assured them this would not occur, as he had experienced a vision showing otherwise. When the enemy forces invaded, one soldier raised his sword to strike the wise old sage. But the attacker's arms remained raised, powerless and unable to either strike or return to his side.

The saint was a man of peace and non-violence, who was able through his cautious thought and visionary gifts to save the lives of numerous people.[27] He chose to live as a vegetarian, as a man of strenuous physical labor, and as a man giving all he could, while taking as little as possible in return. His dedication to non-violence and mercy pervaded his gentle demeanor and were valued by all whose lives he touched.

Saint Winwaloe

Sixth Century
March 3

Although others around him consumed meat, Saint Winwaloe would never touch it saying that the spirit of prayer would sustain him.

sionally ate cheeses and shellfish, Winwaloe would never touch these.[29] He believed wholeheartedly that the spirit of prayer was all one needed to sustain one's soul, and one's soul was able to sustain one's mortal body.

Saint Winwaloe's father was a relative of the Prince of Wales.[28] He promised to consecrate the life of Winwaloe, his youngest son, to God and because of this, gave him to be raised by an Irish monk at the monastery on Green Island. The monastery contained a school for youth. While there, Winwaloe showed such piety and such aptitude for learning that he was soon appointed superior over the other students.

As he grew spiritually, Winwaloe valued a life of austerity and poverty. Shortly after he left his father's home, he began to wear coarse clothes, consumed a simple vegetarian diet of barley bread, boiled herbs and roots, and drank only water. Although the other monks occa-

After completing rigorous spiritual training in prayer, contemplation, and sacrifice for others, Winwaloe journeyed with several other monks to a small monastery. The group was exceptionally devout. When others learned of the group's devotion, the group began to grow, and Winwaloe was chosen to preside over the entire community. His years passed in daily prayer and study. Upon learning he was going to die, he called the others together to share his blessings: "Seek not for peace here, so that you may enjoy peace and tranquility in heaven."[30] He passed on with the same aura of tranquility that had pervaded the entirety of his humble peace loving life.

Saint Kertigan

c. 516 - 601 CE
January 13

When the king threw Saint Kertigan's mother, a young pregnant princess, down a cliff, a wise holy sage found her. He raised both Kertigan and his mother.

Saint Kertigan was said to have been the illegitimate son of Themin, the daughter of the King of Picts,[31] and Eugenius, King of the Scots.[32] When the King of Picts learned that his daughter was pregnant and about to become a mother, he ordered her thrown down a cliff. By God's mercy, she was not injured, and was found by an old hermit who took her into his care. Both Themin and her son grew up under the care and safety of the holy man, who instructed them in the faith of Jesus. Over the years, they became very dear to the hermit and the holy man's other students had become envious of Kertigan. They began to ridicule him and cause him pain he could no longer endure.

Hence, while still a young man, Kertigan ran away to start a new life far from this abuse. The old master pleaded with him to return, but he replied, "It cannot be, my father; return and admonish the disciples, and instruct them in thine example. I must go where the Lord God calls me."[33] Kertigan settled near Glasgow[34] and inhabited a cave there. He converted many people and was eventually declared bishop of Glasgow. In spite of these honors, Kertigan still chose to live within a tiny cell, to use a stone for a pillow, to subject his body to hardships, and to live on a vegetarian diet of bread, cheese and milk.[35]

There was much political instability in the country at this time and as successive petty feuds overthrew governing bodies, Kertigan was driven into exile. He made his way to Wales[36] and eventually to Ireland, where he was consecrated bishop. He is recognized as the first bishop of Glasgow, Scotland,[37] as a man who performed many miracles, and as a humble man dedicated to a life of peaceful, merciful living.

Saint Fintan

c. 520 - 603 CE
February 17

Saint Fintan dreamed he
would create what would
become a famous
monastery and laid the
foundations for it himself.

Saint Fintan was brought up in a life of
piety in the town of Leister, Ireland. During
his youth, he was taught great respect for
spiritual teachings by a wise, holy sage who
helped to raise and guide him. Upon reaching adulthood, he felt drawn toward a religious life and eventually founded a famous
monastery that drew many others to the
faith over the ensuing years. Many disciples
joined him in the hope of learning from his
wise teachings.

The rules he set for himself and his
monks were wise and compassionate. They
were to refrain from consuming all kinds of
meat, butter and milk, and to live solely
upon the vegetation of the land.
All were to perform strenuous
manual labor in the fields and to
till the soil with their own
hands.[38]

Although Fintan was
remembered for many miracles,
some believe tales of these miracles may have evolved as mere legendary
symbols of his many acts of kindness and
mercy, rather than as historically accu-
rate events. Yet it is known that so many
disciples gathered around him to learn
from his wisdom that it was stated,
"There is no room to enumerate them by
reason of their multitude."[39] Fintan was
best known for his humility, kindness,
and wisdom concerning the value of
living free of wants or possessions. He
sought to live a life of austerity, compassion, and peace, seeking to give more to
creation than his humble existence
required taking.

Saint Molua

c. 540 - 608 CE
August 4

Saint Molua was a man with compassion for all beings. He never hurt, frightened, or killed an animal in his life. It was said that when he died, the birds wept.

Saint Molua was born to a family from Limerick, Irelend[40] and during his youth he worked as a herder. Over time, the town's people perceived that miracles seemed to occur when they invoked his name. Because so many sensed that Molua was a spiritually gifted individual, he was sent to study and gain wisdom under the direction of a wise monk in Wales.

After completing his studies, he was ordained a priest and sent to numerous sites to found monasteries. The rules he laid down for his monasteries were strict, yet holy. Molua went to Rome to meet the pope, Saint Gregory the Great, who praised his set of rules stating, "The holy man who drew up this rule has laid a hedge round his family which reaches to Heaven."[41]

It has been written that Saint Molua followed a diet totally devoid of flesh, never killed an animal during his entire life, and that the birds wept when he died. He was a man of peace, and believed in the power of prayer and strenuous work. He urged his monks to cultivate their lands industriously as he felt that with hard work, self-sufficiency would follow and religious understanding would find the soil in which to flourish. His wish for peace reflected his dream that all people have "sufficient food, drink, and clothing. For where there is sufficiency there is stability. Where there is stability, there is true religion. And in the end true religion is everlasting life."[42] Such teachings exemplify his hope that spiritual wisdom be shared with all humans, and compassion with all God's creatures.

Saint Amatus

c. 568 - 630 CE
September 13

Saint Amatus lived in an isolated cave at the edge of a cliff. He gave all that he possessed to the poor and found peace amidst the simple gifts of nature.

Saint Amatus was born into a noble family in Rome. When still a child, his father sent him to a monastery at a precipitous cliff overlooking the Rhone River. He lived thirty years either within the abbey or in an isolated cell on the side of this cliff. He used a small patch of land to supply him with his only source of food, that being water from a tiny spring and barley grown on a thin strip of land. He chose always to go barefoot and to grind the barley with a millstone, as had the slaves of centuries prior.

Amatus was known to have been a man who labored hard, was eloquent of speech, and was gentle in his actions toward others. His noble and serene mannerisms won the hearts of all[43] and he was nominated by other monks to bring the word of God to the cities of Austria. While dining with a nobleman there, Amatus was asked how one achieves eternal life. He replied, "Sell what you have and give the money to the poor, then come and follow me."[44] Taking his words seriously, the nobleman freed his serfs, gave away his goods and his estate to the Church and to the poor. Then he joined the monastery.

Amatus and his fellow monks built a church, seven chapels, and a female monastery in France. In his later years, however, he longed for the solitude of his prior life of contemplation and prayer as a hermit, and built a tiny isolated cell amidst the rocks. Once there, he gave simple religious teachings to a group of monastic nuns who, otherwise, had no means of receiving these. Amatus maintained a meager vegetarian diet of bread and vegetables—sustenance that others dropped down to him by rope over a rocky edge of the cliff.

Saint Guthlac

c. 635 - 714 CE
April 12

Saint Guthlac felt such love for all beings that fish would swim to him and birds would eat from his hand.

Although as a child Saint Guthlac grew up in innocent and pure surroundings, his personality changed drastically as he grew into manhood. During that time, he and his companions engaged in hostile raids during which they wreaked grudges on their enemies, burned cities, raided farms, and ravaged both the goods and the lives of other men.

After living nine years of such a wild lifestyle, Guthlac suddenly awoke one night with a vision telling him that God would spare his life, if he became His servant. Guthlac reflected back upon his wild and destructive life, as well as upon his unnecessary wealth, with contempt. He decided to abandon all material possessions to live as a monk. Leaving his prior life, he embarked upon a spiritually enriched life of prayer, contemplation, and meditation. He developed into a man of wisdom, humility, and patience. With time, he began to long for a life in the wilderness and within a hermitage.[45]

He left the monastery and erected a hermitage on an isolated island, sustaining himself on a diet of barley bread and water. Within this solitude, he developed great respect for and love of nature. The fish in the marshes would swim to him and the birds would perch on his arms and eat from his hands.[46] A holy man of his times once said of Guthlac, "Have you not read that he who elects to be unknown to men becomes known to the wild creatures and is visited by angels? For he who is frequented by men cannot be frequented by the holy angels."

Guthlac lived approximately twenty more years on this island; years of great peace during which he attained gifts of wisdom and prophecy enabling him to assist many.[47] During these pensive and humble years, he greatly appreciated his life of simplicity, peace, and devotion to God.

Saint Joannicus

c. 754-846 CE
November 4

Although initially Saint Joannicus disliked icons, he gradually began to appreciate their value. Eventually he entered the religious life.

Saint Joannicus was born to a poor family in lands now considered part of Turkey. As a youth he was a swine herder, a position he subsequently left to become a somewhat careless and disorderly soldier. He had fallen under the influence of iconoclasts and went on rampages destroying religious symbols. Eventually, however, due to the teachings of a wise hermit sage, Joannicus began to appreciate the holy meanings behind icons and felt pulled toward a religious life.

When he reached the age of forty, he left the military and began a spiritual quest traveling from monastery to monastery, seeking wisdom from various holy monks. His journey led him on a path to enter a monastery on Mount Olympus.[48] There he entered a cavern, led a solitary life, and lived solely on bread and water. After twelve years of living the life of an ascetic, he attained the ability to perform miracles and the gift of prophecy. He became known far and wide for his spiritual wisdom.[49]

His reputation spread throughout the empire. Being of advanced age by then, he preferred to enclose himself in a narrow cell in the monastery and withdraw into silent contemplation. His heart overflowed with forgiveness toward all. When he was asked whether or not errant clergy who destroyed icons should be permitted back into the religious life, in the spirit of love and forgiveness, he advised that all should be received back to their proper rank.[50] Joannicus was an individual of pure compassion and mercy who chose a life of universal peace and non-violence.

Saint Theodore the Studite

c. 759 - 826 CE
November 11

Saint Theodore recognized the plight of women. He was forced into exile when he confronted the emperor for replacing his wife.

Saint Theodore had been the eldest of three brothers. At a young age, he left his family estate near Mount Olympus in Turkey to live as a religious monk. The other monks were so impressed with his piety that they decided to send him to Constantinople for further theological studies. Subsequently, Theodore was ordained as a priest. Within fifteen years he became an abbot.

Life was very tumultuous within the empire during that time as Emperor Constantine VI had put away his wife, replacing her with another woman. When Theodore confronted the emperor concerning this, the emperor banished him. The exile did not last long, however, because the emperor's mother, Irene, overthrew Constantine and claimed the throne herself and permitted Theodore's return. Many chaotic years followed. The monastery fell, became prey to raids, and the religious community was forced to move within the walls of Constantinople.

The monks moved into a run-down monastery at Studios. It was because of Theodore's organizational skills and his natural abilities to understand others, even in these run-down quarters, that he was able to grow their community rapidly to over four hundred men. Theodore was a man of deep understanding. Although he recognized the spiritual benefits of a life of simplicity, he did not ridicule others who were still caught up in the shallowness of a materialistic life. He guided his followers to survive on flesh free diets of vegetation and bread, yet accepted their human frailties if they strayed from such paths.[51]

Theodore's writings, including his sermons, instructions, liturgical hymns, and treatises of monasticism, revealed him to have been a man of deep spiritual and worldly wisdom. He advised his followers to balance their lives with simplicity and non-violence, yet to remain ever understanding of the weaknesses of others.

Saint Lioba

c. 707 - 779 CE
September 28

Saint Lioba's writings were
of such sensitive and spiritual
nature that her superiors
entrusted her to spread
monasticism to the women
of Germany.

Saint Lioba was born in Essex, England,
the only child of parents who had once
considered their marriage barren. She was
baptized Liobgetha, meaning "the dear
one" and placed in a great monastery
while still quite young. While growing up,
she was known for her prudence and sanctity. Her mother trained her to be pious
and to avoid the temptations of worldly
possessions.

After completing her education, she
remained in the monastery and joined the
convent. She was a sensitive woman, as
exemplified by her writings to her cousin,
Saint Boniface, "I am the only child of my
parents and, unworthy though I be, I
should like to look upon you as my brother,
for I can trust you more than anyone else."
She also asked Boniface to protect her with
his prayers, "I beseech you dear brother,
help me with the shield of your prayers in
my conflict against the attack of
the hidden enemy."[52]

Saint Boniface was touched
by Lioba's sincerity and they
began an exchange of letters
with one another that endured
many years. As Boniface began
to learn of Lioba's sincerity, he
felt such confidence in her religious dedication that he entrusted her to lead thirty
nuns in spreading monasticism to the
women of Germany. Lioba was known to
have been very beautiful, to possess the
face of an angel, and to share a pleasant
smile with all. She lived according to
Saint Benedict's austere Rule and ate only
twice a day, these being totally vegetarian
meals of fruits and vegetables.

All the nuns in Lioba's house performed manual work, read the Bible,
prayed, and studied various subjects,
including Latin, that were considered
valuable in the development of one's
mind. Lioba was loved for her patience,
intelligence, and merciful nature. A
steady stream of followers flocked to her
hoping to learn from her gentle compassionate ways, and her radiant sense of
grace and peace.[53]

Saint Euthymius the Younger

c. 820-898 CE
October 15

Saint Euthymius was a man of prayer and compassion. He was endowed with the ability to heal the sick and to give faith to those without.

Saint Euthymius was a holy monk who was esteemed principally in Russia. He was born in Galatia,[54] one of three children. After his father died when he was only seven, he was raised by his mother and two sisters. While still extremely young, he was given in marriage, and he and his young wife had a daughter, Anastasia. By the age of eighteen, however, he felt the need to leave his family to live a life of religious austerity, personal sacrifice, and strenuous labor as a monk. He lived in solitude and silence within an isolated cell and consumed only those foods obtained from tilling the soil, predominantly vegetables. Occasionally, he supplemented these with nuts and herbs.[55]

Euthymius apparently developed the ability to heal people afflicted with a variety of medical disorders. Crowds would flock to hear his preaching and to benefit from his gifts of healing. He alternated his days between healing and preaching, fitting in brief interludes for personal solitude. As word of his abilities spread, enormous numbers of people flocked to benefit from his gifts. After years fulfilling this calling, he was forced to flee to an isolated island to gain the time he needed for contemplation and to communicate with God.[56]

While there, Euthymius received a vision telling him that he must build a monastery. He resolved to do so. Out of the remains of a ruined structure he created a church and several dwellings for other monks. This task took fourteen years and when it was completed, he retired to the desert to spend his remaining years, once again, in quiet solitude.[57] He valued God's simple blessings of peace, solitude, and wisdom, living his final years in non-violence and prayer.

Saint Luke
the Younger

c. 880 - 946 CE
February 7

Saint Luke felt such empathy
for the needy that he would
take clothes right off his back
and give them to beggars.

Saint Luke was the third of seven children born to a family of farmers on the Greek island of Aegina.[58] He was considered a pious and obedient child. Even during his boyhood, Luke felt such sensitive concern for the welfare of all beings that he would never eat cheese or any foods derived from animal flesh. Often he would go without food so that he might give his portions to the hungry. He was even known to have taken his own clothes right off his back to give them to beggars. As a youth, he worked in the fields. But after his father's death, he devoted himself to prayer and contemplation.

With the passing of childhood, he felt a calling to enter religious life. While traveling to join a monastery, Luke was captured by soldiers who assumed he was a runaway slave. He was locked in prison and treated very cruelly. His captors released him only when his identity was finally revealed.[59]

Luke was returned to his mother, who hoped he would remain at home. But the longing for a religious life still filled his thoughts. Finally he was permitted to leave with two passing monks on their way to a monastery. Once there, he built a small cell and lived in religious purity and austerity as a hermit. Throughout all the difficulties encountered during his life he remained full of joy and charity. It had been stated that many altruistic miracles came to fruition through his prayers. It was for this reason that he was often referred to as a wonder worker.[60] Saint Luke wanted nothing more than to live his life in austerity, charity, and prayer. He maintained his vegetarian diet because of his belief in compassionate non-violence and his vision of living at peace with all creation.

Saint Paul of Latros

c.900 - 956 CE
December 15

Saint Paul felt others' pains so deeply that he tried to sell himself into slavery in exchange for the freedom of others.

Saint Paul was still a young child when his father passed away. Shortly after that, his brother, Basil, decided to become a monk and journeyed to the solitary lands of Asia Minor[61] and Mount Latros[62] to lead a life of prayer and meditation. Paul wanted to live with his brother, but Basil recommended that he remain in a monastery until he had grown in years and gained in wisdom, so he would understand the seriousness of his choice. Initially, Paul consented. But within just a few years, he followed his heart and went to live as a hermit in an isolated cave on the rocky cliffs of a mountain. It was also at that time that he resolved to sustain himself solely on foods obtained without harming weaker creatures. He ate only vegetables and acorns. As reputation for his holiness spread, other young men began to join him, and soon, the mountains had become filled with groups of cave dwelling monks.[63]

After twelve years, Paul felt that the peace he had gained in solitude had been lost due to the masses of followers who had joined him. So he withdrew to a remote part of the mountain saying, "When nothing diverts my thoughts from God, my heart overflows with joy, so much so that I often forget my food and everything else."[64]

Yet, try as he did to remain in solitude, masses continued flocking to him to learn from his wisdom, insight, and holiness. Even the emperor, Constantine Porphyrogenitus[65] wrote frequently to Paul requesting advice. Paul felt great concern and compassion for the plight of the poor and often gave them more of his food and clothes than he could spare. Once, he even tried to sell himself into slavery to help some people in distress, and would have succeeded had he not been stopped.[66]

During his later years, Paul spent days in prayer and meditation within his quiet cell. He kept as few possessions as possible and consumed only that vegetation which grew wild, to ensure that he inflicted as little harm upon creation as possible. His main source of solace was prayer—through which he hoped to attain God's blessings for those in need.

Saint Antony of the Caves of Kiev

c. 983 - 1073 CE

July 10

So many wanted to learn from Saint Antony's wisdom that an entire community of disciples grew around him.

Saint Antony of Kiev[67] had been a key figure in the establishment of Russian Orthodox monasticism. Antony was born in the Ukraine and at an early age wanted to live a solitary life emulating the early monastic hermits, the Desert Fathers.[68] He believed he might attain higher levels of spiritual awareness by following their spiritual practices. He embarked upon a pilgrimage to Mount Athos in Greece and became a hermit at the monastery there. He learned much from the holy monks as their site had been the center of Byzantine monasticism.[69] He hoped to remain at that location. But after he had studied under others for several years the abbot directed him to return to his native lands saying, "The Lord has strengthened you in the way of holiness and you must now lead others. You will be the father of many monks."[70]

Antony obeyed. He left the monastery and created his home within a cave high on a wooded cliff. While there, he survived on bread, vegetables and water, and spent his days in contemplation and in tending a small patch of land. Many people reached out to him for counseling and never did he refuse advising anyone—rich or poor.

Gradually, many whom he had advised chose to remain with him. They began to dig out and create caves for themselves. Gradually, the number of followers grew to such great numbers that they were able to build a complete monastery and church. So many sought refuge in the presence of this quiet, unassuming, and gentle man that adjoining monastic communities began to sprout around the initial one. It was said that, "Many monasteries were built with the wealth of princes and nobles, but this was the first built with tears and fasting and prayer."[71] Antony was a man of prayer and wisdom who felt blessed that he wanted no more than a simple cell, a diet attained peacefully, and the ability to advise and assist his fellow beings. He is considered one of the fathers of Ukrainian monasticism.

Saint Theodosius Pechersky

C. 1002 - 1074 CE
July 10

Saint Theodosius' heart went out to those abandoned by society. He worked for the sick and disabled, bringing cartloads of food to prisoners every week.

Saint Theodosius and Saint Antony of the caves of Kiev were instrumental in the establishment of the Russian Orthodox Church. Although Theodosius was born into a wealthy family near Kiev, he believed so strongly in the equality of all men that he sought to humble himself in the eyes of others. He told his mother, "Our Lord Jesus Christ humbled Himself and underwent degradation, and we have to follow His example in that too."[72] So saying, he gave up his inheritance to become one of the early monastic disciples of Antony, who by then was considered a holy sage in the wilderness.

Theodosius felt a strong need to concentrate his works of charity both inside and outside the monastery. He created a hospital for the sick and disabled, and a hostel for travelers alongside the monastery. He also made sure that every week a cartload of food would be sent to a prison near-by. His passion was to evangelize the citizens of Kiev and to educate the poor of the city so that they might become better able to defend themselves from harsh leaders.

For himself, he wanted nothing more than an austere, humble, non-violent life —a life rooted in recognizing the needs of others and in living by the example set by Jesus. Theodosius valued the time he was able to spend in solitary prayer, yet also believed that community prayer possessed great spiritual potential. His goal was to spread his spiritual message beyond his community, believing that Jesus' love was overflowing for all.[73] He worked to spread messages of peace, non-violence, and faith to all to assist in bringing the kingdom of God to earth.

Saint Fantinus

Tenth Century CE
August 30

In a vision, Saint Fantinus
saw foreigners invade his
monastery. The invasion
occurred and Fantinus spent
the remainder of his years serving the poor of foreign lands.

Saint Fantinus had been abbot of a Greek monastery located in Calabria, Italy,[74] when he experienced a vision advising him to leave this monastery and journey overseas. He wandered the countryside prophesying and aiding the masses. For himself, however, he desired only the humblest of lives. He lived out in the open air and nourished himself with the fruits and herbs of the natural plants. While living this life of austerity, Fantinus recognized the blessings of God's natural gifts.

Some time later, Fantinus experienced a vision. Within it, foreign invaders devastated his monastery and he was called upon to journey overseas to Peloponnesus[75] to assist the people of those war-ravaged lands.

The events he had envisioned subsequently came to pass just as he had envisioned them. So he journeyed to that foreign land and remained on its soil for the remainder of his life. While in these lands, he lived the life of a humble monk. His life remained devoid of possessions, of flesh foods, and of material wants. He utilized his spiritual gifts of prophecy and of miracles to help the poorest of the poor.

At no time did he use his gifts to elevate his own position. Consequently, fame of his abilities spread. Masses flocked to him seeking healing and advice.[76] In spite of his being the recipient of praise, Fantinus remained a humble, merciful, and ascetic sage. He sought nothing more from life except that he might live sharing God's peace with all.

Saint Wulfstan

c. 1009 - 1095 CE
January 19

While saying mass, Saint
Wulfstan smelled the odor of
animal flesh from a nearby
slaughterhouse. He vowed
never again to eat meat.

Saint Wulfstan was born near Warwick-shire, England.[77] Even when he was a youth, others noted the purity of his soul. When both of his parents grew older, they entered religious life, his father entering a monastery and his mother a convent. Wulfstan, too, proceeded on his own path following his personal calling toward priesthood, as he felt deeply devoted to a life of prayer and austerity. Although as a youth he had consumed animal flesh, as he attained higher levels of spiritual awareness he felt an overwhelming instinct to live without inflicting suffering upon any of God's creatures.

This occurred one day when he observed a cow being pulled to its slaughter. While saying mass he became distracted by the smell of the animal's flesh being roasted in the kitchen. He suddenly felt that his contributing to the taking of an animal's life by eating its flesh and saying mass were incompatible. He bound himself with a vow never again to eat the flesh of an animal.[78]

During his early years as a priest, Wulfstan was entrusted with the education of children and the running of the monastery. He also served as a night watchman for the church. So that the young men under his care might learn humility, he taught them to carry the dishes and wait on the tables of the poor. Wulfstan's greatest achievement was his ability to persuade the merchants of Bristol to stop their trade in slaves. Enslaved people were being transported to Bristol[79] on their way to Ireland which was then controlled by Vikings.[80] Wulfstan was able to stop this trade and achieve tremendous gains in human rights through the passionate messages of his teachings.[81]

Many accolades had been conferred upon Wulfstan. In spite of all these glories that might easily have swayed one from higher values, Wulfstan remained committed in his dedication to serve the most downtrodden. He felt pain and shed tears witnessing the trials of others as he strived to protect all beings from harm.

Saint Gregory of Makar

c. 960 - 1010 CE
March 16

Saint Gregory was gifted with
abilities to heal the sick.
Many believed he possessed
the ability to perform miracles.

to Orleans, France where
Gregory built a small cell so he
might pattern his life after the
Desert Fathers.

On many days, Gregory
abstained totally from all foods,
and on others ate merely a
handful of lentils. On rare occa-
sions, he supplemented this diet with
barley bread and a few raw roots. A man of
his presence, however, was not destined to
remain in solitude for long, as many
sought him out for his spiritual wisdom
and for his miracles of healing. He was
able to assist numerous people in attaining
inner peace.

When his passing came, peasants
throughout the countryside were filled
with a profound sense of loss.[83] Gregory
had lived a life of inner peace, dignity, and
purpose. He used his innate ability to read
the needs of others so as to assist the
masses, both physically and spiritually.
He was remembered as a peace-loving
messenger of God.

Saint Gregory was born into a large well-
established Armenian family,[82] yet
longed for a life of solitude and prayer.
He found his way to a monastery, joined
the community, and after having been
ordained a priest, felt a deep spiritual
calling to heal the sick. He spent many
years devoting himself to the care of the
sick and the dying. After having
achieved this sense of fulfillment, he recognized that he must return once again to
a life of solitude. He sensed a resurgence
of a need to spend time in solitude, so as
to attain higher levels of understanding
of God. He joined two wandering Greek
monks on a pilgrimage seeking the same
solitude. This spiritual journey led them

Saint Elphege

c. 944 - 1012 CE
April 19

Saint Elphege felt such concern for others that when invaders attacked England, he pleaded with them to take his life instead.

Although Saint Elphege had been born the son of noble parents, he relinquished all his inheritance to enter a monastery in Gloucestershire, England. While in the monastery, he learned to love a life of simplicity and prayer. With the consent of his superiors, he was granted leave to journey to an isolated desert site near Bath so as to lead a life of greater spiritual awareness. While there, he recognized that his spirit was flourishing—sensing that when isolated from all else, he was better able to experience the overwhelming presence of God. Elphege grew tremendously in spiritual wisdom during these years spent in humble, solitary prayer and contemplation.

With time, however, masses of people began to journey to his isolated region of the desert in hopes of learning from his words, spirit, and presence. He felt compelled to build a monastery for the large numbers of followers seeking to join him. He permitted others to live under his guidance if they agreed to adhere to his standards of holiness, honesty, and compassion. A foundational value that he set for his followers, and by which he lived, was that all consume only vegetarian foods—plants and grains.

Recognition of Elphege's piety spread throughout the lands and, although only thirty years of age, he was called upon to accept the position of bishop of Winchester.[84] While serving as bishop, he assisted the poor in attaining necessary skills and values, until there were no longer any beggars in the entire city. When war broke out between England and an invading army, the leading citizens of the town felt that Elphege was so well known that he must flee. But he felt that he could not abandon his flock during this time of danger. The city was taken by storm, with men, women, and children succumbing in fierce and brutal battles.

The English regard Elphege as a holy person and as a martyr. He was a man of humble character who sacrificed his life for the good of his fellow man. His life was simple, gentle and merciful. He was known as a man wishing peace for all people, all creatures, and all creation.

Saint Theobald
of Provins

c. 1017 - 1066 CE
June 30

Saint Theobald chose a
humble life of labor and
prayer. He sacrificed
continually for others until
his weakened body
succumbed to leprosy.

Even as a young man, Saint Theobald was appreciated as a man of sincerity possessing a heart and spirit of great purity. Although his father had been a count with command over many people, young Theobald felt himself being pulled toward a spiritual life. He had read of the lives of the Desert Fathers, and dreamed that he, too, might lead a life of holiness and sanctity. When his father asked him to lead their troops in war, Theobald respectfully admitted that such a path was not right for him, and that he needed to follow a life spreading peace rather than war.[86] Initially, his family found his choice unacceptable. Eventually, however, his father acquiesced to his wishes. Theobald made plans to embark upon a holy life, giving away all his worldly possessions to the less fortunate and beggars.

Along with a similarly motivated friend, Theobald wandered to the forest near Luxembourg[87] to build shelters in a secluded solitary region. The two journeyed barefoot and lived on purely vegetarian diets. Although they suffered from cold, heat, hunger, and fatigue, they found spiritual fulfillment in their lives of solitary prayer and contemplation. They felt that manual labor was essential in enabling one to reach higher levels of spiritual awareness, so they worked the fields, loaded wagons, carried mortar and stones, and made their own charcoal. While working with their hands, they prayed in their hearts.[88]

Their dedication and holiness gave them a reputation for sanctity, and numerous disciples sought to join them. Theobald moved into a deserted, dilapidated chapel near Vicenza in northern Italy, hoping to attain greater solitude. It was while within these lands, that the bishop ordained him as a priest. After many years away from his family, Theobald started on a journey towards home excited at the prospect of meeting his parents once again. Shortly after he began this trip, and after years of austerities, he became afflicted with a painful and deforming skin disorder, either leprosy or a similar condition. It was during this pilgrimage that he met his final days. Theobald died in peace, having found fulfillment in his life as a humble and contemplative man of God.

Saint Stephen of Grandmont

c. 1024 - 1124 CE
February 8

Even as a child, Saint Stephen seemed exceedingly spiritual. So his parents left his upbringing to an aged priest who helped him grow in holiness.

As a young boy, Saint Stephen radiated the presence of a child destined to live a life of spirituality. Because his father was perceptive of Stephen's needs, he located an aged priest to tutor Stephen in religious studies. Stephen lived under the guidance of the priest for many years, growing in both wisdom and insight. After the priest passed on, Stephen was sent to Rome for an additional four years to continue his religious education there. It was during these latter years, that others recognized his distinctive contemplative nature. Stephen preferred a life of holy solitude and longed to follow in the paths of the hermits of Calabria. After receiving Holy Orders, he was granted permission from Pope Gregory VII to lead the life of a spiritual recluse.[89]

Stephen left the city to live a life of contemplation, meditation, and prayer. Within the solitude of nature, amidst the rocks and trees, Stephen spent forty-six years engrossed in prayer and personal sacrifice. Initially, he sustained himself on wild roots and herbs. In his later years, he added coarse bread, a gift that was brought to him regularly by shepherds. He existed upon that meager and humble diet for the remainder of his life.[90] During the days he performed such strenuous manual labor that at night, he would often feel overcome by sleep and collapse onto the boards he used as a bed.

Many disciples came to him expecting to gain spiritual insight from remaining in the presence of his deeply spiritual character. He was a man of gentle nature, who demanded much of himself, yet accepted the frailties of his followers. He thought nothing of his own gain and always took the lowest place among others.[91] Although his life was that of a humble priest committed to poverty, silence, non-violence, and personal sacrifice, he was a pillar of strength to his disciples, as well as to his entire community. Stephen was a man who through dedication was able to focus his entire life toward the service of others.

Saint Henry of Coquet

c. 1055 - 1127 CE
January 16

Saint Henry spent his days in meditation and prayer, eventually gaining the ability to read the minds of others. Masses flocked to learn from the wisdom of this holy sage.

Henry's reputation for holiness had spread and many came to visit him seeking to learn from his gifts of foreknowledge, as well as from his abilities to read the minds of others. The faithful of his native land tried to persuade him to return to Denmark, stating that there were numerous suitable sites available there for him to lead a hermit's life. But he had been given a vision that his fate was to remain on the tiny island of Coquet and fulfill his mission amongst those people.

Saint Henry was a native of Denmark who from the time of his childhood felt a spiritual calling. He set sail to the north of England so that he might join a community of monks living on the tiny island of Coquet off the coast of Northumberland.[92] He felt the need to live in contemplation and austerity so as to attain a higher level of communion with God. To achieve these goals, he lived the simplest of lives within a tiny cell and earned his keep through hard manual labor—planting the crops and tilling the soil. He consumed only one meal daily; a totally vegetarian one of bread and water.[93]

He lived the most peaceful of lives as a contemplative sage filled with wisdom and with an understanding of human nature. Throughout his simple, austere, and peaceful life, Henry was able to advise followers how they might adopt non-violence and compassion towards others, and how they, too, might recognize peace amidst the simple blessings of God.[94]

Saint William of Malavalle

c. 1110 - 1157 CE
February 10

Saint William loved nature. He built a shelter in the forest and lived amongst the animals. He grew to understand them and lived in peace with all.

Not much is known of the early years of Saint William, as there seems to have developed an aura of secrecy surrounding his youth. What is known is that he had been both a Frenchman and a soldier. Ancient writings state that after having fought as a soldier, he felt repentant. He felt such remorse for having spread suffering and violence that he embarked upon a pilgrimage to Rome to ask the pope for Penance.[95] The pope decided both to receive him and to offer his blessing. After receiving this blessing, William went to Tuscany[96] to begin his life as a religious reclusive hermit—away from the pulls of society yet surrounded by the presence of God.

His reputation for holiness gradually began to spread and other holy individuals joined him. Among their ranks, however, were those feigning pious goals. In reality, these men posing as religious contemplatives seeking peace were merely idle vagrants, playing on William's unsuspecting character. When he discovered the dishonorable motives of these followers, he fled the hermitage and went further into the wilderness to an extremely remote region of Siena[97] to find peace in solitude.

Initially, he lived within a mere cavity in the ground barely large enough to give him shelter. Later he built a more substantial shelter out of dense boughs of wood, thatching it with leaves and ferns. There were many wild animals in this region, but William never harmed or took the life of even one of these for consumption. Rather, he sustained himself with the same vegetation and herbs that he observed the animals taking to sustain themselves.[98] Several years later, a sincerely religious hermit, Albert, joined William. Together, they lived spending their time in solitary prayer while embracing nonviolent lifestyles—consuming only vegetables, bread, and herbs.

The depth of William's religious understanding grew over time, as did his gifts of prophecy. Having attained such abilities, he was even able to predict correctly his own death. Throughout his life, William remained resolute in his conviction that to live in the image of God, one must adhere to a life of austerity and peace.[99]

Saint Godric

c. 1085 - 1170 CE
May 21

Saint Godric felt called to a spiritual life. He renounced the world to live in the desert, where he cared for the snakes and fed the ravens.

Saint Godric was born to extremely poor parents near Durham.[100] Because of his family's extreme poverty, even as a small child, he was forced to earn his meager keep by peddling small wares. Over the years, his selling skills improved and he began to travel to larger cities selling his wares because the spirit of adventure had seized him. As his eyes had now become opened to the wonders of the world, he spent his next sixteen years pursuing a life of seafaring.

Then one day, while visiting a holy site, his thoughts turned to higher values. He became able to perceive the deep sense of peace and serenity of the monks and pondered how he might fulfill his own craving for spiritual fulfillment. He felt himself undergoing a conversion of spirit and joined a pilgrimage en route to Jerusalem.[101]

By now, he had decided to give away all his goods and renounce the material-istic world. In Palestine, he joined a group of hermits who had been living in the desert where Saint John the Baptist had walked.[102] He proceeded to spend the following fifty years of his life living as a hermit within that same desert. He sustained himself on roots and berries, and later began to grow vegetables and mill barley to make bread. His home was a small wooden hut, as well as the vast expanse of the desert. It is said that he cared for the snakes and fed the ravens with the crops from his garden.[103]

He was described as a sincere listener, and as a man who was always sympathetic to those with troubles. He spent much of his time in prayer and in silent contemplation of God, from which he gained understanding of divine mysteries. After his passing, miracles of healing were experienced by those who invoked his name, particularly by women seeking help for female disorders.[104] He was a man who loved all, cared for the most misunderstood and despised creatures, and showed unlimited compassion for all.

Saint Stephen of Obazine

c. 1100 - 1159 CE
March 8

Saint Stephen lived in an isolated forest with other holy sages. Their religious community never partook of animal flesh.

Even from his early childhood years in France, Saint Stephen appeared to be an individual immersed in spiritual thoughts and acts of charity. As he grew in maturity, he renounced the materialistic world of possessions because he felt drawn to a life in the clergy. He prayed, meditating upon the question of how he might live in divine poverty, and even consulted a saintly sage-like priest concerning this question. The priest gave him the supportive advice he needed to go forth in search of God.

Following his advice, Stephen and his friend, Peter, called several other friends together and distributed the last of their worldly possessions among them. At dawn of the next day, the two friends set out barefoot to the forest of Obazine, an uncultivated region, where they built a rough shelter.[105] They resolved that never would they take the life of any animal. They would survive the remainder of their lives on plant-based diets.

In spite of their simple, disciplined lifestyles and prayerful quietness, many others seeking to become their disciples soon joined them. They accepted many faithful disciples into their group and eventually built a monastery for this growing community. Life in the community was austere. Their days were filled with manual labor and their nights with prayer and religious communal discussions. Yet during these difficult times, Stephen showed a gentle and kindly nature toward all. To ensure the spiritual stability of his community, Stephen brought all his disciples into the fellowship of the Cistercian Order, so they might all follow in the same pattern of sacrificial lifestyles and vegetarianism. Stephen's followers grew in numbers and in devotion, and he survived to see his values flourish until he was called to his Creator, twelve years later.[106]

Saint William
of Bourges

c. 1147 - 1209 CE
January 10

Though he sought a simple life,
Saint William was appointed
bishop. Even in this position,
he never took the life of an
innocent creature.

Saint William was born into a distin-guished family in a small French town near the Loire River. During childhood, he found no enjoyment in the extravagance and emptiness of riches and withdrew to pursue his passions—those of piety and academic studies. When old enough, he joined the Cistercian Order of monks so that he might embark upon a life of con-templation, austerity, and prayer.[107]

When the archbishop of Bourges[108] died, a successor was sought from among the Cistercian abbots, and the elders of the church elected William. He might have refused the appointment had he not received direct orders from Pope Innocent III to accept it. While serving in that posi-tion, William proved to be a model bishop, while in his pri-vate life, he proved to be a model of Cistercian principles. He wore coarse clothes, never ate any meat, and attended to his parishioners in sincerity—stating that his mission was to assist those poor in body and spirit.[109]

According to the responsibilities of his position, William effectively defended the rights of the Church, especially its lands, against their being taken over by secular authorities. He even presented his case to the king, obtaining a successful outcome. He converted many people throughout the land to Christianity and even passed his last breath while teaching the masses. Shortly after giving his last sermon, he developed a high fever, and succumbed.[110] He was a man who defended the poor, pro-tected the rights of those less fortunate, and lived causing no harm to any being. His life was one of gentleness and compas-sion toward all.

Saint Humility
of Florence

c. 1226 - 1310 CE
May 22

After suffering the loss of
their own infant children,
Saint Humility and her
husband devoted their
lives to God.

Saint Humility was born to a respected
and wealthy Italian family. At the age of
fifteen, she was forced to marry a local
nobleman. She subsequently bore two
sons in the marriage. Both of their children died in infancy and her marriage
went through many troubled years due
to its shaky foundation and those tragic
events. After her husband suffered an
almost fatal illness, she was able to convince him that they should both devote
their lives to the ministry—he as a lay
brother and she as a nun.[111] Her husband agreed to do so, and they both
embarked on paths devoting their lives
to sharing God's blessings with those
less fortunate.

Humility was twenty-four
years of age when she began her
new life as a solitary and austere
sister. Initially she served in a
convent of Poor Clare sisters
and later in a small cell attached
to a church. She subsisted on
vegetables, bread, and water.
She would never eat the flesh of animals.
Her husband was located in another
abbey, where he died three years later,
without meeting Humility ever again.[112]

After spending twelve years in reclusive contemplation, during which time
she had grown in grace and wisdom,
Humility was persuaded to found a convent for women. She was quite successful
in this endeavor and went on to found a
second convent in Florence. Over these
years, she remained completely unassuming, simple in her needs, and as always,
humble in character. She lived the
remainder of her life committed to sharing
her values of peace and compassionate
love with all.

Saint Simon Stock

c. 1165 - 1265 CE
May 16

Saint Simon felt concern for all creatures. When others served him fish, he ordered that the poor creature be thrown back into the sea.

Even as a child, Saint Simon seemed to possess a very serious and thoughtful nature. In his home in Kent, England[113] he enjoyed time spent in prayerful activities as much as he did in play and academic studies. By the age of twelve, Simon left his home to live in the wilderness. While in the forest, he created a shelter for himself in the hollow of a great oak tree. This was the reason for his having been nicknamed 'stock.' He spent his time in prayer and solitary contemplation, preferring to live under harsh conditions, drinking only water, and never consuming any foods that were not vegetarian. He sustained himself on herbs, roots, and wild apples.

It seemed that during this time, the holy Patriarch of Jerusalem had sent monks to England to teach others their holy ways. By the time the holy men came, in 1212, Simon had been living in the forest for twenty years. Yet it was inevitable that a man such as Simon was destined to meet other men of similarly holy natures. Before the year ended, they had met and Simon joined their company. Simon left the forest to learn from these holy men and also to further his religious education at Oxford University. After his education was completed, he journeyed to Mount Carmel[114] in the Holy Lands to learn the practices of the wise men by living among them.[115]

The order of holy individuals Simon joined was the Carmelites and it was his destiny to bring their teachings back to Europe. When he returned to Europe, he established Carmelite houses in university towns and other large cities, including Paris, Bologna, Oxford, Cambridge, and London.[116]

His deep concern for all creatures is best exemplified by the course of action he followed when he was offered a meal of fish. He felt deeply saddened thinking of the tragedy that had befallen the fish and ordered for it to be thrown back into the river. When the cooked fish was thrown into the water, it regained its life fully and was able to swim away.[117] Simon spent the remainder of his years teaching his followers paths of holiness, non-violence, and compassion for all.

Saint Agnes of Montepulciano

1268 - 1317 CE
April 20

Saint Agnes was permitted to enter the convent at age nine. Over the years she developed the gift of prophecy and the ability to perform miracles.

Saint Agnes was born in a small village in Tuscany, Italy[118] to a well-to-do couple. Even during her early childhood, her spiritual character led others to anticipate she would choose a religious life. She seemed to delight in prayer and would spend hours on her knees giving thanks. At the age of nine, she induced her parents to place her in a convent of austere nuns. While there, she demonstrated a sense of wisdom beyond her years, and by the age of fourteen, she was made prioress. When a new convent was being formed, Pope Nicholas IV authorized a special dispensation to permit Agnes to become abbess of this convent.

For fifteen years, Agnes lived on bread and water, and slept on the ground. She witnessed numerous visions during that time, and other nuns testified that they saw her levitate and perform miracles. The citizens of her previous town wanted her to come back, so they erected a new convent to house her community, which would be under Dominican patronage. Agnes went to work for this community. Through her remarkable abilities of prophecy, she was able to aid those who were hopelessly in need.

Agnes continued her dedicated, holy, and austere life until illness took her at the age of forty-nine. Even at the time of death, her thoughts were always focused upon the welfare of others, as exemplified by her final words to her sisters: "Do not grieve over much at my departure. I shall not lose sight of you from above. You will discover that I have not abandoned you and you will possess me forever."[119]

Saint Laurence Justinian

1380 - 1455 CE
September 5

Saint Laurence wore ragged clothes and begged for alms in the streets so that he might truly understand the plight of the poor.

Saint Laurence grew up in a particularly spiritual environment, as both of his parents were pious individuals. His father died when he was quite young, leaving his mother with several small children to raise. His mother found peace in her religion and prayed often, an action that enriched her children. In addition to raising her children, Laurence's mother also dedicated herself to helping the poor. Of all her children, Laurence always seemed to possess a generous soul. Even as a child, he told his mother that his only desire was to become a saint.

By the age of nineteen, Laurence joined the priesthood. He sensed that if one sought to be drawn closer to God, one must live a life of personal austerity, remain free of wants, and sacrifice for the welfare of others. He went to live in a monastery, so as to remove himself from worldly distractions. During his novitiate, he became afflicted with tuberculosis of his lymph nodes. It became necessary that he have surgery on these infected lymph nodes. He never cried out in pain, but rather prayed to Jesus.

In 1433, Pope Eugenius IV appointed him bishop of Venice. Laurence attempted to decline this position, as he preferred the life of a humble monk, but to no avail. Even after he had become bishop, Laurence still longed to understand the suffering of the poor. So when he was able to free himself from the view of others, he would put on his most ragged clothes and go begging for alms in the streets. By this means, he kept in spiritual touch with the needs of those disenfranchised within society.

Throughout all of these times, Laurence never consumed more than a humble vegetarian diet of bread. He felt that his living in poverty and simplicity, as well as maintaining his diet obtained through non-violence, brought him closer to God. Laurence continually treated all with equality and compassion, and particularly sought to aid those with wounded hearts.[120]

Saint Herculanus of Piegaro

c. 1380 - 1451 CE
June 2

When war ravaged the city, Saint Herculanus went begging door-to-door for alms to help the poor survive.

Saint Herculanus was born in Italy on the borders of Umbria[121] and Tuscany. He entered the Franciscan monastery where, for some time, he maintained a life of contemplation and prayer. While in the monastery, he became the disciple of an older priest with whom he traveled to the Holy Lands and to Egypt. Upon his return, he initially spent some time in contemplative meditation. Later he felt the need to go forth preaching to others, recognizing that this was his strength.[122]

He became one of the foremost preachers of the fifteenth century, speaking eloquently to others of the need to reform their lives, to follow holy examples, and to seek salvation. His personal life remained one of great austerity. He consumed only vegetarian foods— predominantly small quantities of bread and vegetables. Some days he went totally without food, to ensure that he never consumed more than he needed. Herculanus had been preaching in Lucca[123] at a time when the Florentines[124] besieged the city. During the time of the seizure, the people had begun to run out of provisions. Herculanus promised the citizens that if they prayed, the city would be saved. His prophecy was fulfilled.

His personal missions were steeped in compassion, such as his begging door to door to raise alms for the city's poor. The citizens of Lucca were so impressed with his dedication toward the indigent that they joined him and raised enough funds to create two new Franciscan monasteries.[125] Herculanus was a man of gentle ways who strove to possess no more than needed for survival and to consume no foods if such repasts meant the loss of life of any creatures. He sought to share his humble messages of peace and to live sharing God's blessings with all.

Chapter 5

Mystic Saints

Mystic Saints are those saints who sense the soul, spirit, and essence of God in all creation. To them, God is present in every human, animal, insect, plant, rock, and planet. Because they consider all as manifestations of God and God's presence, they seek to protect all from harm and suffering. Saint Francis of Assisi has been the most well known of the mystic saints, as he truly lived his life recognizing the presence of God in all creation—from the largest of the celestial bodies to the smallest of creatures.

Because mystic saints sense God's presence in all beings, they also recognize the right of each of them to live in dignity and safety—be that being of animal, fish, bird, or insect form. Many such saints could not bring themselves to take the life of another animal for their own personal gain—hence, they chose to live as vege-

tarians. Had many of these saints lived today, they might have lived as vegans, animal rights activists, and members of humane societies. The hearts of these saints went out to all forms of life that suffer, so much so, that they often sacrificed their own well-being and safety to help even the weakest and meanest of creatures.

The mystic saints viewed all life as one family flowing in a stream of infinitely perpetual and interconnected life. This was similar to the Hindu view of all life representing a manifestation of God. They saw creation as a continuum of life begetting life in a unified cycle of existence in which the death of one life leads to the formation of a future life. With such beliefs, the mystic saints tried to live without disrupting that which God created. Having respect for all life, these saints lived in simplicity and austerity, never harming or taking more from creation than what was essential for their existence.

Mystic saints sought to live without material possessions in the belief that quests for possessions led people on paths to seek further riches and power. They felt that once people gained material possessions, they were destined to entrapment in a cycle of fear and mistrust of others, as others might take such possessions from them.[1] Hence, they valued a simple life.

Mystic vegetarian saints saw God's imprint upon all facets of creation. This is expressed in the words of Alban Butler, "Thou are truly a hidden God, who dwellest in inaccessible light, unknown to the world; but thou impartest thyself abundantly and lovingly to those who, having purified their souls…express and show forth in their hearts and bodies, Jesus Christ."[2]

Saint Francis of Assisi

1182-1226 CE
October 4

Saint Francis loved all God's creation , even the roadside worms. He sought to share God's blessings with all that walked, swam, flew, and crawled.

Saint Francis was a man who felt love and compassion for all creation. He was definitely a vegetarian for at least a portion of his life. Uncertainty exists, however, as to whether or not he was a vegetarian during his entire life. This was because Saint Francis was trying to uphold several religious and humanitarian principles simultaneously and sometimes had to compromise if these principles conflicted.

One of the principles was that his monks and he must not own any possessions. This meant that their very survival depended upon food for which they begged. The other principle was that because he, personally, saw God in every being, he sought never to harm or take life from any being. As a compromise, although he preferred his monks to be vegetarian, he permitted them to accept any foods offered them, even if such foods were non-vegetarian.

Francis was born in the quaint town of Assisi, Italy,[3] the son of a successful cloth merchant. As a young man, he learned his father's trade and led the life of a wealthy aristocrat. In spite of this wealth, he was different from the other aristocrats in that his heart went out to the poor. When the city of Assisi became involved in war, Francis joined the army, only to be taken as a prisoner of war for over a year. After he was released, he returned home very seriously ill and required a year of bed rest to regain his strength. It was during this year, while bedridden and isolated, that his sense of deep religious compassion for others evolved.

Thenceforth, he embarked upon a life of prayer and meditation, and spoke of experiences in which he felt he left the world. After one of these visions, Francis began what was to become his life-long mission of visiting homes of the poor and hospitals for the lepers. He shared clothes and money with the downtrodden and compassion with the sick.[4]

Francis' compassion for the poor became so encompassing that one day he sold some of his father's wares to help them. In retaliation, his father threatened him with disinheritance. Francis' conscience left him with only one path—to renounce his inheritance. He left home, spending two years living in solitary prayer, giving his own clothes to another in greater need, helping the poor, wandering around the city caring for the sick, and performing strenuous manual labor to rebuild dilapidated churches.[5]

Many began to admire Francis and desired to become his companions. These young men joined together and lived in a small cottage, thus initiating the inception of a holy Order in which they would live in poverty, eat meager, coarse meals, work at manual trades, and when work was lacking, beg for food. They gave freely to all in need, loved no earthly possessions, and vowed never to touch money.[6] Out of humility, Francis gave his Order the name Friars Minor.[7]

Francis was a "man overflowing with sympathy for man, beast, and all God's creation—wherever and howsoever he encountered them. Not only was every man his brother, but also every animal, every sheep in the fields, every bird in the branches, every mule on which he rode, and every bumblebee. All took refuge in his protection."[8] It has been stated that Francis' heart melted when he saw even the tiniest or ugliest creature suffer.

In reference to Francis' diet, "He scarcely or only seldom allowed himself the pleasure of cooked food." Once after he ate a few bites of chicken, he felt such remorse for the chicken that he had his companion tie a rope around him and drag him in the streets.[9] It was also documented that, "On his missionary journeys, in preaching the Gospel, he always took whatever was put before him by those who gave him hospitality. But when he returned home, he kept strictly to the rule of fasting."[10] When Francis was teaching the Gospel of God, "If he were invited to dinner by great princes, he would taste a bit of the meat in observance of the Holy Gospel" so as not to refuse gifts given with God's love, and then "Making a pretense of eating by raising his hand to his mouth, lest anyone should perceive what he was doing, he would drop the rest in his lap."[11]

Saint Francis did not restrict his friars to the same personal commitment to vegetarianism that he held for himself. He set rules for his friars, such as Saint Francis' *Rule of 1221*, Chapter 3, stating that in conformance with the Gospel, friars might eat any food put before them, "Whenever you enter a town and they receive you, eat what is set before you"[12] (Luke 10.8). This Rule did not disallow consumption of animal flesh, as its intent was to encourage poverty, rather than animal non-violence. In Chapter 15 of Saint Francis' Rule, however, he advised his friars that they were, "forbidden to have animals of any kind…forbidden to ride horseback, unless they are forced to by sickness or real necessity."[13] Some have stated that Saint Francis permitted his brothers to accept eggs, bread and milk when they begged for food, but nothing else.[14]

Saint Francis loved all God's creatures and showed unselfish love to birds, beasts, and all created things. He felt a spiritual communion with all facets of nature, no matter how small or outwardly insignificant.[15] Existing in his state of universal love and understanding, he felt such tender concern for all God's creatures that he freed rabbits caught in traps, paid to free sheep being led to slaughter, and threw fish back into the water.[16]

Saint Francis' concepts of Franciscan Teachings included his vision of the Lord being shared in some measure amongst all created things.[17] He sensed that all nature "was a vast brotherhood and he felt himself borne upon the stream of universal life; and in all this life he saw a kinship with the sacred humanity of Jesus Christ."[18] He felt that careless destruction of nature was sacrilegious, and because of his beliefs in merciful compassion, he was known to have picked up worms from the road and placed them in safer places so they would not be run over and killed. He possessed an unselfish love of birds and beasts and all created life, and felt that all beings had a life akin to his own. According to his beliefs, man should not enslave nature to his own sin nor take away its freedom—stating it is, "Lust of dominion which destroys the freedom of life."[19]

Saint Francis spent his final years in prayer and contemplation in a small cell on Mount Alvernia. He received the miracle of stigmata,[20] but humbly tried to conceal these wounds by covering his hands. For over two years, his health progressively weakened, with the stigmata being a source of constant pain. He passed on in 1226 at the age of forty-four, yet his vision of God's presence in all creation and all creatures has remained as a lasting legacy of his great compassion.[21] Because of his love for all creation, Saint Francis has become a symbol of compassion for all of Christianity.

Saint Clare of Assisi

Founder of the Poor Clares
1193-1253 CE
August 11

Saint Clare left her home to dedicate her life to God. She felt compassion for all beings – from the greatest to the smallest.

Saint Clare was born of noble birth in Assisi, Italy, at a time of great economic upheaval and warfare. When she was eighteen, Saint Francis had come to preach at the church in Assisi where she had been studying, and she was inspired by his words. She felt drawn to seek him out and pleaded for his assistance so that she, too, might live "after the manner of the Holy Gospel."[22] The evening after Palm Sunday procession, Clare ran away to the little town where Saint Francis lived with his community. They met her at the door and in front of the alter of the Blessed Virgin. She had Saint Francis cut off her hair and accepted a penitent habit of sackcloth to tie around her with a cord. She was then placed, and well received, in a Benedictine convent.

When this event was made public, her friends and relations came to drag her bodily from the retreat, but she would not budge. She said that God had called her to His service, and the more others tried to persuade her from her convictions, the more God would give her strength to resist and overcome them. Saint Francis soon removed her to another convent and eventually to a poor house contiguous with the church. Eventually, all accepted the meaningful nature of her sacrifice, and her sister, Agnes, her widowed mother, and a total of sixteen other women joined her.

Saint Clare and her followers wore no shoes or stockings, or any covering on their feet. They did not speak when it was not necessary to do so as Clare believed that holy silence prevented sins of the tongue and also left one's mind free to contemplate God. They observed perpetual abstinence from meat. When others sought to give material possessions to her sisters and her as gifts, Saint Clare would not accept these. Pope Gregory IX permitted her the privilege of poverty so she might refuse such gifts, issuing the statement, "He who feeds the birds in the air and gives raiment and nourishment to the lilies of the field will not leave you in want of clothing or of food until he comes Himself to minister to you for eternity."[23]

Clare prayed intently, and legend has it that her prayers before the Blessed Sacrament stopped an invading army of Saracens that sought to plunder Assisi. This humble woman was able to lead her convent for forty years and continually sought to be a servant to all who joined. She washed the feet of the lay sisters when they had returned from begging, served at table, and looked after the sick. In the tradition of Saint Francis, she possessed great love of the natural world and an appreciation of god's creation manifest in nature.

Saint Clare died at the age of sixty after enduring sickness for many years. Following her devoted and courageous example, there were nearly 22,000 Franciscan sisters by the end of the twentieth century. Clare was ever faithful and when she met her final days she accepted her fate, saying, "Go in peace; you have been on the right road."[24] Saint Clare was a woman of sacrifice and humility who lived without consuming flesh so as to share the privilege of life with all God's creatures.

Saint Aventine
of Troyes

c. 470 - 538 CE
February 4
Saint Aventine worked to
earn funds to free slaves.
He protected snakes
and birds, and risked his own
life to hide a hunted
deer in his cave.

Saint Aventine was a man of gentle soul who would neither hurt nor destroy any animal whatsoever. He saw God's presence in all people and all beings. While he served as abbot of a monastery at Troyes,[25] Aventine dispensed all the abbey's collected funds to redeem captive slaves. He once paid to free a small boy who was being led away by captives, brought him up as his own son, and helped him through his studies to become a monk. As Saint Aventine grew older, he decided to leave the monastery hoping to spend his later years as a spiritual sage living in a forest cave.

Aventine was a man of such great compassion, that when he would see small fish entrapped in pitchers of water brought from the river, he would return them to the stream. He would also aid snakes that his cart had rolled over, and cared for them until they returned to health. He would thrust forth his palm with crumbs for the birds and they would reciprocate by perching upon his fingers. Once he even hid a deer that was being pursued by hunters within his own cave, until such time as the hunters had passed further along and the deer was out of danger.

In works of art, Saint Aventine is frequently portrayed as a kindly, humble saint taking a splinter out of a bear's foot. The bear had been a wild one, suffering pain from a wood splinter embedded in its paw. After the saint removed the splinter, he apologized to the animal for his own inability to recognize his pain sooner.[26] This kindly saint loved all God's creatures as himself. He lived as a compassionate vegetarian and showed concern for each and every humble being he encountered.

Saint Felix of Cantalice

c. 1520 - 1587 CE
May 18

Saint Felix spent his life begging for food and alms so he might help those rejected by the rest of society.

Saint Felix was born into a very devout peasant family. At the age of twelve, he had been hired out as a shepherd and also as a ploughman. While working in the fields, he suffered a severe accident. He was plowing with two young bullocks, when they became frightened, bolted, and ran the plough over his fragile little body. Others thought that definitely he would die from such severe trauma, yet his life was spared. In gratitude for the miraculous sparing of his life, he resolved to live in a monastery and repay God for His mercy.

Felix spent the next forty years of his life begging for food and alms, obtaining rations that enabled the older and infirm friars to exist. Any extra alms he received, he shared with the poor. He often suffered insults, discomfort, and fatigue in this capacity, yet he never swayed from performing these worthwhile deeds.[27] He was a man of great spirituality and sensed that God was always present with him. He shared concern for everyone and everything, saying "All earth's creatures can lift us up to God...if we know how to look at them with an eye that is single."[28]

He sought a life of poverty and humility, assisting the poor with alms, tending to the sick with his own hands, and consoling the dying with his peaceful words. For a good part of his life, he lived on no more than bread and water, and always offered thanks to God for these meager gifts. Most of all, Felix loved creation as one unified whole, and lived a life of nonviolence in the sincere belief that all creatures are one in the eyes of God.

Saint Joseph of Cupertino

c. 1603 - 1663 CE
September 18

Saint Joseph was blessed with powers of healing and of levitation. The pope was concerned, saying one Saint Francis of Assisi was enough. Joseph was forced to live in seclusion.

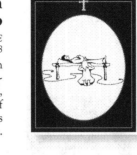

Saint Joseph was born into an exceptionally poor family. His mother actually had to give birth to him in a shed because his father had sold their house to pay debts. To add to these tragedies, his father died while he was still an infant. Joseph suffered an unspecified illness for three years, after which he remained lethargic and absent-minded. At the age of seventeen he sought to lead a religious life, but was refused admission to a religious Order. But Franciscans, moved by compassion, received Joseph into their monastery, where he gained great admiration because of his commitment to prayer, penance, and sincere devotion.

After entering the priesthood, Joseph decided to spend the rest of his life existing on only herbs and dried fruit.[29] His scholastic aptitude was weak, yet he seemed to have been gifted with great spiritual powers of levitation. Many people, including dukes and princes, swore under oath to having witnessed these actions. In addition, Joseph possessed the power to heal others through his prayers.

His superiors were frightened of his gifts, and although Pope Urban III cleared Joseph of any attempts to feign holiness, Joseph was removed from his parish, not allowed to say mass, and not even permitted to give advice. Pope Alexander VII said one Saint Francis of Assisi was enough! Joseph was forced to live in seclusion. He subsequently suffered depression due to this rejection. Joseph died a humble death, without having been restored to his full position.[30] The memory, however, of this spiritual, compassionate, and non-violent man has remained a legacy of the power attainable by one who sees God in all and seeks to share God's love with all creation.

Chapter 6

Founders of Monastic Orders

A wealth of spiritual wisdom and compassion lies hidden behind the silent walls, rules, and traditions of the ancient Christian monastic Orders. This wisdom, however, has often been of such profound depth and such subtle nature, that few have grasped its messages. The men and women who founded and lived by the principles of these religious Orders adhered to their principles so as to cultivate their minds, their sensitivities, and their insight to understand the meanings of life, death, the hereafter, and God.

Mahatma Gandhi has spoken of the wisdom he gained while visiting a Cistercian monastery in South Africa. He described the monastery as a beautiful, deeply spiritual facility in which most followers observed silence. One of the monks said that silence helped each to listen to the small voice that is always speaking within us, as it will not be heard if we continually speak. Gandhi understood the meaning of this statement, and began to live by it. He recognized an inner voice within each individual stating that "The 'Inner Voice' may mean a message from God or from the devil, for both are wrestling for the human breast."[1] It was during times of silence that he felt he was better able to communicate with God, stating "The music of life is in danger of being lost in the music of the voice."[2]

Many of the foundational rules and values among those leading monastic lives within the various vegetarian monastic communities were quite similar. These included silence, as well as total sacrifice of self, an emptying of the ego, the elimination of material possessions, and the conviction to live without harming or killing any of God's creatures.

Much of the knowledge concerning the ancient vegetarian traditions within Christianity has been preserved through out the tumultuous centuries of religious transition as a result of the organized documentation within these religious Orders. Founders of these Orders, as well as the thousands of individuals who lived according to their values, have helped to preserve Christianity's ancient spiritual meanings. Such individuals have shared their values of simplicity, obedience, sincerity, and austerity, as well as the important principle of not abusing the rest of creation. Their respect for the entirety of humanity, concern for all nature, and commitment to prayer and contemplation, are all powerful examples of the depth of their insight. They lived as vegetarians for reasons that varied from one Order to another, yet all reasons were meaningful. These reasons include those of personal sacrifice, ethics, ecology, nonviolence, and the desire to live in the image of God.

Saint Benedict

Order of the Benedictine Monks
480-550 CE
March 21
Saint Benedict sought a life of peace, prayer, and non-violence. He lived in a tiny hillside cave, but so many disciples joined him, that he formed a religious Order of the Benedictines.

Little is known of the early years of Saint Benedict except that he was born in central Italy and began his studies in Rome. While he was still a young man, pagan and Arian tribes overran his world, and the entire countryside experienced pillage and devastation due to this war. Benedict had become so discouraged at witnessing the level of immorality that followed the war that he felt the need to leave the city and to live in solitude abandoning worldly values. To find such peace, he traveled to an isolated region with bleak terrain to live as a hermit. It was during these years, in the wild and rocky countryside of Subiaco, east of Rome, that he met a monk, Romanus, to whom he opened his heart. Romanus secretly brought bread daily to Benedict, then a young recluse, by hoisting this sustenance down a rope over the rocks to his tiny cave.[1]

Benedict lived in this cave for many years, until eventually shepherds found his tiny hidden cell and began to visit him. They brought him food and listened to his words of enlightenment. They greatly admired his spiritual wisdom, saying that what he said to them they took back in their hearts as nourishment for life.[2] Disciples began to gather around him and with the passage of time there were so many followers that Benedict actually founded twelve monasteries to accommodate all of these holy disciples. Each monastery was inhabited by twelve monks, and all aspired to gain wisdom from his presence. Benedict's austerity, however, evoked envy from those of less fervent discipline than himself, and these jealous enemies attempted to poison him. He needed to flee from these persecutors. While seeking refuge in another region, he found a land thriving in paganism. He dedicated the next fourteen years of his life as a missionary and apostle to these people.[3]

So many of the young men within this village became his disciples that Benedict needed to create an official Rule for his followers concerning monastic life. In an attempt to encourage others to live in accordance with his Rule, Benedict became the primary embodiment of it. All his followers were required to labor as brethren to cultivate the soil and to build the monasteries. He was a tolerant man concerning various shortcomings within his followers, but never would he accept violence amongst members of the group.[4]

Benedict created a set of rules for members of the monastery to follow. In chapter Thirty-nine of his Rule, termed the *Rule of Saint Benedict*, he describes guidelines concerning consumption of food. For their daily meal, his monks were to eat two cooked dishes. So if someone was intolerant of one of the foods, he might eat the other. If fresh fruit or vegetables were available, a third dish of one of these could be added. A pound of bread would be sufficient for each person per day and over-indulgence was to be avoided. Finally, the meals were to be vegetarian, "Except the sick who are very weak, let all abstain entirely from the flesh of four-footed animals."[5]

By the ninth century, Saint Benedict's Rule became the dominant monastic Rule in the western world, a status it still holds today. Benedict created this Rule as he felt it was God's wish. Even Saint Gregory stated that, "Benedict possesses the spirit of one man only, the Savior, who fills the heart of the faithful."[6] Benedict believed that good works flowed from uttering truth, giving charity, relieving the poor, naked and sick, living a life of non-violence, and attributing to God, whatever good one sees in oneself.[7] Eventually, he extended his ministries to the people of the surrounding country— curing their sick, relieving their distressed, distributing alms, and aiding their poor. It was said that he was able to foretell many events and was even able to predict his own death. Benedict lived as a non-violent man of peace and founded his Order, committed to living in the image of God.

Saint Bruno

Order of the Carthusian Monks
c. 925-965 CE
October 11
Saint Bruno lived a life
of prayer high on the craggy
rocks of a desert mountain
range. A group of hermits
joined him to learn
from his holy ways.

Saint Bruno was descended from an ancient and honorable family in Cologne, Germany. He was the youngest child of Henry the Fowler, king of the Germans, and his wife, Saint Matilda. As a child, he exhibited great earnestness, and nothing childish or frivolous ever appeared in his mannerisms. He also seemed to possess a distinct orientation toward religious life.[8] He rose to distinction, taught philosophy, and embarked upon the study of theology, a path that eventually led him to receive minor orders. Upon entering the clergy, he remained in a monastery for eighteen years until such time when he left with several friends in search of a more strenuous, sparse existence of even fewer attachments.[9]

These young hermits left in search of a place where they might serve God away from worldly affairs. They chose a site in the desert of Chartreuse[10]—a site difficult to access because of its remote location high in the mountains. Its terrain was beset with high craggy rocks, and its climatic conditions harsh. It was covered with snow and thick fog almost all year long. Saint Bruno and his companions recognized this site as the perfect location and began to build an oratory, as well as several small cells. It was from these humble beginnings that the Carthusian Order began, taking its name from the desert of Chartreuse.[11]

This small group of monks lived in tiny cells, ate only one meal a day, kept everything among them very poor, wore simple garments, and performed strenuous manual labor following every prayer. They ate only vegetarian foods, mostly bran bread, and never would they consume the flesh of animal or fish. In addition, they would not permit any person among them to hunt, fish, or even drive cattle. Their constant occupation was that of praying, reading, performing manual labor, and transcribing books.[12] The abbot wrote of them: "Their dress is meager and poorer than that of other monks. They fast almost perpetually; eat only bran bread; never touch flesh. They never touch fish but will eat it if given them as alms."[13]

The inspiration for the Order was drawn from the ancient hermit monks of the early Church in the desert of Egypt. Saint Bruno had never anticipated that he would be creating a new Order; he merely wished to follow a life of greater austerity and simplicity.[14] Although Saint Bruno found his greatest peace in the solitude of the desert, Pope Urban II convinced of Bruno's prudence and learning, ordered him to Rome to assist him in the government of the Church. To the humble monk, his greatest pleasures were his austerities, and going to Rome was a severe trial of his obedience. With inexpressible grief he left his disciples and journeyed to Rome.

Once in Rome, the pope recognized Bruno's holiness and consulted him in all affairs of religion and conscience. After many years, the pope finally permitted Saint Bruno to return once again to the solitude and simplicity of the wilderness, where he died peacefully in the presence of his monastic brethren.[15] Saint Bruno lived with the belief that a life of austerity and prayer, untarnished by the goods of the world, and without inflicting suffering upon another being, was a path that would lead one closer to fulfilling one's service to God.

Saint Alberic

Order of the Cistercians
c. 1040 - 1109 CE
January 26

Saint Alberic left a religious Order in which he sensed a lack of religious fervor to help form a new one.

The events of Saint Alberic's childhood are unknown. But it is known that as a young man, he became one of the three individuals credited with founding the Monastic Order of the Cistercians, the two others being Saint Robert of Molesme and Saint Stephen Harding. The story of Alberic's life unfolds with his having been a prior in the Benedictine monastery of Molesme.

He and the abbot, Robert, sensed an increasing loss of religious fervor among the monks. So Robert decided to leave the group. Alberic, and another individual, Stephen Harding initially remained. They had hoped to stimulate religious dedication within the group, only to end up being forced to leave the community after all. All three met once again in an isolated forest of Burgundy, France and formed the 'New Monastery', which later became Citeaux.

Robert, Alberic, and Stephen were elected abbot, prior, and sub-prior of the new foundation, respectively. Shortly thereafter, the Pope required Robert to return to Molesme, the community he had left. Alberic became abbot of the New Monastery in his place.[16] Alberic guided the new community to seek spirituality through poverty, simplicity, prayer, contemplation, and constant devotion to God. Members of the group were to live devoid of possessions, to serve the needy, and to maintain diets free of animal flesh. All personal luxuries, even those items devoted to liturgical use were rejected, as were feudal sources of revenues such as rents from outside churches or monasteries. Because of the remoteness of their chosen site, self-sufficiency became imperative. Alberic continued guiding his followers in the ways of service, austerity, holiness, and vegetarianism throughout the remaining nine years of his life.[17]

Saint Robert of Molesme

Order of the Cistercians
1027-1100 CE
April 29

Saint Robert's teachings were so wise, that twenty-one Monks followed him to the forest, as a tribe following Moses, to start a new Order of monks.

Saint Robert was born to a well-respected family in Champagne[18] and was brought up to value learning and piety. It was at the young age of fifteen that he decided to become a Benedictine monk. Within a very short time period, and in spite of his youth, he was chosen prior. Shortly thereafter he was made abbot. He did not feel fulfilled, however, within such a large community and left the monastery to join a small group of religious hermits living in cells in the desert of Colan.

As these hermits had no superior to guide them, they requested Robert to fill this role. They recognized his inherent holiness, and even when their situation in the desert became physically unbearable, they followed Robert, as a tribe following Moses, to the forest of Molesme.[19] There, they built small cells from the boughs of trees, and chose to live in great simplicity, as well as in religious dedication. In addition to prayer and meditation, all members of the group performed difficult physical labor. Meanwhile, the monks back at the monastery recognized that they had not prospered well after Robert left, and obtained orders from the bishop and pope stating that Robert must return there. Robert was forced to leave his humble cell and to return to the monks in the monastery, who still did not prosper because their motives were not spiritually pure.

Some monks, however, did recognize that the true essence of Robert's ways lay in his deep religious commitment. This group of approximately twenty-one monks left the monastery to follow Robert. They traveled to an uninhabited forest covered with brambles and woods where they lived in total fidelity to the Rule of Saint Benedict. They built themselves tiny abodes of wood, spent their days working and praying, and maintained the simplest of vegetarian diets—roots and herbs. From these humble beginnings began the Cistercian Order.[20] Saint Robert was a deeply spiritual individual who wanted nothing more than a life of simplicity in reverence to God. His austerity, vegetarianism, and humble non-assuming nature were all symbolic of the holiness of this man of God.

Saint Stephen Harding

Order of the Cistercians
c. 1060 - 1134 CE
January 26
Saint Stephen was a deeply religious man. He correctly foresaw the coming of thirty men to his monastery sharing his desire for selfless sacrifice.

Saint Stephen Harding was an Englishman who helped found the Order of Cistercians. Little is known of his parentage or family, except that during his childhood he was placed in an abbey in Dorsetshire[21] where he was educated well. He seems to have left the abbey without any idea of becoming a monk and journeyed to Scotland, Paris, and then Rome - possibly to study. On the way back, he passed a forest in Burgundy and came upon a grouping of rough huts inhabited by monks. The monks spent their days in manual labor, prayer, and poverty. They subsisted on but a few vegetables each day.[22] Stephen found kindred spirits in the priors, Robert and Alberic, and rejoiced at the chance of being able to live with such holy individuals devoted to lives of poverty and prayer.

After several years, many others joined the group, but not all were as committed to lives of humility and self-sacrifice. In 1098, Stephen, Robert, and Alberic journeyed to Lyons and received permission from the Archbishop of France to start their own community. With only the clothes they were wearing, plus vessels and vestments to celebrate mass, they journeyed to the remote forest of Citeaux, the loneliest and most uncultivated region in the countryside. They began to build a monastery there, but superiors in Rome ordered Robert back to the Monastery of Molesme. It was with much difficulty that they converted the forest into arable lands, and with much dedication did they adhere to the Rule of Saint Benedict.

In 1109, Alberic died and Stephen was elected abbot in his place. Stephen formulated rules that the monastery was to survive without outside support and that no costly goods were to be used in the service of God. The days were difficult for the monks, and grew even more challenging when a mysterious disease began to take their lives, one by one.

Stephen asked one dying monk to give him word from beyond the grave informing him if he was performing the will of God. Soon after the monk's death, his spirit appeared to Stephen telling him that recruits would be coming, "like bees swarming in haste and overflowing the hive, would fly away and spread themselves through many parts of the world."[23] Shortly thereafter, a group of thirty men arrived at the monastery to offer themselves to religious life. The numbers of new members continued to swell. Committed to their vegetarian lifestyles, all monks undertook agricultural work with great fervor and became pioneers in agrarian reform.

By the time of Stephen's death, the Order had spread beyond France, and with its later (seventeenth-century) Trappist reform and the inclusion of nuns, the Order spread to five continents.[24] Throughout the ensuing years, Stephen and the other monks remained committed to their lives of poverty, non-violence, and prayer so as to serve God best with all their hearts.

Saint Gilbert of Sempringham

Order of the Gilbertines
c. 1100 - 1189 CE
February 4

Saint Gilbert spent his life teaching the poor in a free school. Although he received a meager stipend, he gave all away to the indigent.

Saint Gilbert was born in Lincolnshire, England[25] where he received a religious education. He felt a calling and a commitment to live a religious life, and was subsequently ordained priest by the Bishop of London. Gilbert would teach the poor in a free school and then give his entire stipend away to the indigent. Those who followed him grew in sanctity, and as their numbers increased, Gilbert framed a set of Rules for these young men and women to help direct their lives. Gilbert sustained himself solely on vegetarian foods—roots and pulse—and always shared a plate of food from each of his meals with the poor.[26]

Initially, he fashioned the patterns of religious life for himself and his followers after the Rule of Saint Benedict.

Saint Gilbert and the sisters incurred the displeasure of King Henry II (reign 1154-1189), who accused them of assisting Thomas Becket[27] in his escape to France. Gilbert was summoned by the King to answer questions, but subsequently obtained a pardon from all charges. By the time of his death, there were over fifteen hundred members within his monasteries—all living by the Rule he envisioned for those seeking a life of holiness and dedication.[28] Gilbert chose to live in simplicity, in sacrifice for others, and in never taking more from this earth than he needed. His humble life was but one example of his gentle soul—a soul that was devoted to the spiritual service of God.

Saint Dominic

Order of the Dominicans
1170-1221 CE
August 8
Saint Dominic crossed
the Alps on foot to preach
at friaries in Spain, Poland,
Scandinavia, Italy, Germany,
Hungary, Palestine,
and Morocco.

Saint Dominic was noted to have been a devout child during his youth in Old Castile, Spain.[29] By the age of fourteen, he had decided to enter the university to study theology. He was a man of such concern for others, that when famine broke out, he sold all his books to buy food for the needy. Dominic asked God to help him in his desire to assist others achieve salvation and in directing his own life in attaining higher states of contemplation.

By the age of thirty-one, he was elevated to a high position within the Church. While in this position, he observed that people were not following the teachings of those priests they felt were not committed. To rectify this, he set himself as an example, one he hoped others would follow. As such an example, he chose to live on purely vegetarian sustenance. He rarely ate more than bread and soup.[30]

Whenever he found people being led astray, he would be there to help them with instruction, patience, penance, fasting, tears, and prayer. After having been a preacher for ten years, he desired to become a new type of church minister - one who lived without material worldly possessions. He felt that as long as people had love of worldly possessions, these would fill their hearts and would replace any room potentially available for the Holy Spirit. With this concept in mind, Dominic contemplated the creation of an Order of religious men. These men would dedicate themselves to preaching and live in extreme poverty, maintain perpetual abstinence from meat, and receive sustenance in the form of alms from the faithful. Saint Dominic envisioned a Church in which the spirit and the example of the preachers would spread the light of the Church.[31]

By 1216, Pope Innocent III gave Dominic approval to formulate rules for the religious order he would be permitted to form. After many political and religious challenges, his Order, the Paris Dominicans, were given a church, as well as another building for their monastery. Dominic crossed the Alps on foot (his usual practice) and met his spiritual brothers at Bologna. He preached wherever he traveled and bid his friars to act similarly— in the spirit of prayer, humility, self-denial, and obedience. Soon, his Order consisted of sixty friaries, with friars in Poland, Scandinavia, Germany, Hungary, Palestine, and Morocco.

Many noted that Dominic's face radiated inner peace. At fifty-one years of age, however, exhausted from his years of work, he knew he was approaching death.

He told his friars, "My dear sons, these are my bequests: practice charity in common; remain humble; stay poor willingly."[32] Saint Dominic maintained visions of a world in which people were guided by values and prayer, rather than by possessions. His desire to live in total commitment to God led him to live as an ascetic, as a vegetarian, and as a man maintaining his focus on devotion and prayer toward God.

Saint John of Matha

Order of the Trinitarians
c. 1167 - 1213 CE
December 17
Saint John risked his life to meet with the King of Morocco and was able to secure freedom for hundreds of Christian slaves from Morocco, Tunis and Spain.

Although Saint John was born into a well-to-do family in Provence, France[33] he found himself being called to the solitude and contemplative atmosphere of a hermitage. He asked his father for permission to study theology, and was able to do so in Paris. He completed his doctorate studies and subsequently was ordained as a priest. His instincts led him to the quietude of prayer and to perform merciful acts for those in need. He gave away his entire inheritance to the poor and frequently visited hospitals to care for the sick.

After many years had passed, John heard tales of a holy hermit. He felt compelled to seek him out. When he did, he begged the hermit to admit him to the solitude of his hermitage so he might be instructed in his ways of perfection. The two holy men grew in spiritual strength in one another's presence and eventually devised a plan to ransom and rescue Christians being held as prisoners of war.[34]

They obtained the benediction of Pope Innocent III to follow through with their mission, and formed the Order of Holy Trinity to do so.[35] The first Rule of the Order was that the priests must not consume any foods that were not vegetarian. For their sustenance, they were permitted bread, pulse, herbs, eggs, oil, milk, cheese, and fruit. It was only during high festivals that if others offered them flesh or fish, that they might consume these, and only specifically on the condition that these were donated to them.[36] They received funds to build convents so that numerous holy individuals who wished to join them were able to do so.

The priests were able to meet with the king of Morocco and free one hundred and eighty-six Christian slaves from Morocco, and several hundred more from Tunis and Spain. In spite of much hostility against the priests from enemy ships, the priests successfully completed every voyage and were able to save the lives of innumerable people.[37] Saint John lived his entire life as a man of peace and gentleness, held no malice toward either human or animal, and lived in constant devotion toward his fellow beings.

Saint Albert
of Jerusalem

Order of the Carmelites
c. 1149 - 1214 CE
September 14
Saint Albert possessed the ability
to read the feelings of others.
He was called upon to facilitate
communication between
the governments, the pope,
and the Islamic community.

Saint Albert came from a well-established family in Parma, Italy.[38] Little is known of his early life except that he completed studies in both theology and law, and then joined the priesthood. He seemed to possess a natural ability to resolve conflicts diplomatically and subsequently became an invaluable mediator. By the age of thirty-five, he was made bishop. He was chosen to mediate a dispute between the government and Pope Clement III, as well as between Pope Innocent III and leaders of two other cities in their attempts to secure peace. Eventually, when others recognized his abilities in understanding human nature, he was sent to become patriarch of Jerusalem.[39]

By this time, the third crusade was over, and Albert's talents in diplomacy and reconciliation had been very advantageous in securing peace between Christians and Moslems. Albert was most remembered, however, for his hermitic endeavors. The prior of the hermits who lived in Mount Carmel[40] asked Albert to translate their way of life into a set of rules. He defined sixteen rules concerning obedience to superiors, accommodations for each hermit, sharing of facilities, manual work for all, silence from unnecessary words, living in constant prayer, and perpetual abstinence from meat.

His defining rules made Albert the first legislator, if not the founder, of the Carmelite Order.[41] Although it is not specifically stated whether Albert lived by the same dietary standards that he set for his monks, his apparent reverence for the value of vegetarianism amongst Carmelites demonstrated his support and respect for this principle.

Saint Angela Merici

Order of the Ursulines
1470 - 1540 CE
January 27

Saint Angela felt such compassion for the poor that she created a free school. She gathered the poorer girls of the town and educated them herself.

Saint Angela was born to a family of farmers in Lombard, Italy[42] the fifth of six children. While still exceptionally young, she witnessed the death of her older brother and three sisters, and shortly thereafter, both her parents. She and her surviving sister became wards of her uncle. Not much is known concerning the rest of her childhood except that she was a pious child and was fascinated by stories of Saint Ursula. The deaths of her family members obviously came as a great shock to her.

One day, she received a vision from her beloved older sister, and decided to consecrate her life to God. She followed a life of extreme austerity, modeled after the life of Saint Francis, taking no possessions as her own and living entirely as a vegetarian—consuming only bread, vegetables, and water.[43]

After the death of her uncle, when Angela was but twenty-two years of age, she took it upon herself to educate the poorer children of the town. She gathered together the little girls of the neighborhood and gave them regular and systematic instructions. This work that started humbly began to flourish, and soon, the leading families of the town brought their daughters to her for education.[44] Her works of charity became widely recognized throughout the city.

Angela recognized that these young women of poverty would be forced into the most menial of services, prostitution, or begging. To remedy this, she began by setting up refuges for these poor women who had not found husbands. Then she created homes for them, run by older matrons, often widows, to protect them. Finally, she made sure that neither the younger women were exploited sexually, nor the older women exploited financially.

Although Angela had her ardent supporters, she also had many enemies. Through all her trials, she held firm in her commitment to educate and protect the young women of her city as if they were her own. In 1535, she, and twenty-eight other young women, consecrated themselves to the service of God. She placed these women under the protective blessing of Saint Ursula, the patroness of medieval universities who was venerated as a leader of women. Hence evolved the name Ursulines for her followers, the name under which her Order was born. Going about in her Franciscan habit, she became a well-respected figure, known for her compassion toward all in need, her belief in non-violence toward all creatures, her physical austerities, her devout religious convictions, and her life saving assistance to all women in need.[45]

Chapter 7

Patron Saints

Over the centuries, specific saints from among the vast and diverse categories of saints have been chosen as special protectors, or patrons, over various professions, events, diseases, and regions of the world. Some of these patron saints have been protectors of those who need healing, especially from illness, poverty, isolation, humility, starvation, and despair. Some patron saints are considered protectors of geographic regions with these regions ranging from local church communities to entire countries to large landmasses. Saints are chosen as patrons for protecting specific people performing family and community functions and for protecting people working in various professions. In general, patron saints are considered holy individuals who fulfill the role of protecting needs and causes that are important to humanity.

As early as the fourth century, local churches had already begun to select specific saints to be their patrons. Even as late as the time of Alexander III (1159-1181) bishops were permitted to declare saints as patrons. More recently, however, only the pope and his designated groups have chosen saints as patrons from among those saints who performed certain skills to those who excelled in dedicated professions. Generally, the professions chosen for patron saint protection have been those in which much sacrifice is needed, and those who provide great service to the community. Names of these patron saints are invoked with great frequency during intercessory prayer and during times of dire need.

Just as these saints represent a wide range of individuals from numerous walks of life, the reasons each chose to be vegetarian are similarly varied.

Saint Paula

Patron Saint of Widows
347 - 404 CE
January 25

After the death of her husband and child, Saint Paula raised her four remaining children alone, created homes for the poor, convents, and a hospital.

Saint Paula was born into a well-respected family in Rome where her parents gave her in marriage while she was still quite young. Her actions and grace indicated that she was a woman of virtue, and she was recognized as such by the people of that city. Through her early years of marriage, she was blessed with one son and four daughters. When Paula was only thirty-two years of age her young husband died suddenly. Paula was heart-broken. When her first daughter developed a fever and also passed on, she fell into an even greater state of sorrow.

After these losses, Paula decided to dedicate the remainder of her life to the will of God. She dressed simply, gave her possessions away to the poor, and abstained from all foods derived from the flesh of animals, eggs, and fish.[1]

She sought out those in need, sharing their burden of suffering and anguish. After raising her children in holiness, Paula felt a calling to live in the desert and maintain a serene contemplative existence in a hermitage. She traveled to Jerusalem, moving later to Bethlehem. There, she opened a house to aid the poor and a resting place for pilgrims. She built a well-equipped hospital for the infirm as well as three convents for women similarly called to lives of devotion. In these humble quarters, the religious women worked by weaving clothes for themselves and for countless indigent individuals.[2]

Paula spent her later years sharing worldly and spiritual wisdom with other pious women, making pilgrimages throughout Jerusalem, and bringing the word of God to the masses. Throughout her life, she remained true to her principles of austerity, prayer, commitment to non-violence, and dedication to all in need.[3]

Saint Genevieve

Chief Patroness of the City of Paris
c. 420 - c. 500 CE
January 2

Saint Genevieve believed prayer could save Paris from an attack by Attila the Hun. She inspired the entire city to pray and the invaders miraculously changed their plans and retreated.

Saint Genevieve was born in a small village close to Paris. As a child, she radiated such a sense of holiness that while Saint Germanus was traveling through France, he predicted the coming of Genevieve's future sanctity. When she was only seven years of age, she decided to dedicate her life to God and to give herself totally with devotion and sacrifice to God accepting whatever He planned for her. One day, when she was begging her mother's permission to enter the church, her mother struck her on the face. Suddenly, her mother lost her own vision, only to recover two months later by washing her eyes twice or thrice with water that Genevieve fetched from the well and blessed with the sign of the cross.[4]

Genevieve joined the convent by age fifteen. From that time forward, she limited both the quantity and the types of foods she consumed—choosing to exist on a diet solely of barley bread with a few beans. She adhered to this humble vegetarian diet for thirty-five years. Only at the age of fifty, by the command of certain bishops, did she modify her diet by adding a small amount of fish and milk.[5] After Genevieve was transferred to Paris, she filled her life with continual prayer interspersed with journeys to serve others in the name of charity. During these years, others were jealous of her and tried to discredit her works. With the passage of time, however, their envy turned to veneration.

When pagan King Childeric[6] captured Paris, the citizens of the city were reduced to a state of famine. Saint Genevieve ventured out as the head of a group of volunteers to find food. She was so overwhelmingly successful that she was able to bring back several boats filled with corn. The king, though originally a pagan, developed such great respect for Genevieve's courage that he prayed to her, performed many acts of generosity, spared the lives of many prisoners, and became a Christian himself.

Saint Genevieve's reputation for holiness spread far and wide. Even the king frequently sought her advice. When word came that Attila the Hun was preparing to march troops into Paris, people throughout the city made plans to abandon it.

Saint Genevieve motivated them to have faith that they could avert disaster by fasting and praying. Many devout followers passed whole days in prayer in the baptistery with Saint Genevieve as she assured them that heaven would not abandon them. Her faith came to fruition when the invaders suddenly changed their aggressive course of action. They withdrew from their invasion, sparing the city of Paris.

Saint Genevieve passed on while in her eighties, after having lived a holy, simple, spiritual and merciful life. Many miracles were said to have occurred through prayers appealing to her after her death. The most famous of these was the miracle *des Ardens*, in the year 1129, also called the miracle of the burning fever. During the reign of Louis VI, an epidemic spread throughout France and England due to people's eating rye bread infected with a dark violet fungus. The infection caused a raging fever that led to the death of fourteen thousand people. When the shrine of Saint Genevieve was carried into the cathedral, many sick people touched the shrine and recovered. Miraculously, the entire epidemic suddenly ceased, with no others becoming ill.[7]

The name of Saint Genevieve has been invoked against drought, excessive rain, flooding, and other natural disasters. Because of her work ensuring the safety of Paris, Pope John XXIII declared her patron saint of the French Security Forces. Saint Genevieve lived as a vegetarian because she felt compassion for all beings.

Saint David

Patron Saint of Wales
c.520 - 589 CE
March 1

Saint David created twelve monasteries and several churches. He assisted in the conversion of unhealthy water into potable water for his entire community

Saint David has been perhaps the most celebrated of the British saints. Unfortunately, very little is known of his early years. According to legend, he was born to a Prince from North Wales. David was educated in both secular matters as well as in the psalms. He joined the priesthood and was sent to live on a small island so that he might continue his studies in peace and simplicity. It was said that, while still a student, he restored sight to one of his teachers who had become blind from much weeping.[8]

David embarked upon a life of great purpose—building twelve monasteries, several churches, and treating water to make it potable. He founded his principal abbey in southwestern Wales. The abbey community lived in great austerity, imitating the Egyptian monks of the early Church. David and his fellow members within this community believed hard manual labor was the duty of all, thus preferring not to use cattle to help them plow the fields. They resolved to maintain a diet of bread and vegetables, with just a sprinkling of salt, so as not to inflict unnecessary suffering upon any creature by taking its life for food. The only liquid David consumed was water, sometimes mingled with a small amount of milk; hence he was given his nickname, Aquatis, a man of water.[9]

It is written that because David was a man of eloquent speech and deep wisdom, the patriarch of Jerusalem consecrated him archbishop of his region in Europe. He accepted this position only on the terms that he might function in a site of quietness and solitude.

Saint David lived maintaining a strict vigil of continuous prayer from Friday through Sunday. At the time of his death, his last words to his monks and neighbors were, "Be joyful, brothers and sisters. Keep your faith, and do the little things that you have seen and learned with me."[10] David sought a path of sacrifice, prayer, and constant toil in devotion to God. Never would he allow his followers to abuse animals as beasts of burden. David lived a life of peace, mercy, and concern for all creation.

Saint Leonard of Noblac

Patron Saint against Burglaries
Sixth Century
November 6

When the queen of Franks went into labor in the forest, Saint Leonard prayed unceasingly. It was believed his prayers saved both mother and child.

Although not much is known concerning the early history of Saint Leonard, he eventually became one of the most popular saints of Western Europe. He was believed to have been of Frankish noble birth and to have converted to Christianity at a later age. Although he was offered the position of bishop, he chose, instead, to lead a life of simple anonymity and of humility. He moved to a remote forest, rid himself of all worldly possessions, and began his life of spiritual dedication in an isolated cell. His days were filled with prayer. His diet consisted merely of fruits and vegetables. Never would he consume meat or foods of animal origin.[11]

One day when the king of the Franks had been hunting in the forest, the queen who was with him suddenly went into labor. The labor became very difficult and all feared the queen might lose her life. As the labor progressed, Saint Leonard prayed intently and unceasingly. The queen delivered safely: both she and her child were spared. All in attendance, the king included, felt marked gratitude toward the peaceful saint.[12]

Many disciples came to learn from the manner of this quiet saint, and eventually, a community of dedicated followers formed around him. This community grew in numbers and formed a monastery. By the time of his death, Leonard was revered for his holiness and his miracles, particularly his prayers that seemed to facilitate the release of prisoners.

The church at Noblac had become the site of many pilgrimages, especially by pregnant women anticipating labor and by those released as prisoners of war.[13] This saint's gentle mannerisms and sensitivity to all in need were reflected in his life of non-violence, of compassion to both man and beast, and in the successes of his merciful, spiritual prayers.

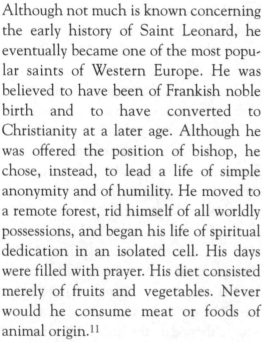

Saint Kevin

Patron Saint of Dublin
c. 498 - 618 CE
June 3

Saint Kevin lived in the forest and learned of foods, such as berries and apples, which he used to help others attain health

Although little is known concerning the early life of Saint Kevin, it is believed that he was of royal descent. Writings indicate that when he was seven years of age, his devoutly religious parents sent him to be educated by monks. These monks cared for him throughout his youth until he reached adulthood. After he was ordained, Kevin moved away to live secretly in solitude. While in the forest, he lived on green vegetation and brush, avoiding animal flesh. He began a study of various forms of vegetation, such as blackberries and apples, so that he might understand their healing power.[14] When he had attained sufficient knowledge, he embarked upon a ministry of healing, making use of plants to heal those suffering from illness.

After he had lived for years in this humble manner, a farmer discovered the tremendous value of his knowledge and persuaded him to share his gifts with society. Once the wisdom and patience of this holy man were made known to others, numerous disciples flocked to him, seeking to lead similarly austere and dedicated lives with him, and to learn from his teachings.[15] Even the king sent his infant son to live with Saint Kevin so the young prince might develop character from being in the presence of such a holy man.[16]

Tales concerning Saint Kevin's understanding and compassion for animals abound. He was often depicted throughout Ireland with a blackbird perched on his outstretched hand. Legend has it that birds would settle on his hands while he remained engrossed in prayer and contemplation. He said, "I have no wish that the creatures of God should be moved because of me. All the wild creatures of these mountains are my house mates, gentle and familiar with me."[17] Kevin served, prayed, and shared his humble retreat with all creatures. He lived his peaceful life in one small, quiet site following the words of a wise man who once said, "Birds do not hatch their eggs when they are on the wing."[18] Saint Kevin's life was one of compassion, concern, and love for all beings, all people, and all creation.

Saint Anskar

Patron Saint of Denmark
801 - 865 CE
February 3

Saint Anskar organized missions to spread his teachings throughout Denmark, Norway, Sweden, and Germany.

Saint Anskar was born in a small town near Amiens, France[19] and was educated at a nearby monastery. While still quite young, he entered directly into monastic life, and gradually attained the ability to assist others in developing their religious faith. Eventually, Anskar created a school of religious education and continued, for the next thirteen years, to organize spiritual missions in Denmark, Norway, Sweden, and Germany. While on these journeys, he built churches and founded libraries.

Unfortunately, most of the religious schools he formed were totally destroyed when invaders from northern lands marched on Hamburg.[20] During this phase of history, the entire region lapsed into idolatry. Eventually, Anskar was able to return to Sweden and Denmark, with the assistance of Pope Nicholas I, to reconstruct some of these churches and rebuild the faith.[21]

Saint Anskar had a remarkable talent for preaching and his charity toward the poor knew no bounds. He sought no gain for himself, desired no possessions, wore the coarsest of clothes, and lived in contentment on bread and water. He said his only wish was that God would make him a good man.

His Nordic mission, however, was not destined to attain the lasting success that he sought. The Vikings invaded once again. The monarchy of Denmark that had aided his mission fell from the throne in 864, and the entire region fell to the Vikings. Sweden remained under their domination for the next three hundred years, and Denmark for the next two hundred. The memory of this dedicated saint has been preserved throughout the Scandinavian nations. His simple lifestyle and peaceful principles attest to the selfless nature of this gentle man of God.[22]

Saint Ulrich

Patron Saint of Augsburg
890 - 973 CE
July 4

When invaders approached Augsburg, Saint Ulrich helped create a strong protective wall around the city. He motivated the people to pray for peace. Their prayers were answered.

During his youth, Saint Ulrich had been deeply inspired by one of his uncles who had become a priest and eventually rose to the status of bishop. He had also been motivated by a young woman recluse, Wilborada, who lived beside a monastery near his home in southern Germany. At the age of seven, Ulrich had been sent to live in the monastery to be educated. While growing up, he was recognized as a young man of genius, innocence, and sincere piety, and at the age of sixteen, he was transferred to another school so that he might work with a bishop and spend most of his days in prayer and study. Ulrich eventually joined the priesthood.[23]

In the year 926, Magyars invaded the region. They plundered Augsburg, burned the city, and killed the young female recluse, Wilborada. Ulrich was emotionally devastated, but developed resolve to correct many of the wrongs of the world. He believed in total non-violence of thought and action, and would tell others, "Take away the fuel, and you take away the flame."[24] The king of Germany, Henry the Fowler, nominated Ulrich, then age thirty-two, as bishop of Augsburg.[25] Ulrich placed his heart and soul into this responsibility. He restored order, restored people's confidence, helped the city achieve prosperity, and remained a devout pastor and preacher.

Throughout these many years, Ulrich could have achieved power and distinction, yet chose to remain a simple holy man. He rose at three every morning to pray, went to the hospital daily to comfort the sick, washed the feet of twelve poor people daily, and gave alms liberally to all in need. He took his frugal meal only in the evening, and never consumed the flesh of animals.[26]

In order to protect his people against invasion by barbarians, Ulrich saw to it that the city created a strong fenced wall around it. He saw to the erection of several fortresses and prayed incessantly for his people to be spared. His prayers seemed to have been heard, as the invading barbarians suddenly panicked in their attack of Augsburg and fled in great confusion. Ulrich was remembered for his devotion to his people and for his faith in the ability of prayer and non-violence to attain just outcomes.

Saint Yvo

Patron Saint of Abandoned People
and Orphans
c. 1040 - 1115 CE
May 23

Saint Yvo protected the king's wife when the king wanted to leave her. The saint was imprisoned for these acts of compassion.

Saint Yvo seemed to have been destined to an unswerving life of religious dedication and sanctity. He was born into a well-respected family near Chartres,[27] studied theology, and joined the clergy at a monastery. While there, the superiors recognized his aptitude for scholarship and sent him for studies in theology, canon law, and scripture. After he completed his studies, his superiors made him the director of his religious community.

During those years, he oriented his teachings to helping the community attain higher levels of religious insight and dedication. He taught his followers that they were to remain silent unless they had words of value to express - words that would be helpful to another human being or that callings of charity motivated them to speak. Yvo also believed it to be of the highest importance that neither he, nor any of his followers, consumed the flesh of fish or animal.[28]

Many recognized Yvo's piety and wisdom, and when the city was in need of a new bishop, the clergy and people demanded that he be placed in this position. Although Yvo much preferred a life of humility and anonymity, Pope Urban II and King Philip both mandated that he fill this role. While serving in his position as bishop, a conflict arose. The king wanted to divorce his wife and marry another woman. Yvo felt great concern for the fate of women and children affected by such separations and he spoke out against this. So the king placed him in prison.

Fortunately, the pope was able to secure his release. For the remainder of his years, Yvo continued to speak his mind as an independent individual—always in the interest of honesty, morality, and with concern for those vulnerable within society. For himself, Yvo remained at peace in his life of simplicity and non-violence toward all. He was able to lead the simple, humble life for which he longed; a life sharing God's mercy with all.

Saint Laurence O'Toole

Patron Saint of the Archdiocese of Dublin
1123 -1180 CE
November 14

Saint Laurence spent his days comforting those needing spiritual support, including those who had been raped, maimed, or who had lost family members.

Saint Laurence was born into a family of royalty near Dublin. When he was ten years of age, violent men raided his family's home, and family members were forced to turn Laurence over as a hostage to these abductors. For two years, Laurence was badly treated, and when his father was able to gain sufficient backing, he forced the abductors to give his son back to the bishop of Glendalough. Laurence asked to remain with the Bishop, voicing his wish to live as a monk, saying: "It is my desire to have for my inheritance the service of God in the Church."[29]

When he reached twenty-five years of age, Laurence was chosen abbot of Glendalough.[30] He had become known for his virtue and prudence and for the zeal with which he reformed the Church. In his personal life, he remained merely a man of simplicity and of prayer. Laurence prayed fervently, never ate foods containing animal flesh, fasted all day Friday, and often ate no food at all. With distinct regularity, he served food to thirty poor people at his table daily.[31]

When war broke out between England and Ireland, Laurence spent his time comforting those who had been raped or maimed, had lost members of their families, or who generally needed support. He also acted as a mediator in discussions between King Henry II of England and the Irish princes. When Pope Alexander learned of Laurence's ability to deal justly with people, he gave him charge over the entire Church of Dublin.[32]

Laurence was considered a father by all, and when famine broke out after the war, he made sure that three hundred people were fed every day, and that they were furnished with clothes and other necessities of life. Laurence had given so much to everyone else that at the time of his death he was able to state in total peace, "I thank God I have not a penny left in this world to dispose of."[33] His life was one of austerity, sacrifice, and the striving to secure the blessings of peace and mercy for all others.

Saint Hedwig

Patron Saint of Brides
1174 - 1243 CE
October 17

Saint Hedwig spent her
life teaching the poor.
She maintained a home for
impoverished and abandoned
women, saving them
from living in squalor.

Saint Hedwig was born into a royal family in the year 1174. At the age of 12, she was given in marriage to Henry I, Duke of Silensa. Although she had given birth to three daughters and three sons, she chose not to communicate much with her husband. For thirty years, she occupied a different part of the castle, and often visited a convent where she slept in a common dormitory with the religious sisters. During a battle in which Henry fought, his troops were victorious in overthrowing the throne of Poland and he assumed control of the government. A sequence of events, however, led to a turn of fate in Henry's life. Following his rise to power, one of his sons overthrew him. He was also excommunicated by the church.[34] He lived the remainder of his life almost as a

monk, and Hedwig accepted his death as the will of God.

Hedwig was a composed and calm person with great inner peace. She would not wear rich clothing and resolved never to eat red meat. She maintained a diet of vegetables, bread and water, only occasionally eating fish or salad.[35] She recommended fasting as a means to live a holier life, saying that fasting could "master concupiscence, lift up the soul, firmly implant one on a path of virtue, and prepare a final reward for the Christian."

After her husband's death, Hedwig took the habit, but did not take religious vows, as she wanted to administer her property for the good of the poor. She taught the uneducated, continually supplied a home for women living in squalor with food and clothes, attended women in childbirth, visited prisoners, and interceded on behalf of those condemned to death. She is said to have performed many miracles, and has been remembered as a woman of mercy and kindness towards all.[36]

Saint Mary of Onigines

Patron Saint of Women in Labor
c. 1180-1213 CE
June 23

Mary opened her home to the destitute, abandoned, and abused. Eventually, she turned her entire home into a house for lepers.

Saint Mary was born to a wealthy family in Flanders[37] and was given in marriage at a young age to a gentleman known for his piety. Both Mary and her husband were devout in their prayers, lived simple austere private lives, and devoted themselves to serving the lepers in a section of the town called Villembroke. Although their worldly friends held them in contempt, the holy couple did not succumb to the temptations of either praise or respect.

Mary was assiduous in her meditation. She believed in hard physical work and spinning, permitted herself no more food than her body needed, and resolved to consume only vegetarian foods - black dry bread and a few herbs. She did not permit herself to eat in excess and took meals only once daily. She was said to have a remarkably tender personality and just the sound of her words were able to free bitterness from the hearts of others. After hearing of her spiritual discourses and her humble character, many disciples were drawn to her teachings.

Mary did not believe her existence was of higher worth or rank than that of any other creature. She counseled all who needed consolation concerning the mercy of the Lord, gave all her worldly possessions to the poor, and spent her years sacrificing for those afflicted with leprosy. She actually turned her house into a home for lepers.[38] After years of sacrifice, Mary left this world during her thirties. Her brief, austere and totally peaceful life had been rich in holiness, devotion to God, and sacrifice to all creation. She embodied the essence of one sharing God's wish for peace and mercy for all.[39]

Saint Elizabeth of Hungary

Patron Saint of Charity Workers
1207-1231 CE
November 17

Saint Elizabeth's heart went out to all. She organized the feeding of nine hundred people daily, provided for orphans, founded a hospital, and personally spun wool to clothe the poor.

Saint Elizabeth was the daughter of Andrew II of Hungary. At the age of four, she was betrothed to Ludwig, the eldest son of the king of Thuringia.[40] She was sent to live with her husband's family and was treated unkindly by some members of the Court who envied her kind and generous ways. Her marriage was solemnized when she was fourteen. When others tried to persuade Ludwig to send her back to Hungary, he said that he would rather forfeit a mountain of gold than give her up.

Elizabeth's needs were simple. Her days were filled with long periods of prayer and many works of charity. When others criticized her charity, her husband said, "As for her charities, they will bring upon us divine blessings. We shall not want as long as we let her relieve the poor as she does."[41] She spun coarse wool to be used by the poor, provided for all orphans at her own expense, was the founder of a hospital, fed nine hundred people daily at her own gate, and even brought a person inflicted with leprosy into her home.

Her personal needs were few. She abstained from flesh foods at all times. Her meals generally consisted of bread and honey, or dry crust. She did not like to wear rich apparel, preferring coarse undyed cloth such as those worn by the poor people.[42] While he was at war, Elizabeth's husband became afflicted with the plague and succumbed to an early death. Elizabeth's brother-in-law, Henry, overthrew her reign.

Having been illegally deposed from her royal reign, she continued helping the poor during her few unassuming and austere remaining years. She died at the age of twenty-four due to poor health, as she had become worn down after continually sacrificing herself for the welfare of others. Legends concerning the mercy of this gentle, self-effacing and pacific young woman abound and attest to the love all felt for this woman of pure holiness and grace.

Saint Ivo Helory

Patron Saint of Lawyers and Judges
1235-1303 CE
May 19

Saint Ivo was a highly skilled
attorney who always defended
the poor. He was known to
have given his bed to vagrants,
while he slept on the floor.

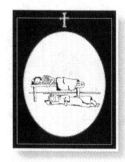

Saint Ivo Helory, also called Saint Yves of
Kermartin, had been a lawyer. He was
born in Kermartin, near Brittany,[43] and
studied canon law and theology in Paris
for ten years. While an attorney, he won a
reputation for complete impartiality and
incorruptibility, and for giving special
care to indigent clients.[44] He protected
orphans, defended the poor, and adminis-
tered justice with kindness—even earn-
ing the goodwill of the opposing side.
Never would he accept bribes, and if possible, he always tried to reconcile differences between parties to settle disputes
out of court. His defending the
plights of the downtrodden won
him the name, "the poor man's
advocate."[45]

During his middle-aged
years, he chose to leave his
career as an attorney to become
a priest. Saint Ivo believed in
simplicity and austerity. He abstained
totally from consumption of meat and
spent most of his time working for the
needy. He helped build hospitals with his
own hands, gave clothes off his back to
beggars, and even gave his bed to
vagrants, while he slept on the floor. He
was compassionate in his preaching and
shared his personal example of honesty,
compassion, and mercy with all.[46] He
chose to live in as humble and peaceful a
manner as possible, and also as a vegetarian. He shared his wish for mercy and
peace amongst all.

Saint Philip Benizi

Patron Saint of the Philippines
1233 - 1285 CE
August 22

Saint Philip chose to live in a tiny cave behind the church. He possessed great wisdom of human nature and helped those in disputes attain mutual understanding.

Saint Philip was born to a respected couple that had been childless for many years. At the age of thirteen, he was sent to Paris to study medicine, and by the age of nineteen, had earned degrees in both medicine and philosophy. After years of practicing medicine in Florence, he began to study the Bible, as well as the lives of the saints. It was then that he began to feel a religious calling. He left his career as a physician to join a group of seven Servites, a new religious Order, who had chosen to live in great austerity in small cells surviving mostly on alms.[47]

Philip had a vision that he had been called to work on a high hill. He went to a mountain church, and began performing manual labor, working there as a gardener. He lived cheerfully and obscurely in a tiny cave behind the church, until people began to recognize his innate ability to settle disputes between others. They also began to notice that he had a positive effect on sinners. After Pope Nicholas III was told of Philip's abilities, he sent him on missions to help facilitate peace between warring factions.

Upon the death of the Pope, it was rumored that the local cardinal had proposed Philip as successor to him. When word of this reached Philip, he ran away to the mountains to live the life he preferred—one of austerity consuming only vegetation and water. When the danger of fame passed, Philip returned to his humble, austere, non-violent lifestyle and continued his teachings of brotherly love, saying, "Love one another, reverence one another, and bear with one another."[48]

Saint Albert
of Trapani

Patron Saint of Carmelite Schools
1240 - 1306 CE
August 7

When war broke out, enemy ships blockaded the ports. The people were starving and called upon Saint Albert to pray. One by one, the enemy ships scattered and the food supply reached the city.

Saint Albert was born on the island of Sicily. When quite young, Albert felt a calling to become a Carmelite priest. He lived a life of humility and simplicity, making all his religious visitations on foot. He never consumed any foods the taking of which necessitated the loss of life of an animal. Rather, he sustained himself merely on bread and water. Over the years, many individuals had been converted to Christianity because of Albert's teachings and his examples of piety.

Eventually, war had broken out and the king of Naples besieged and blockaded the city's harbor. The people were not able to obtain food or water and were in imminent danger of starvation. The city's leaders, as well as the common people, came to Albert beseeching his assistance through prayer. He prayed incessantly, and suddenly, three ships arrived and successfully ran through the blockade. This miracle saved the city and was attributed directly to Albert's prayers.[49]

During the final years of his life, Saint Albert lived peacefully as a hermit near Messina and was able to live out his life of simplicity, total non-violence, and peaceful holiness.[50]

Saint Nicholas of Tolentino

Patron Saint of Animals and Babies
1245-1305 CE
September 10

Saint Nicholas spent his days in the slums – comforting the dying, healing the sick, sheltering the abandoned, and sharing his love with all children who knew none.

Saint Nicholas was born in the small town of Fermo, Italy[51] to elderly parents of very poor means. His parents considered him an answer to their prayers. It was after they had made a pilgrimage to the shrine of Saint Nicholas that they were able to conceive. His mother named him Nicholas. When still quite young, Nicholas was trained at an Augustinian friary.

From the age of fourteen on, Nicholas resolved to live a life of prayer and austerity. He avoided animal flesh, milk, fish, and eggs.[52] When he reached eighteen years of age, he eventually joined the Friary's monastic community.[53] He remained there for the remainder of his life.

His concern for the poor was so overwhelming that he was entrusted with the daily distribution of food to the poor at the monastery gate. Oftentimes, he took food meant for the clergy and dispensed it to the poor. It was at one such time that the first of his healing ministries occurred. He put his hands on the head of a diseased child saying, "The good God will heal you", and the boy was immediately cured.[54]

Nicholas would meander around the slums of Torentino, comforting the dying, waiting on (and sometimes miraculously curing) the sick and bed-ridden, watching over the children, ministering to criminals, and settling conflicts among those in quarrels and those estranged. When he performed miracles of healing, he would usually ask others to refrain telling of these miracles to others, stating, "Give thanks to God, not to me. I am only an earthen vessel, a poor sinner."[55]

In his later years, when ill and weak, his superiors tried to order him to consume meat. He felt torn, concerned about the conflicts of his obligation to be obedient and his own conscience. One night, Nicholas witnessed a vision of Mary telling him to ask for a piece of bread, dip it in water, and eat it—and he would recover. Nicolas followed this command and fully recovered. In grateful memory, Nicholas would always bless pieces of bread and give them to the sick, thus originating this act, which would become a traditional custom of Augustinian monks.[56]

Saint Rita
of Cascia

Patron Saint of Victims of Spousal Abuse
1377 - 1457 CE
May 22

Saint Rita suffered abuse from a violent husband and two violent sons. After her sons died in her arms, she dedicated her life to praying for the welfare of others.

The humble peasant parents of Saint Rita recognized when she was a child that Rita was destined to lead a holy and religious life. When she had reached the age for girls to marry, she preferred to remain single so as to follow a religious life. Her parents, however, were not able to understand or to accept her desire to follow such a life, and gave her in marriage to a brutal man.

For eighteen years, she withstood his physical and verbal abusive behavior, as well as his infidelities. He was known to be so violent that his temper was the terror of the neighborhood. As occurs often in abusive families, her two sons followed in the ways of their father and were equally violent to her, as well as to strangers. Rita would cry and pray for all of them, but was unable to change the situation.[57]

Rita's husband succumbed to his own weaknesses. He entered into a fight with another man and lost his own life. Her two sons, on the verge of avenging their father's assailant, both contracted an illness and succumbed in their mother's arms.[58] Rita was now deeply saddened, yet free to pursue her original calling. She felt a passionate desire to join a religious order. Initially, the clergy thrice rejected her because she was not a virgin. On her fourth application, Rita was admitted into the convent.

Once there, she lived in simplicity and prayer, avoiding consumption of all flesh foods. She chose to sustain herself on a humble vegetarian diet of bread and water.[59] Rita had suffered so much herself that she did not need excesses to give her joy; she needed only peace. She lived the remainder of her holy life in prayer, simplicity of wants, non-violence, gentleness, and in prayerful thanks to God.

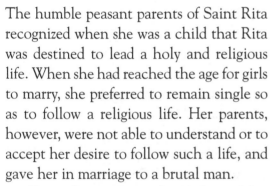

Saint Francis
of Paola

Patron Saint of Italian Seafarers
1416 -1507 CE
April 2

The king of France sought Saint Francis' help for a fatal illness. Francis told him that lives of kings, as of all men, were in God's hands.

Saint Francis was born in Paola, a small town in Calabria, Italy.[60] His parents were hard working and prayerful people who, after having been childless for many years, prayed for a child, and conceived Francis. After he was born, they chose to name him after Saint Francis of Assisi whose intercession they had sought to help them conceive. In Francis' thirteenth year, he was sent to be educated in a Franciscan friary, where he was guided to lead the humble and austere life he was to value for the remainder of his years. When he reached the age of fifteen, his parents permitted him to move to a remote town by the sea, where he lived in seclusion in a cave.[61] While there, he used no bed other than a rock and ate no food other than herbs.[62]

After seventeen years spent in contemplative seclusion, he founded his Holy Order and quickly attracted so many disciples that a church and monastery needed to be built to accommodate all of them.

Because the people of the entire countryside felt such great love for him, they assisted him in construction of a church. Even after the church was completed, however, Saint Francis continued to live the simplest of lives. He slept on a plank of wood or on the bare ground, believed in the rules of penance, charity and humility, and followed the simplest of diets. He abstained not only from all foods derived from animal flesh, but also from eggs and all products obtained from milk.[63]

Saint Francis was endowed with the gifts of miracles and prophecy. He foretold of the capture of Constantinople by the Turks,[64] as well as the fall of the kingdom of Naples. He possessed the gift of healing and because of this, wherever he traveled, people brought the sick into the streets for him to touch. Many were cured.

King Ferdinand of Naples, who had become annoyed at a reprimanding he received from Saint Francis, gave orders to have the humble saint arrested and imprisoned. The official sent to carry out these orders was so deeply touched by the saint's mannerism that he left awestruck and dissuaded King Ferdinand from carrying out such an action.[65]

Years later, Louis XI, king of France was diagnosed with a disorder of his nervous system. He was destined to succumb to a slow and difficult death. He besought the holy man to come to him, and Francis obeyed. While traveling through France to meet the king, Francis healed many of the sick along the way. When Francis finally arrived, the king fell on his knees and pleaded with Saint Francis to heal him. Francis replied, however, that the lives of kings, as of all men, were in the hands of God and all have their appointed time limits to which it behooved all to be resigned. His words were full of wisdom and his prayers brought great solace to the king who died in the arms of the saint in perfect peace.[66]

Through his self-sacrifice and humility, and by totally surrendering his life, Francis was able to live in the image of God. He drew lessons from the austere lives of the desert saints for inspiration, living his life in simplicity, kindness, nonviolence, and in appreciation and prayer to God.[67]

Saint John of Capistrano

Patron Saint of Judges and Juries
1386 - 1456 CE
March 27

The king feared his army
would lose in the war.
He called upon Saint John to
lead the forces.

Saint John settled down in the small town of Capistrano,[68] near Naples, Italy. It is not known whether he had originally come from France or Germany. It is known, however, that he studied civil and canon law in Perugia, Italy[69] where he married the daughter of one of the region's principal inhabitants and later became governor of that city. Although he had the reputation of being a man of perfect integrity, that did not protect him from becoming the victim of political resentment. A powerful, jealous family had him imprisoned as a political prisoner. After he attempted to escape, they captured him and treated him brutally in an underground dungeon. Eventually, he was able to escape. Although no mention was made as to the dissolution of his marriage, this must have occurred as John began a study of theology.

John was imbued with a deeply religious spirit. He chose to live a life of extreme austerity, to walk without sandals, to sleep but a few hours a night, and to consume only foods that did not contain the flesh of animals. During that time, Italy had been going through an era of political unrest. Saint John's sermons were a welcome source of refuge to the people. Whole towns and villages flocked to hear his sermons.

During the later years of John's life, Pope Nicholas V summoned him, under the appeal of Emperor Frederick III,[70] to assist them in the war against the Turks. The Turks had captured Constantinople and were advancing to Belgrade.[71] John himself led the troops to Belgrade. It was believed that his prayers, as well as the military expertise of their commander, motivated the advancing forces to suddenly and totally abandon their siege, hence saving all of Europe.

Unfortunately, an infection that had been caused by the thousands of unburied corpses led to the death of their leader, Commander Hunyady.[72] Only a brief month or two later, after years of toil and austerities, Saint John himself passed on. His prayers, guidance, bravery, and self-sacrifice helped to save a nation.[73] John wished no ill upon any being, felt compassion for both friend and foe, and left a lasting legacy of the power of prayer.

Saint John of Kanti

Patron Saint of Lithuania and Poland
1390 - 1473 CE
December 23

Saint John gave away all he possessed to the poor. Once when he gave away his only meal, he returned to find his plate full.

Saint John of Kanti was born into a fairly affluent family in Poland and studied at the university in Krakow. He was ordained a priest soon after he completed his studies. When he was advised to modify the strictness of his life, lest these might adversely affect his health, he pointed to the Desert Fathers of the Church as examples of those who lived long lives and thrived as a result of their spiritual and ascetic practices. John gave away all his goods and money to the poor, slept on the floor, and resolved never to eat meat.[74] When traveling to Rome, a journey he made four times in his life, he walked the entire distance carrying his luggage on his back.

While still a young priest, John had been dining and noticed a famished-looking beggar pass the door. John jumped up to give his entire meal to this man. When he returned, his plate was miraculously full again. Unfortunately, John's success as a teacher and a preacher created envy in the hearts of others who then sidelined him to a position as a parish priest. He persevered there for eight years during which time he won the hearts of the local people who then accompanied him on his journey when he was again recalled as a teacher.

He became professor of sacred Scripture at a university and held that position for the remainder of his life. He advised his pupils, "Fight all false opinions, but let your weapons be patience, sweetness, and love. Roughness is bad for your own soul and spoils the best cause."[75] When John lay dying, all felt sorrow, as his teachings and self-sacrificial actions had been appreciated and loved by many. Saint John sought to live in austerity and without inflicting even the slightest harm, physically or spiritually, upon any being.

Saint Peter
of Alcantara

Patron Saint of Night Watchmen
1499 - 1562 CE
October 19

Saint Peter felt all change must
come from within. He believed
one must correct one's own
faults before criticizing the
faults of others or of society.

Saint Peter was born in a small Spanish
town where his father held the position of
governor. His father died while Peter was
still a youth. At the age of sixteen, he
joined an Order of strict Franciscan friars.
He was a man who believed individuals
must exercise control over their own
actions. It was because he had trained
himself to require little sleep, that he subsequently became known as the patron
saint of night watchmen.[76] He refrained
from owning or desiring possessions, kept
only one habit, went barefoot, and never
consumed either meat or wine. He prayed
three hours every day, and forbid the friars
under him from accepting stipends at
Mass, stating that all their needs would be
met by alms.

When other people lamented about
the ills of society, Peter would say: "The
remedy is simple. You and I must first be
what we ought to be; then we shall have
cured what concerns ourselves. Let each
one do the same, and all will be well. The
trouble is that we talk of reform-
ing others without ever reform-
ing ourselves."[77] He was very
concerned about several ills in
the Church.

Much information about
Saint Peter's spiritual life has
been preserved in the writings
of Saint Teresa of Avila, a similarly motivated religious reformer. Saint Peter first
met Saint Teresa in 1560. Teresa stated
that he was the person who actually
inspired her to stand behind her principles
of religious reform. She described Peter as
a man whose "Poverty was as extreme as
his mortification, even from his
youth....He spoke little unless questions
were asked of him; and he answered in a
few words, but in these he was worth hearing, for he had an excellent understanding."[78]

Peter had such love of solitary contemplation, that after spending hours in
prayerful deep thought, he was often able
to instill great spiritual knowledge in others. Teresa stated that the book on prayer
that Peter had written had given her the
strength she needed to carry her cross.
Peter's life was one of self-sacrifice, devotion to God, austerity, and one totally
devoid of animal flesh. He believed that
in his simplicity, he had found God.

Saint Francis Xavier

Patron Saint of Foreign Missions
1506-1552 CE
December 3

Saint Francis was chosen by Saint Ignatius of Loyola to spread Jesus' teachings to India. Francis grew to love the people of India and felt as one with them.

Saint Francis Xavier was born in a castle in Spain, the youngest child of quite a large family. At the age of seventeen, he began his studies at the University of Paris where he met another Spaniard of noble birth, Ignatius of Loyola. Xavier, however, did not at first recognize the influence this holy man, Ignatius, would exert on him during these impressionable years. Eventually, Francis became one of the original seven Jesuit (Society of Jesus) priests, along with its founder Ignatius, who made vows of chastity and poverty in the service of God. Years later, when King John III asked Saint Ignatius to choose a priest to send on the first missionary expedition to India, Ignatius appointed Saint Francis.

Saint Francis was thirty-five years old at the time. His six-month voyage on a vessel filled with nine hundred Portuguese sailors, soldiers, and passengers, was a challenge for him. He heard confessions regularly, and cared for those with scurvy—even giving up his cabin to the sick.[79]

Upon reaching Goa,[80] a mixed Portuguese-Indian community on the west coast of India, he found the people in such need of spiritual support that he began his teaching by example. He lived with great austerity and in continual prayer, and always came before the people as one of them. His mission took him on a journey to the lower tip of India thirteen times. He decided to follow the same diet as the poorest of people—a strictly vegetarian diet of rice and water. He gave all his time and energy to those he was serving—sleeping but three hours a night on the ground in a native hut.[81]

Life was very difficult for the people in southern India at that time. Francis described their suffering as "a permanent bruise on my soul."[82] Saint Francis fell ill on one of his journeys, developed a high fever, and died at the age of forty-six. During his eleven years' ministering, he had opened Southern India, Sri Lanka, the Malay Peninsula,[84] and Japan to the teachings of Christianity.

Saint Francis Xavier was a man of the people, of the poor, and of all God's creatures.

Saint Philip Neri

Patron Saint of the United States Army
Special Forces
1515-1595 CE
May 26

Saint Philip recognized that tangibles of the world were fleeting. He shared all his earnings, as well as his knowledge, with impoverished children.

Saint Philip was born in Florence, Italy one of four children. Unfortunately, their mother died when all of the children were still very young. An excellent stepmother raised them and Philip grew to be a child of docile and sweet disposition. His first religious teachers were the Dominicans whose dedication made a lasting impression upon him. Philip went through a spiritual transformation, recognizing that the tangibles of the world were not of value. He spent his days teaching children, while he personally lived in austerity in one room with a simple bed, a chair, some books, and a line for his clothes. He resolved to sustain himself on purely vegetarian foods, consuming only bread, water, a few olives, and vegetables.

Philip spent much of his time as a recluse, spending whole days and nights in prayer. With time, he began taking classes in philosophy and theology, as he felt determined to strengthen his bond with God. Fate, however, changed the course of his plans and led him to become an apostle for the people. During this era, the masses had lapsed into a semi-pagan state of indifference to the teachings of Jesus, due to abuses and corruption within the Church.[85] Elections within the Church had fallen into the hands of the rich. Most of the cardinals were now princes of the states, rather than of the Church. Philip's mission began in a very small and humble fashion. He would stand on street corners and enter into conversations with people concerning the ways in which they were living. Then gradually, he would attempt to bring them back to God.[86]

By the time Philip was ordained a priest, word of both his abounding kindness, and of his clairvoyance, had attracted countless followers. Many were attracted to his sermons. He would teach others, only on the condition that they would serve in the hospitals and beg alms for the poor. Every day for the remaining forty-five years of his life, he taught, encouraged, and guided his followers.[87] During the later years of his life, Philip immersed himself in contemplative solitude and prayer. In spite of his achievements, he remained a man of simplicity, a believer in non-violence to all beings, and a man who felt humble gratitude for even the most meager of blessings.

Saint Mary Magdalen of Pazzi

Patron Saint of Bodily Ills
1566-1607 CE
May 25
Saint Mary always thought
of others before herself. Even as
a young child, she would
deprive herself of meals to give
her food to beggars.

Saint Mary was born in Pazzi, in the Republic of Florence, and was related to the sovereign house of the Medicis.[88] She was of such compassionate nature that even at the age of seven, she would deprive herself of meals so she could give her food to poor beggars. As a child, she would teach other children how to pray and would console all those who had suffered scorn or exclusion from their peers. By the time she reached her teens, she was placed as a boarder in a monastery. There she recognized her need to follow a life of meditation and prayer. When her parents proposed marriage for her with several desirable suitors, she could not accept the proposals as she felt a calling to lead a religious life.

While still very young, Mary embarked upon a life of contemplation, prayer, and austerity. She resolved to exist purely on vegetarian foods of bread and water, rarely deviating from this diet. Although she was tempted toward gluttony and pride, she was able to ward these off with prayer, austerity, and meditation.[89] Through all her trials, she felt she had become stronger and also had become gifted with the ability to prophesy. She foretold the accession of Pope Leo XI to the papacy, and his death soon after his election.[90]

She considered her gifts to have been given by God. Mary never considered herself superior to the most disenfranchised of society. She did not even feel higher than the lowest of creatures. An illness involving violent headaches, fevers, sweats, pains, and the coughing up of blood began to consume her. She died quietly and calmly, having lived a humble, peaceful life of simplicity, gentleness, and appreciation of God's blessings.

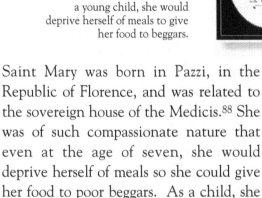

Saint John Francis Regis

Patron Saint of Lace Workers
1597 - 1640 CE
June 16

Saint John would search out
those inflicted with illness and
personally care for their most
loathsome of sores.

Even as a child, Saint John Francis was noted to be a serious and dedicated student. When Jesuits opened a school, they petitioned him to enroll in their school. Once he entered, John Francis excelled in piety and devotion, choosing to spend even his weekends in prayer. When he reached eighteen years of age, he developed a dangerous illness, which brought him closer to God and toward the ministry of healing others.

John Francis was a man who was austere and hard on himself, yet tender toward all others. He exemplified simplicity, humility, and honesty. His virtues were revered through his sermons which became powerful inspirations for the entire congregation. Many times, he would beg in the streets to help the poor, would procure medical care and other necessities to help those afflicted with illnesses, and would personally care for their most loathsome sores. Although he often drew insults when begging, others admired him for his acceptance of abuse.

John Francis lived on a vegetarian diet of bread and water, occasionally drinking milk. He refrained at all times from consumption of animal flesh, fish, eggs, and wine. He would allow himself only minimal rest and no possessions. Yet as hard as he was on himself, he would consistently run to aid the sick during their times of need. Neither storms, snow, rains nor flood daunted him nor stopped him from his mission to aid others. He devoted himself particularly to the service of those afflicted with infection from whom others fled in fear of succumbing to the same disease. He lived by the sentiment, "We are created by God, and for him alone; and must direct all things to his glory."[91] He remained personally drawn to aid all people, animals, and the most humble of beings.

Saint Leonard of Porto-Maurizio

Patron Saint of Parish Missions
1676 - 1751 CE
November 26

Plague tore through the town, sparing no family. Saint Leonard spent his days giving solace to the survivors whose hearts were broken after losing loved ones.

Saint Leonardo of Porto-Maurizio[92] was born into a well-to-do family. Unfortunately, his mother died when he was two years of age. His father remarried, subsequently having four more children with his second wife. As a child, Leonardo had a religious orientation and would parade his younger siblings in ecclesiastic reverence as though they were attending church. He was sent to study in Rome with his uncle. While there, he joined several religious societies. Leonard felt that he gained much inspiration from a book written by Saint Francis de Sales entitled, "Introduction to a Devout Life." After completing his education, he chose to follow an austere life path—sleeping on boards, consuming a diet purely of vegetation such as fruit and vegetables, and never consuming fish or flesh.[93]

By the age of twenty-one he was ordained and applied himself to the study of theology, becoming a gifted and eloquent preacher. He inspired an immense congregation of faithful followers and helped heal the hearts of survivors after a plague had torn through their town. He labored at a mission in Tuscany, where he lived in great austerity—eating only vegetables, wearing a ragged and patched habit, and sleeping on hard boards.

He organized a hermitage of religious followers of similar calling. He would have preferred to remain living in such solitude but was called upon to fill positions aiding large communities of followers. This occurred because his reputation as a man of wisdom had spread far and many sought to learn from his teachings. Once when called to examine the case of a young girl condemned to death, Leonardo was able to satisfy the magistrate that the girl was innocent. It was often stated that for twenty-five years, Leonardo never uttered a complaint unless such was necessary to secure the welfare of others. He lived a life of total service in whichever direction God led him.[94]

Saint Jean-Marie Vianney

Patron Saint of Parochial Schools
1786-1859 CE
August 4

Saint John Vianney was sent to preach in Ars, a town others considered worthless. His love proved so strong, that over three hundred people made pilgrimages daily to receive his blessings.

Saint Jean-Marie (John) Vianney (Cure d'Ars) was born in a small town close to Lyon, France.[95] As a child, he was exceptionally concerned about the welfare of others and showed signs of charity that appeared quite precocious for his age. He even invited beggars to his father's house for care.[96] The French Revolution broke out when he was three years of age and after its onset, his family was not able to attend Mass, except in secret. When he reached thirteen years of age, Jean-Marie asked permission from his father to become a priest. His father could not agree to his request, because he needed Jean-Marie to work on the family farm. Two years later, however, Jean-Marie was permitted to follow his calling.

Jean-Marie had great difficulty with his studies, particularly when it came to the subject of Latin. In spite of private tutoring, the examiners could not accept him for ordination. The vicar general governing the diocese was told of Jean-Marie's holiness and was also told that he was the most unlearned but most devout seminarian at Lyon. The vicar general decided to ordain him saying, "Let him be ordained. The grace of God will do the rest." The vicar said that the church wanted not only learned priests – but also holy ones.[97]

In 1817 Jean-Marie was made parish priest of a remote, neglected, ordinary town of 230 people, Ars-en-Dombes. As the new pastor, Jean-Marie sought to sacrifice himself to atone for the shortcomings of his flock. To do so, he lived on practically nothing but potatoes for six years. He felt that if the people of Ars would not pray or fast for themselves, he would do so for them.

Jean-Marie personally visited every family in the village, provided regular catechism classes for the children, and laboriously prepared his sermons. He waged a personal war against the taverns in the town, and because of his preaching, every one of them eventually closed for lack of business. He then preached against blasphemy, profanity and obscenity.

His reputation for holiness and achievement spread. He organized the opening of a free school for girls to help raise their level of education. He sketched

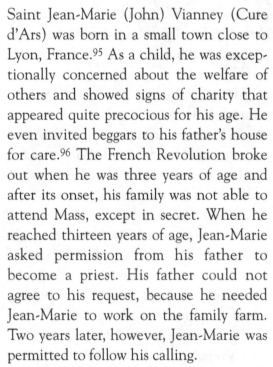

the plans, dragged the stones, and mixed the mortar for the construction of the school all by himself. His life remained focused on the poor and he opened a shelter for orphans and other homeless or deserted children—all run as charities on alms.[98] Stories of miracles were attributed to Jean-Marie, including having created twenty loaves of bread from a few pounds of flour. The people of the village felt they had a saint in their midst. It was said that whatever he had for himself, he gave away, living his life as a continual example to others.

Between the years 1830 and 1845, people began to make pilgrimages to Ars to receive his blessings and guidance. Within a short time, over three hundred people were visiting the city daily. Jean-Marie was often credited with the gift of prophecy, the ability to know the past, and the vision to predict the future. He also developed the ability to perform miracles of physical healing.[99] For Jean-Marie, this recognition of his gifts meant that he had to spend twelve to sixteen hours every day in the confessional, so that he might guide all who journeyed to see him. He slept, at most, four hours a night and ate only one meal a day, usually bread, or one or two, often moldy, potatoes. Once, when he was not well, the doctor prescribed veal, chicken, fresh butter and honey, but Jean-Marie merely brushed these aside.[100]

For himself, he longed for solitude and quiet, yet he was compelled to remain in his ministry of healing others and of bringing the word of God to Ars for forty-one years. By the time he was seventy-three years of age, the strain was too much for him and he passed on, with people still kneeling around him to finish their confessions.[101]

The life of Saint Jean-Marie Vianney, Cure d'Ars, was a life "dedicated with a wholeness…to the service of God. What He lived on and lived by and lived for— was to do His Father's will who had sent him 'to seek and save.' "[102] Saint Jean-Marie Vianney lived in total simplicity, free of wants or thoughts of personal gain, and as a humble vegetarian, his heart overflowing with compassion toward all.

Chapter 8

Doctors of the Church

Over the centuries, dedi-
cated individuals have
used their literary abilities to preserve and expand the
writings and teachings of the
faith. Without such individuals,
many of the values of the Church would
have been all but lost. Therefore, the
Church has honored each such individual
with canonization, as well as with the title
of Doctor of the Church. The writings of
these individuals were generally of such
value that the entire Church derived wisdom from them for generations to follow.

In 1298, Pope Boniface VIII decreed
that the entire Church recognize the four
initial Doctors of the Church—Saint
Gregory the Great, Saint Ambrose, Saint
Augustine, and Saint Jerome. This was in
gratitude for the wisdom and scholarship
their teachings offered their followers. The
process by which these individuals were
conferred the title of Doctor of the Church
involved careful examination of all of their
writings, as well as final approval by the

Pope. There are presently thir-
ty-three Doctors of the Church,
including three female saints—
Saint Theresa of Avila, Saint
Catherine of Siena, and Saint
Theresa of Lisieux.

Those saints venerated as Doctors of
the Church were learned theologians as
well as deeply spiritual individuals. The
values one gains from reading the teachings of these scholarly and holy individuals
have remained as spiritual legacies for millions. They embody teachings on such
issues as: freeing oneself of worldly temptations, achieving inner peace, developing
powers of contemplation, feeling love for
all creatures and all creation, and living in
peace, austerity, and non-violence.

The Doctors of the Church shared
God's wisdom and teachings with others.
Because these saints placed their thoughts
in writing, we have the opportunity, today,
to understand the values that led many
holy individuals to choose vegetarian
lifestyles.

Saint Basil the Great

Doctor of the Church
c. 329-379 CE
January 2

When a devastating drought swept the lands, Saint Basil worked ceaselessly organizing soup kitchens, giving food to the poor, and healing the hearts of survivors.

Saint Basil was born in Caesarea, which was the capital of the Roman province of Cappadocia during that time. His family was well known and well respected for its virtue. Many other saints were included in his family lineage, including his grandmother, both his parents, and three of his siblings. Initially, he studied academic subjects at major centers of learning in Constantinople and Athens, and then went on to study the essence of religious life at various monasteries, including those in Syria, Palestine, Egypt, and Mesopotamia.[1]

Basil was adept in all the liberal arts and sciences, and excelled in poetry, philosophy, and literature. In his passion to spread the wisdom of his religious teachings, he felt that those who were called to care for souls should expend their utmost efforts to educate themselves so as to be most effective when teaching others. To fulfill his own mission, Basil developed skills as a scholar and a great orator.[2]

After he had achieved the skill of eloquence, his following began to flourish and his fame spread. With time, however, he felt that his achievements might lead him on a path toward ambition and pride. So he decided to renounce the world entirely and embark upon the sacrificial and laborious life of a monk. He also chose only those older monks who had proven themselves to be dedicated holy men as his spiritual guides.

Basil retreated into the desert and sustained himself on bread and water alone, barring holidays during which he would add a few herbs. He felt such a diet would rid him of worldly thoughts. He slept on the ground, kept no possessions, and wore only the coarsest of clothes. All who met him remarked that he was astonishingly meek and radiated a sense of gentleness toward others. He divided his deeply spiritual days among prayer, meditation, and manual labor.[3]

Saint Basil was a man who harbored deep emotions concerning social issues. He organized soup kitchens, distributed food to the hungry after a devastating drought led to a great famine, gave away his personal inheritance to benefit the poor, and extended his pastoral care to thieves and prostitutes. Although Christian monasticism was born in the deserts of Egypt, it was the Cappadonians[4] —Saint Basil, Saint Gregory, and Saint Gregory of Nyssa—who fully transformed it into a theological and intellectual movement.

Basil integrated monasticism into the Church, and also saw to it that orphanages and schools were incorporated into various monasteries. In his schools, children were prepared both for lives of monasticism as well as for lives within the secular world. Worn out from a life of service and dedication, Basil died at the age of forty-nine. He left the legacy of a man of humility, simplicity, and compassion, who lived by the principle, "We must obey God rather than men."[5]

He lived as a vegetarian in simplicity and felt that such a diet could rid an individual of worldly thoughts, help him reach higher levels of contemplation, and bring him closer to God.

Saint Jerome

Doctor of the Church
345-420 CE
August 30

Saint Jerome sought deep understanding of the scriptures. He studied Hebrew from an aged Jewish scholar to attain the wisdom he needed to share God's word.

Many people were impressed by Jerome's holiness, learning and truthfulness. Yet his blunt honesty often drew him into conflicts and left him vulnerable to those who sought to attack his reputation. He embarked upon a search for a quiet retreat in Palestine. Upon finding one, he decided to live and work in a tiny cell formed within a large rock close to Jesus' birthplace.

He opened a free school and a hospice for the community, and found peace for himself. He wrote of his life in the desert, "Bread, our own vegetables, and milk—country fare—provide us with a plain but healthy diet. In summer the trees give us shade; in autumn the air is cool and the fallen leaves are restful; in spring our chanting of the psalms is made sweeter by the singing of the birds."[8]

Saint Jerome was born to a well-to-do Italian family and was sent to Rome for his education. After three years of schooling, Jerome felt the need to learn more of life through experience. He traveled throughout Europe and happened to meet a priest from Antioch who influenced him to travel further east. Jerome set off with three friends to reach Antioch, but illness took the lives of two of his friends and left Jerome seriously ill.

After a meeting with Saint Malchus, Jerome decided to travel to a barren desert southeast of Antioch[6] where he remained in solitude and contemplation for four years. To draw himself further from the temptations of the world, he began to study Hebrew from an older Jewish monk who converted to Christianity. He found these studies extremely difficult, but afterwards, thanked the Lord because with knowledge of Hebrew, he had become equipped to work as a biblical scholar, translator, and writer.[7]

It was Saint Jerome's critical scholarship concerning the Holy Scriptures that has given his name the high level of respect it maintains. Because he lived less than four centuries after Jesus, he was able to trace names and lineages so as to shed understanding upon the names of ancient places, people, and customs described in the Bible and other texts of antiquity. As Greek and Aramaic were still living languages during his time, Jerome was able to interpret many ancient treatises. His writings have contributed greatly to our understanding of many passages of the Bible —more than would have been possible were he not dedicated to this endeavor.

Because Saint Jerome was a man of prayer and piety, it seemed to follow that he became a devout interpreter of the Bible. During his years of retreat at Bethlehem, he was able to revise correctly numerous translations of the Psalms, New Testament, and most of the Hebrew Scriptures.[9] However, after a series of sad events, including the sacking of Rome, loss of life of many of his friends, assault on his monastery in Bethlehem, and diminution of his eyesight, Saint Jerome met his passing. Prior to his death, he voiced the humble words, "For today we must translate the words of the Scriptures into deeds, and instead of speaking saintly words we must act them." Saint Jerome was a gifted, peaceful man who was blessed with the special mission of bringing God's word to humankind. Because Jerome wanted to be at peace with all of God's creation, he chose to live as a vegetarian.

Saint Ephraem

Doctor of the Church
c.300 - 373 CE
June 18

When famine swept the lands, Saint Ephraem was the only man trusted to distribute grain fairly to rich and poor alike. His fairness saved the lives of many.

Lay me not with sweet spices,
For this honor avails me not.
Burn ye incense in the holy place;
As for me, escort me only with
your prayers.
Instead of perfume and spices
Be mindful of me in your
intercessions.[11]

Saint Ephraem was born in the early part of the fourth century in Mesopotamia when the entire region was under Roman rule. His parents were Christian and he was raised to value truth and to have reverence for the Lord. At the age of eighteen, he aligned himself with the bishop of his region and became head of their school. Thrice, the Persians tried to capture the city in which he lived and finally won control of it through a negotiated conquest. All Christians were forced to abandon the city and Saint Ephraem fled to live in a secluded cave in the rocky cliffs overlooking the city of Edessa. Such a lifestyle suited his humble needs well, as all he sought had been a life of austerity. He lived on a scant vegetarian diet consisting of a few vegetables and small quantities of barley bread daily. It was during such times of solitude and contemplation that Saint Ephraem wrote the major portion of his spiritual works.

In the year 372, famine swept the entire country and Ephraem was overwhelmed with a sense of pity at the plight of the suffering poor. The granary owners entrusted him to distribute their limited supply of grain to those in need. He completed this mission of mercy with every bit of strength left in him; yet this so depleted his frail body that he survived but one month after completion of this mission. He was barely able to return to his cave before he passed on.

Saint Ephraem was the only Syrian priest to have been honored by all branches of the Christian Church. He possessed deep insight concerning the mysteries of God, the value of sacred song, and the need for humankind to remain sympathetic toward all others. He lived as a vegetarian to avoid desiring possessions of any sort and to avoid inflicting harm upon weaker beings. He was a man who truly sought nothing from this world but the opportunity to contribute to it.

Saint Peter Damian

Doctor of the Church
1007 - 1072 CE
February 23

Saint Peter Damian would bring the poor and starving into his home. He fed those who were too weak to eat.

Saint Peter Damian was born into a large but relatively poor family. Both his parents died when he was young and he was given to be raised by a brother who treated him more like a slave than as family. Another brother, seeing this injustice, took Peter away and saw to it that he received an education, the attainment of which subsequently became his forte. Shortly after Peter had completed his education, he was asked to return to the school to become a professor. By this time, he felt the need to lead an austere life. After long hours of prayer, he would consistently beg for alms that he would distribute to the poor. He would also invite the poor into his home so that he might serve them food with his own hands.[12]

After some time, Peter Damian decided to abandon the world of earthly possessions and embrace a monastic way of life. He joined two Benedictine monks and went to live in a small cell. He sustained himself on a totally vegetarian diet of coarse bread and grains. He went barefoot, wore a threadbare habit, and spent long days in contemplation and prayer. Seeing his deeply spiritual nature, his superior permitted him to devote much time to the study of sacred scriptures and religious literature.[13]

Saint Peter's religious spirit and writings helped restore peace to the nation after the death of their emperor. He taught the ideals of the desert fathers to his hermits, advising them to constantly guard against temptation and to find God within themselves - particularly through practices that conferred a sense of inner peace. His commitment to vegetarianism was grounded in his beliefs in a life of simplicity, non-violence, and preservation of nature's gifts. In his spiritual writings, he advised followers to pray without ceasing, to fast, to live on a simple vegetarian diet, to sacrifice for the good of others, to constantly recall passages from the scripture, and to share such teachings with others. By living the practices that he preached, he hoped that the seeds of all of such principles would become firmly planted in society, and would blossom into reality.[14]

Saint Bernard

Doctor and Abbot of the Church
1090-1153 CE
August 20

During the Second Crusade, Saint Bernard grieved at the atrocities committed upon the Jews. He traveled, pleading to stop such persecution.

Saint Bernard was one of seven children born into an aristocratic and peace-loving family in France. When his mother died, he was only seventeen years of age and felt this loss deeply. By the age of twenty-two, he was received into a strict Benedictine monastery and together with twelve other monks, founded a religious house at Clairvaux.[15] This religious center became one of the main houses of the Cistercian monks and was strictly vegetarian at that time.[16] Life in the monastery was poor, austere and the diet sparse, consisting of coarse barley and beech leaves.

Bernard was dedicated to the religious Order and because of his purist ideology, he soon commanded a great influence on Christian monasticism. The depth of his spiritual faith left such a deep imprint upon others that years later, even Bernard's aged father and youngest brother joined the Order. Within the monastery, Bernard opposed the use of images, baroque architecture, and elaborate iconography. He felt churches should be austere, glass should be plain, and architecture should be simple. He believed that a setting of simplicity was one in which a seeker might find God. Although Bernard oversaw the establishment of many other religious centers, it remained his writings that elevated his reputation and brought his messages to the world.

Several years later, the Turks captured Edessa, a city near Jerusalem. The Christians there appealed to Pope Eugenius for help. The Pope persuaded Bernard to go to this region and preach the Second Crusade.[17] Bernard found himself preaching peace and non-violence to those oriented toward violence such as the monk, Raoul, who had been inciting people to massacre Jews.

Bernard abhorred Christian persecution of Jews and did all he could to protect them. He wrote to the Archbishop and other clergy, "The Jews are not to be persecuted, killed or even put to flight...The Jews are for us the living words of the Scripture...We are told by the Apostle that when the time is ripe all Israel shall be saved...It is an act of Christian piety both to 'vanquish the proud' and also to 'spare the subjected,' especially those for whom we have a law and a promise, and whose flesh was shared by Jesus whose name be forever blessed" (*Letters*, pp.460-6).[18]

In addition to being an excellent theologian, Bernard was a mystic and a worker of miracles. Once his reputation for these gifts had become known, the sick and maimed would line the streets upon which he was traveling so they might receive the blessings of this holy man. Often, the crowds seeking his blessings were so numerous that he was forced to flee to prevent riots. In 1153, shortly after

he successfully convinced two warring groups to reconcile their differences and lay down their arms, Bernard passed away.

Saint Bernard's love for all people and all creatures was abundant and his abilities facilitated the growth of the Cistercian Order. His belief in vegetarianism, as well as his belief that non-violence toward all creation is the will of God can be felt within the words he shared in his book *De Consideratione*:

> God's love knows no bounds, for he hates nothing he has created.[19]

Saint Catherine of Siena

Doctor of the Church
1347-1380 CE
April 29
Saint Catherine possessed tremendous ability to preach the word of God. Although the men tried to stop her, people came by the hundreds to hear her.

Saint Catherine was born into a large family in Siena, Italy[20] the twenty-fourth of twenty-five children. Her family was one of comfortable means, piety, and concern for the welfare of others. At the age of six, she experienced a vision of the Lord and afterwards resolved to dedicate her life to God. Catherine's decision led to numerous arguments with her mother, particularly when Catherine refused an arrangement of marriage. Because she refused to follow her parents' wishes, Catherine was reduced to the status of a servant within her own home.[21]

Her life's commitment to serve others was solidified when her sister, the youngest in the family, died in childbirth. Catherine resolved to live a life of austerity and of service to others. This strong commitment remained with her for the remainder of her life. It was at this time that Catherine resolved to live as a vegetarian, consuming only bread, raw vegetables, and water.[22]

After living three years at home in contemplative solitude and prayer, Catherine experienced a mystical union with Jesus. She received a calling to perform active service within the world. She embarked upon her journey to serve the community and began to perform both works of charity and assistance to others seeking God. During the famine of 1370, Catherine concentrated all her efforts to helping the ill and the dying. She faced considerable opposition from the men of her time when she tried to preach, as only men had traditionally carried out such ministries. Her confessor and first biographer, Brother Raymund of Capua, encouraged her to continue in this mission, as he felt it conferred strength upon those women to whom she preached and also humbled the men.

Although those in Church authority would not listen to her, hundreds of lay people crowded from mountains and country districts just to see and hear her. She converted so many people that the Church needed to hire more priests to hear their confessions. Catherine refused to be deterred by any conventions or obstacles placed before her and preached to the thousands who now came to hear her words.[23] She said that God had taught her to build a private cell around her soul so she might radiate the peacefulness others needed to absorb during their times of tribulation.[24]

In 1373, Catherine assisted a young political prisoner who faced execution. She knelt on the block with him, gave him Communion, and received his severed head into her hands. It was then that she began her inner journey of writings, *The Dialogue*, which were to become the essence of her deep mystical experiences of God. She also wrote of her concern that Church leaders needed to reform abuses of ambition, immorality, and personal pretentiousness. These writings led to her suffering disenfranchisement by those in authority within the Church, yet elevated her to gain a position of integrity and hope among the masses.

Catherine's life as a vegetarian, living on herbs, vegetables, fruits, bread, and water was regarded as a holy act, if not a miraculous one.[25] Some felt that her wish to imitate her idols, the Desert Saints, as well as her mystical bond with God gave her the strength to survive her austere physical and dietary lifestyle.[27] Catherine died at the age of thirty-three, after fasting to plead for reform within the Church.

In 1970, Pope Paul VI honored her with the title of Doctor of the Church, a title never before given to a layperson or to a woman.[26] Saint Catherine was a woman of the highest integrity and religious commitment, who truly lived her teachings through her actions. She lived as a vegetarian so as to reject worldly possessions and overindulgence, and to show the peace that one might attain through a life of compassion and personal sacrifice.

Saint Robert Bellarmine

Doctor of the Church
1542 - 1621 CE
September 17

Although he was obliged to accept the position of cardinal, Saint Robert worked daily, rounding up surplus food to give to the poor.

Saint Robert Bellarmine has been recognized as one of the greatest theologians the Church has ever produced. He was born in Tuscany, Italy to a noble, but impoverished, family. As a child, he demonstrated exceptional skills, particularly within his academic studies of Latin and in his playing the violin. Yet he felt an inner longing for a religious life, so he entered a school run by the Jesuits to help others develop religious values. He studied there three years and at the age of eighteen, began theological studies that would eventually lead to his ordination.

His natural abilities led him to a position as a theology professor within a university, where he laid out his philosophical and theological concepts for what was to become known later as "controversial theology." This philosophy focused on controversial concepts that had been dividing the church. His work was of such scholastic breath and depth that many assumed a team of scholars had compiled it. His preaching skills were of such equally high caliber that crowds of two thousand people filled his churches weekly.[28]

Robert had been serving as head of the Society of Jesuits in Naples at the time the Pope's theologian, also a Jesuit, died. Although Robert had no inclination to serve at such a high level, Pope Clement VIII appointed him cardinal. Outwardly, Robert went along with the external formalities, such as the red robes and the use of servants, but inwardly he remained the simplest of Jesuits. He maintained a personal life of austerity, refused a personal pension, gave surplus funds to the poor, denied himself the warmth of a fire even in winter, and sustained himself on a meager vegetarian diet of bread and garlic.[29]

Saint Robert preached incessantly, considering himself a shepherd to his flock. His status within the church changed several times and he served as both archbishop of Capua and then prefect to the Vatican library. When Pope Leo XI suddenly died, Robert narrowly escaped having been appointed Pope himself.

Robert was a personal friend of Galileo Galilei, who had been championing Copernicus' theory that the earth travels around the sun, against the polemic idea that the earth was the center of the universe. During the first stage of the trials against Galileo, Robert was instrumental in preventing him from being condemned, but in the end, neither Robert nor Galileo were able to break free from those enforcing the rigid interpretation of the scriptures discrediting Galileo's findings.[30]

Robert's wisdom in interpretation of the scriptures, his theological principles, his scientific understanding, and his ability to convey the word of God were invaluable to the growth of the Church. His personal convictions to live a life of austerity, non-violence, and integrity have remained the legacy of this holy man of God.

Chapter 9

The Vegetarian Pope

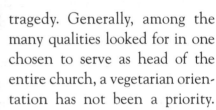

The Catholic Church has honored all popes with canonization. As a group, popes were not specifically oriented toward vegetarian or ascetic lifestyles, as their strengths often resided within leadership and legislative abilities. To fill such an important position, most popes have needed the ability to guide the masses, to unite dissenting parties, and to lead the faithful in times of turmoil and tragedy. Generally, among the many qualities looked for in one chosen to serve as head of the entire church, a vegetarian orientation has not been a priority. Hence, most popes were not so oriented. Pope Peter Celestine V, however, was an individual who, among other achievements, left his legacy as a man of nonviolence who felt compassion for even the most vulnerable of God's creatures.

Saint Peter Celestine

Pope
1210 - 1296 CE

May 19

The people rejoiced when a humble hermit, Saint Peter Celestine, was chosen pope.

Saint Peter Celestine was born to peasant parents, the eleventh of twelve children. Because he demonstrated unusual piety as a child, his mother, though left a widow at a young age, worked to send him to be educated by holy individuals so he might develop similar traits. She felt Peter innately possessed capabilities to gain from the wisdom of holy men. Peter seems to have been gifted with visions and by the age of twenty he withdrew from the world to live as a contemplative hermit. He lived a life of great austerity, valuing time spent in solitude and sustaining himself on vegetarian foods, never consuming flesh.

Although Peter longed to live alone, so many disciples arrived hoping to learn under his direction that he resigned himself to the fate of becoming head of a large community of hermits. Initially, these hermits lived in scattered cells around him but eventually they joined together to live in a communal monastery. Peter lived to see thirty-six communities of monks form under the guidelines and values of his teachings. These communities contained a total of six hundred monks and nuns.[1]

After the death of Pope Nicholas IV, the position of Pope remained vacant for three years. Saint Peter Celestine's name was mentioned with reverence as a choice to fill this position. With a common impulse, the conclave instinctively rose up to choose him, a humble hermit, for this position of honor. When people climbed the mountain to notify him officially of his victory, they found that news of the election had reached him and he was already weeping. He attempted to flee, hoping to hold on to his life of prayer and contemplation. He was prevailed upon to accept the council's position as the will of God. The people expressed boundless enthusiasm that a man of such piety, holiness, and unworldly characteristics had been chosen as Pope (Pope Celestine V).[2]

Peter was eight-five years old at this time and had no orientation towards Papal government, canon law, advanced Latin, or public ceremonies. While serving as Pope, he desired to please all and to offend none. He gave away treasures that might have been of value to others but were of no use to a man of his spiritual depth. It was not Peter's nature to govern or to lead, but rather to retire into prayerful solitude within the Vatican. Eventually, he asked permission to abdicate his position as head of the Church. The assembly, deeply moved by his humility, accepted his resignation and permitted him to return to his hermitage.

His successor, Pope Boniface VIII, however, found himself in a bitter political battle and feared that his opponents would bring back Pope Celestine to create a schism. Pope Celestine tried to run away from this political entanglement, but the ship in which he was traveling was captured by misguided religious-political leaders who placed him in prison. In prison, the aged sage suffered many indignities, yet never complained. In a voice of tranquility, he said, "I wanted nothing more in this world than a cell, and a cell they have given me."[3] Being a man of many years, his frail body succumbed to the harshness of prison life. He became ill with fever, and died shortly thereafter.

Saint Peter Celestine was a man of pure love who sought a life of simplicity, prayer, and solitude. His choice to sustain himself upon a vegetarian diet exemplified the soul of this humble man seeking mercy, compassion, and peace for all.

Chapter 10

Vegetarian Ascetic Saints

Throughout the history of Christianity, various holy and spiritually oriented individuals have been defined as ascetics. Among these have been those Christians who sought lives of inward contemplation and spiritual awareness. Those individuals preferred to sacrifice personal desire for the welfare of others. Rather than expending energy toward rewards within the outer world, they sought riches of the soul. Often, their ascetic and religious values were similar to those of the ancient desert saints and the European monastic saints, yet their habitats varied and their callings were often quite distinct.

Although they maintained personal convictions of simplicity, sacrifice, and spiritual wisdom, they frequently lived among the populace. Some shared their spiritual wisdom with others and became well-known and revered sages, gurus and leaders, while others sought to serve by living simple austere lives in personal contemplative prayer, setting examples for others.

As a group and as a spiritual force, the vegetarian ascetic saints sought to live taking from the earth only that which they absolutely needed. They did not hoard that which they might never use and had no desire to build up their own stores at the expense of other people or beings. Effectively, they lived in a state of spiritual, humanitarian and ecological awareness, with their primary practice focused upon overcoming themselves and their primary goal focused upon sharing God's love:[1]

Solitude, prayer, love, and abstinence
are the four wheels
of the vehicle that carries our spirit
heavenward.

Saint Serafim of Sarov[2]

Saint Olympias

c. 368-410 CE
July 25

Saint Olympias hid Saint John of the Cross when he was being persecuted. She was exiled for life for this act of mercy.

It was shortly after Saint Olympias' birth, that both her parents died and she was left an orphan. A concerned woman, Theodosia, said to have possessed a virtuous and prudent soul, volunteered to raise Olympias for her entire youth. As was custom, Olympias was given in marriage at a very young age, only to have her new husband die twenty days after their marriage. Several other men asked for her hand in marriage, but she modestly declared that she resolved to remain unmarried for the rest of her life and sacrifice herself for the welfare of others.

In attempting to force Olympias to change her mind, one of her suitors with political power commanded that she not be permitted to attend church or to dispose of her estate until the age of thirty. Although forced to accept this lifestyle, Olympias embraced her life of prayer and penance with even greater fervor. It was then that she resolved to live as a vegetarian so that she might not consume the flesh of any animal or take the breath from any creature.[3]

When Olympias regained control of her money and her estate, she divided it among the poor and the church. She performed numerous charitable acts, established a convent for herself and a number of other women who also chose to devote themselves to God, and founded a hospital and an orphanage. She was a woman of great principle, who not only helped Saint John of the Cross during his times of tribulation, but also peacefully accepted the persecution levied against her for aiding him during his exile.

Olympias accepted her sentence of exile for having aided Saint John of the Cross, suffering this fate for the remainder of her life. She was a woman who stood by ethical and humanitarian principles, and faced her final days knowing that she had lived in the image of God.[4]

Saint Publius

290 - 380 CE
January 25

Saint Publius attracted many religious followers and founded numerous monasteries throughout Greece. He taught the spiritual value of living as a vegetarian.

Saint Publius was a fourth-century ascetic abbot who has been venerated by the Greeks as a saint. He had been the son of a senator who lived near the Euphrates River.[5] When his parents passed on and their estate given to him, he sold all the property and goods so as to give the proceeds to the poor. Initially, Publius left society to live as a hermit as he sought to live in solitary contemplation. He longed to grow spiritually by assimilating the religious values that he had been taught into a life of austerity, prayer, and contemplation.

Eventually, however, so many disciples came to join him that he became the leader of a large religious community.[6] Publius believed strongly in the value of one's personally sacrificing for the sake of others. He spent his days in manual labor, penance, and prayer. For both his followers and himself, he decided that the entire community must consume only vegetarian meals. These meals consisted of coarse bread and vegetables, no liquid other then water, and no cheese, grapes, vinegar, or oil.

Knowledge of his teachings and wisdom spread, and Publius became the founder of monasteries throughout Greece and Syria. Publius' life was one of prayer, and of sharing his vision of ethics with others.[7] He was strongly humanitarian, believed in avoiding ecological abuse and waste, and avoided the taking of an animal's life. His was an appreciation of the simple blessings of life.

Saint Malchus

Fourth Century
October 21

Saint Malchus possessed a spiritual bond with animals. When captured by Bedouins, he was able to secure his release and that of a woman captive through the aid of a lion who loved him dearly.

Saint Malchus had been born in the town of Nisibis, the only son of his parents. When his parents wanted him to marry, he felt he could not do so as he had been drawn to a life of religious contemplation and devotion among the desert monks. So he left home and journeyed to seek his fate. Some years later, he heard of his father's death and decided to return home to look after his mother. The superior of his monastic community feared he might be tempted to leave religious life due to the pulls of the secular world. Malchus had resolved, however, to see his mother, so he left without permission.

While attempting the journey home, the caravan to which he became attached was raided and plundered by Bedouin.[8] A chieftain carried off Malchus and a young woman. They were brought to the desert beyond the Euphrates where Malchus was forced to work as a goat herd. He lived on dates, cheese, and milk, engaged endlessly in silent prayer, and sang the spiritual songs he had learned among the monks. He was not unhappy and accepted living among his captors, remembering that both Jacob and Moses had been shepherds in the wilderness.

His captives told him he must marry the other woman captive. He knew he could never do so as he had resolved to live as a celibate monk and also because the woman had been married to another man. Both Malchus and the woman pretended to live as a married couple. After living some time in captivity, Malchus decided to attempt an escape from his captives. He was able to successfully maneuver the escape of both himself and the captive woman. They hid safely in a cave and when their captors approached them, a lioness that had acted peacefully toward them left the cave and took the lives of their captors.

Eventually, Saint Malchus returned to his hermit colony, thankful once again to return to his quiet, dedicated, and simple life as a prayerful hermit. He survived to an old age and taught many others his values.[9] He lived as a vegetarian for the remainder of his years, avoiding harm to even the humblest of beings.

Saint Asella

c. 355 - 410 CE
December 6

Saint Asella felt love for even the weakest and homeliest of creatures. She spent her life in prayer seeking peace for all creation.

When only ten years of age, Saint Asella knew she must follow a religious path. By the age of twelve she chose to live as a contemplative solitary ascetic. She lived in Rome during the time when Saint Jerome was assisting a number of women enter religious life, and her path was facilitated through his guidance. She found such peace in her religious lifestyle that she never again desired any of the material possessions that others in the secular world sought to acquire. She felt fully at peace and spiritually fulfilled living with-

in a tiny cell carved out of the side of a cliff. She slept upon the earth and ate a diet of purely vegetarian foods, bread and water.

Saint Asella dressed with extreme modesty, wearing only sackcloth. She continually tried to avoid all attention to herself so that she might live in quiet simplicity. She spent her years in prayer and contemplation, feeling at peace with God and all His creation.[10] Others recognized that Asella possessed a purity of soul and that she felt compassion toward all beings that God placed upon this earth. She lived as a vegetarian seeking to live in simplicity and to share peace with all. Desiring no possessions and wishing peace for all, Asella spent the remainder of her years in contemplative prayer.

Saint Sulpicius Severus

c. 372 - 425 CE
January 29

Saint Sulpicius freed every one of the slaves he inherited through his family rights and taught them to read and write himself.

Saint Sulpicius was born into a wealthy and illustrious Roman family. He spent his youth studying texts written by the best Roman authors, and subsequently went on to study law. He married a woman he loved dearly, but she died shortly after their marriage. Her death contributed to his desire to wean himself from all worldly wants. Sulpicius owned a great estate, and used all the revenues he derived from it to aid the poor and to facilitate other pious deeds. In spite of the condemnation of his friends, Sulpicius joined the priesthood, retreating to a life of solitude and prayer.[11]

Sulpicius visited Saint Martin at Tours[12] and learned much during his discipleship under this holy man who imbued him with wisdom and courage that sustained him for the remainder of his life. He tried to imitate Saint Martin's achievements, and in so doing, built two churches and emancipated his slaves. He treated these slaves and other servants as his equals and engaged in numerous discourses with them.

For himself, his wants were minimal. For his sleep, he slept on a bed of straw laid upon the ground. In his kitchen, he never permitted any foods that were not vegetarian. He personally consumed only coarse bread, grains, and herbs that had been boiled. He used no seasoning other than vinegar. He said that monks who prayed and fasted for long periods of time developed the ability to taste the essence of boiled herbs they had gathered with their own hands.[13]

Sulpicius' most important work was his summary of the sacred history of the world from the beginning of creation until the year 400 CE. His life was an example of austerity, of vegetarian peacefulness and of love for the beauty that God had created.

Saint Maxentius

448-515 CE
June 26

Although Saint Maxentius sought a life of solitary prayer and meditation, the village people recognized his spiritual abilities and attributed all sorts of cosmic events to his prayers.

Saint Maxentius was born in a small town near Lyon, France.[14] When he was still a child, his parents entrusted his upbringing to an older abbot under whose care he grew in an environment of piety and religious dedication. Many others extolled his virtues, but Maxentius found this praise distasteful and left for two years to practice his beliefs in solitude.

Just at the time when Maxentius decided to return home, a great drought had just ended, and others attributed this cosmic event to his return. He was acclaimed as a savior and wonder worker. Hence, Maxentius could find no peace or solitude as masses of people flocked to him. Because of this, he realized he must leave his prior life behind. He changed his name, and embarked upon a journey to a distant town to live in obscurity.

Although he was able to conceal his identity, he was not able to conceal his sanctity, as his was a life of pure sacrifice and austerity. He consumed only foods whose preparation did not require acts of violence toward other creatures, and sustained himself predominantly on barley bread and water. Although in this new village he spent his days in solitary devout prayer, when positive events occurred, the townspeople credited these to miracles emanating from his holy nature. When soldiers approached the monastery, Maxentius reassured the other monks and then personally opened the door unarmed. As a soldier raised his arms to strike the holy man, he became unable to lower them until the aged monk rubbed holy oil onto his limbs.[15]

When Maxentius reached old age, he retired gracefully to live in a tiny cell outside the monastery. Yet even when he was quite aged, other monks continued to consult him for spiritual guidance. He remained a man filled with wisdom who found fulfillment in a life of sacrifice, prayer, and love for all beings.

Saint Monegundis

c. 520 - 570 CE
July 2

After the death of her two young daughters, Saint Monegundis spent her life helping others. She became blessed with the ability to heal through prayer.

Saint Monegundis lived in Chartres, France with her husband and two young daughters.[16] Her daughters were the joy of her life, yet fate took their lives when they were both still young. This tragedy affected her so deeply, that with her husband's approval, Monegundis decided to leave the secular world and enter the religious life. She felt that if she did not abandon the world and give herself entirely to God's service, she might live thinking only of her own tragedy. She left the world with the belief that, "Lest in her grief she should become so centered in herself as not be mindful of God."[17]

She built a tiny cell on the side of a cliff, slept on a small mat, and ate only foods she might obtain that did not harm the lives of other beings. These were primarily oat bread with water. She resolved to eliminate all animal flesh from her diet. She led a prayerful, contemplative life and, gradually, seemed to develop powers of healing. With time, many others came to benefit from her gifts and, in her humility, she was obliged to move away to avoid being overcome with vanity from too much praise. A large number of women came to join her so they, too, might dedicate themselves to God. Monegundis became the nucleus of a convent.

Monegundis remained dedicated to her life of austerity, contemplation, vegetarian non-violence, and prayer. In return, she was blessed with the power to heal and to share God's mercy with others. After her death, her tomb became a place for healing pilgrimages by the sick, and many cures were attributed to her intercession.[18]

Saint Paul Aurelian

c. 480 - 573 CE
March 12

Although the king appointed him bishop, Saint Paul spent every free moment in his tiny hillside cave praying for the poor.

Saint Paul was born in Wales and received his religious education in a monastery, along with several others who had been chosen for their holiness. When sixteen years of age, Paul chose the life of a solitary hermit so he might grow through prayer and study. His headmaster arranged for him to live in a small cell created on the side of a hill, and arranged to have a quaint chapel constructed in which Paul might preach. Paul remained there for many years until he eventually joined the priesthood.

After several years during which he felt he had grown spiritually, he sensed a need to travel to distant lands and fulfill his ministry elsewhere. So, along with twelve of his companions, Paul traveled to Brittany. It is said that he taught numerous individuals while there, and performed many miracles as well.[19]

The people in these new lands felt they had grown in spirituality under Paul's guidance and sought to make him bishop. Paul protested with tears, because he loved his humble life of simplicity and humility. His pleadings were to no avail, however, as the king appointed him bishop anyway. Although Paul much preferred a simpler lifestyle, he served his congregation to the best of his ability.

Through all these years, he never lost his values of humility and self-sacrifice. He maintained his staple diet of simple vegetarian foods, bread and water, and lived in tiny quarters. When possible, he would silently steal away for contemplation and prayer.[20] It is understandable that this man of humble simplicity, and sacrificial nature towards others, would live peacefully as a vegetarian, seeking to spread gentleness and peace through all his actions.

Saint Coleman of Kilmacduagh

c. 550 - 632 CE
October 29

Saint Coleman founded a monastery where he was able to live amongst the wild animals. They befriended him and helped him with his daily chores.

Saint Coleman was born in Kitartan, Ireland during the middle of the sixth century. He was deeply spiritual and preferred a life of solitude, simplicity, and humility, devoid of the complexities and distractions of the world. Others began to recognize that his was a soul of inner wisdom. He seemed to be guided by a force emanating from a higher level. Although he sensed that these spiritual gifts seemed to have developed within him while he was living as a wise and pensive ascetic, those of superior status within the church did not. They forced him to leave his world of personal spiritual growth, and to become a leader of others within the church.

Against his will, Coleman was made bishop. Yet he knew that this was not his calling, and also sensed that he would lose his spiritual ability to understand life within such a position. Therefore, he abandoned the organized church and sequestered himself away as a hermit in a mountainous region where he was able to find solitude. He chose to live on the simplest of vegetarian diets of vegetables and water, and found solace in the company of the creatures of the wild, amidst nature.[21]

Eventually, Coleman founded a monastery called Kilmacduagh. After his many years in the countryside, it was said that he befriended animals, who then assisted him in his simple daily chores in the forest.[22] Saint Coleman was a lover of contemplation, prayer, and of all creation. He showed kindness to all God's creatures and valued his time living peacefully among all of nature as the greatest gift God had given him.

Saint Bavo

c. 580 - 655 CE
October 1
Saint Bavo gave away all his possessions and traveled throughout France and Flanders helping the destitute.

Saint Bavo had been a nobleman living in Brabant[23] in Western Europe. After the death of his wife, he began a personal quest to find both truth and the meaning of life. He had been gifted with the innate ability to recognize the shallowness of his prior life of possessions, power, and money. He converted to a life of prayer and penance, and within his newfound closeness to God, he found solace.

He gave away his wealth to the poor, became a monk, and traveled on missionary journeys helping the most pitiful and destitute throughout France and Flanders.[24] His hope was merely that he might live a life of quiet solitude as a hermit. At first he sought shelter in the trunk of a tree, and later moved to a cell in a cave.

Despite his wish for seclusion and personal simplicity, word of his insight, sacrificial nature, and wisdom spread.[25] Others sought him out so they might learn from his inner wisdom and spirituality. Yet through all of this, Bavo remained a man devoid of pride and a man pure in his dedication to others.

He chose to sustain himself on a flesh-free diet of vegetables and water. It had been said by his superior that his was, "a soul which has had the happiness to see the nothingness of the world and the depth of her spiritual mysteries….[He] approaches near to God."[26] Saint Bavo was a man of unswerving spiritual commitment, who lived as a missionary, a contemplative hermit, and an austere vegetarian, finding peace in taking as little as possible from that which God created, and in sharing all he possessed with others.

Saint Amandus

c. 600 - 684 CE
February 6

The King of Germany
imprisoned Saint Amandus.
Yet when the king had a son,
he released him saying he was
the only man with sufficient
integrity to teach his son.

Saint Amandus was born to a wealthy family in Flanders. Yet as he grew to understand life, he chose to renounce his wealth and embrace a religious life within a monastery. When he made this decision, he experienced pressures from his family. But Amandus said, "My father, I do not care for thy property; all I ask of thee is to suffer me to follow Jesus Christ, who is my true heritage."[27] With many tears, he thought it best that he flee to a distant island. While there, he built a small cell, lived with the simplest of contents, and remained there for fifteen years. He spent his days in prayer and meditation, choosing to eat only vegetarian meals, generally barley bread and water.

After many years of developing his faith, he requested permission to teach the Gospel to the people of Germany. Once there, he found the people not yet able to receive the Word. At that time, the king of the Frankish people, Dagobert, had three wives and numerous concubines. When Amandus rebuked the king for his actions, the king imprisoned him. He remained imprisoned until one of the king's wives gave birth to a son and the king wished to have the child baptized. So the king called for Amandus, by then an aged imprisoned cleric. The king promised that if Amandus baptized the child, he would permit Amandus to be the spiritual father and teacher of the child.

The child, Sigebert, grew in spirituality and loved Amandus as though he were the father. When Sigebert eventually became King of Austria, Amandus was permitted leave to do missionary work over all the territories under the monarchy and was able to found numerous monasteries.[28] After years of service, and of advanced age, Amandus met his death. He has been remembered for his peaceful, calm holiness, as a man who wished no harm to any being, and as the great Apostle of Flanders.[29]

Saint Giles

c. 633 - 712 CE
September 1

Upon seeing a hunter about
to shoot a doe he had
befriended, Saint Giles ran
in front of the arrow
and saved the doe's life.

doe and one of the huntsmen shot an arrow at her. When Giles was attempting to protect the frightened animal, the arrow landed in his chest. Giles refused medical treatment, thinking only of his need to protect the deer.[31]

The legend of Saint Giles had been one of the most famous tales of the Middle Ages. Giles had been Athenian from birth, born into a distinguished family. His piety and spiritual wisdom were obvious and drew the admiration of many. Even as a youth, Giles, by laying a cloak over a sick beggar was said to have cured him. Giles did not wish to receive the praise of others, so he sailed to Marseilles[30] to live quietly in the woods near the Rhone River. He remained there in solitude for three years, consuming only vegetation, such as wild herbs and roots.

While in the forest, he befriended a deer and the peaceful animal took refuge with Giles in his cave. One day, hounds of King Flavius had begun to chase the

The King was so touched when he saw this old, almost naked, man protecting the doe that he returned to talk with him often. Eventually, the king convinced Giles to consent to the building of a monastery so that others might be guided by his spiritual wisdom.[32] The monastery was constructed and functioned to serve many. Centuries later, this site became an important destination for pilgrimages. The name of Saint Giles has been invoked as the patron saint of beggars, lepers, the physically handicapped, and of nursing mothers.[33] The Saint was a man with the kindest of souls, who sought to live his meager life immersed in unconditional love and with the willingness to sacrifice himself for any being in harm's way.

Saint Silvin

c. 655 - 720 CE
February 17
Saint Silvin built churches
and used the donated money
to ransom slaves.

Even in his earlier years, Saint Silvin seemed destined to lead a religious life. Not much is known of his early youth. Yet it is believed that he grew up in an economically advantaged situation, because as a young man he was involved with the courts of two kings. His family had arranged for him to be married so as to conform with the norm of his times. But Silvin felt a calling to lead a religious life of poverty and celibacy. He decided that he must be true to his callings and left the court of the monarchy so as to journey to Rome. While there, he prepared to join the clergy and, eventually, received holy orders.[34]

Some years after Silvin initially entered the clergy, he was elevated to the position of bishop. Records remain unclear as to whether his territory was in Toulouse, France[35] or whether Silvin remained in the countryside preaching to convert those without any religion. It is known, however, that whatever his status might have been, Silvin worked unceasingly to preach and teach both uneducated Christians and others without religion. It is also known that he expended his entire personal fortune to ransom slaves, build churches, and give charity to the impoverished.

For himself, he wanted nothing of the materialistic world. He wore the simplest and coarsest of clothing, lived in an exceedingly humble shelter, practiced personal austerities, and lived on a simple vegetarian diet of raw herbs and fruits. He was much loved for his holiness and charity, and revered for his gift of healing.[36] His desire to live in simplicity and humility, to remain always as a peaceful man, and to share all of his energy helping the slaves and the indigent, have remained as the legacy of this holy man.

Saint Benedict of Aniane

c. 751-821 CE
February 21

Saint Benedict sought fairness for all. Because he possessed such integrity, he became one of the most trusted counselors of King Louis, the Pious.

Saint Benedict was son of the cupbearer[37] of both King Pepin of France and his son Charlemagne.[38] At the age of twenty, Benedict resolved to live a religious life so that he might gain understanding of the essence of God. He sought to live a simple life by eating sparingly, sleeping little, and eventually joining an abbey to become a monk. He lived his life consuming only vegetarian foods of bread and water. He enjoyed living a life of abstinence.[39] When the other monks noted his piety and sought to make him abbot, he refused the abbacy, venturing out to sustain himself by doing simple manual labor.[40]

He remained alone for many years and was later joined by others who sought to learn from his direction and devotion.

They worked with the simplest of materials and lived with the most modest of possessions. The number of disciples who chose to follow him increased and Benedict eventually needed to build a monastery and a church.

As his influence grew, he was appointed overseer of numerous monasteries and developed a close relationship with King Louis the Pious, heir to Charlemagne's throne. Louis was a deeply religious man whose main interest was theology. Benedict became one of Louis' most trusted counselors, and was given the responsibility of presiding over governmental committees and assemblies concerning particular issues.[41]

Saint Benedict helped to initiate a revival of monasticism in the Western Church after it had been declining over the generations. Through his simple vegetarian lifestyle, he adhered to his belief in sharing compassion with all life. Benedict died at the age of seventy-one, a man of inner tranquility and a man at peace with God.[42]

Saint Aybert

c. 1060 - 1140 CE
April 7

Saint Aybert was a man of austerity. He built a hermitage in barren lands and lived solely on vegetation. He developed the gift of healing and blessed the lives of many.

Saint Aybert was the son of a well-to-do gentleman in a village in Tournai.[43] As a child, Aybert was serious and pious, and would frequently slip away in the evenings to pray in the sheep folds. Often, he would be discovered there in the mornings, having fallen asleep while praying. As he grew older, he also grew in piety. He sought to live a life of prayerful meditation and contemplation, and to progress internally in the ways of holiness. Eventually, he left the villages so that he might retreat to an austere life with a reclusive priest in a solitary cell outside an abbey.

Aybert and the other reclusive priest consumed only non-flesh foods. Wild herbs made up their ordinary meal and only seldom did they even taste bread, as they chose to eat neither foods of animal origin, nor foods that had been cooked. Eventually Aybert joined the abbey, and worked there as provost for twenty-five years. He dispensed hospitality and kind words to all, yet never modified his desire to live an austere, and inwardly spiritual, existence.

Again, the time came when Aybert felt he must return to a solitary, contemplative and prayerful life - lest he would lose his spiritual footing. He built a hermitage in a barren region, and remained there for twenty-five years existing on only roots and herbs.[44] He began to attract visitors who found themselves healed and enlightened by his kind words of advice. He met his death at eighty years of age. It was said that he had found his greatest solace while living this peaceful vegetarian spiritual life amidst the abundant gifts of nature.[45]

Saint Dominic Loricatus

c. 1015 - 1060 CE
October 14

When Saint Dominic entered the clergy, his parents sacrificed a goat for him. He felt such remorse that he aided weaker creatures for the remainder of his life.

Saint Dominic's parents had aspirations for their son to enter a religious life. In order to accomplish this, they gave the bishop a present of goatskin, in exchange for Dominic's gaining admission to the priesthood. When Dominic, still a young man, obtained knowledge of this transaction, he was filled with remorse that the life of a goat had been taken in exchange for his admission. Knowing this, he felt he could no longer celebrate Mass in good conscience. He felt overwhelmed with sadness and guilt that another of God's creatures, a weak and peaceful one, had lost its life for his personal gain.

He begged his superiors to let him follow the austere life of a hermit in one of the small cells created by a well-respected holy man in the mountains of Umbria,[46] Italy. Seeing his sense of sorrow and his longing to seek penance for the sacrifice of the goat, his superiors acquiesced.

For the remainder of his life, Dominic consumed only that amount of vegetarian food needed to sustain him—his meals consisting of bread, herbs, and water. During his lifetime, he never hurt, ridiculed, or took advantage of any other being, human or otherwise. He lived the remaining years of his unassuming and humble life in the peaceful and contemplative isolation of the hermitage.[47] His personal wish to sacrifice himself for the sake of any weaker creatures was but one example of his compassionate, peaceful soul.

Saint Richard of Wyche

c. 1197 - 1253 CE
April 3

Saint Richard felt such sadness seeing chickens and other young animals being brought for slaughter that he cried to others to spare the lives of these innocent beings.

Saint Richard's parents had been fairly wealthy landowners in Worcestershire, England. But, sadly, both of them died when their children were quite young. Their estate was left in the hands of a negligent guardian who let the lands go to waste. Richard was the youngest son. He was naturally drawn to a life of studies. When he came of age and realized what had happened, he took matters into his own hands. He literally began to work as a laborer and ploughed the field so as to bring the estate back to its prior level of functioning. His brother wanted to deed the lands to Richard. But when he recognized that he did not want to live a life of material possessions, Richard turned over his portion of lands to his siblings.[48]

Richard decided to leave the estate, almost penniless, to study at Oxford, Paris, and Bologna. After gaining recognition as a scholar and a teacher, he became chancellor of Oxford University. He studied two years for admission to the clergy and succeeded in becoming a Dominican priest. Shortly thereafter, because he had developed a reputation for refusing bribes, Pope Innocent IV consecrated him bishop. Others wrote of Richard that throughout his years as bishop, he was a man of wisdom to his disciples and a healer to his people.

Throughout this lifetime, although he had achieved positions of great honor, Richard remained humble and austere in his personal life. His diet was simple and he rigorously excluded animal flesh from it. When he saw poultry or other young animals being conveyed to the kitchen he would say, "Poor little innocent creatures, if you were reasoning beings and could speak, how you would curse us! For we are the cause of your death, and what have you done to deserve it?"[49]

If classified in present day terms, Richard might have fallen into the category of being a compassionate vegetarian, if not an animal rights activist. His ability to feel pity for the life and soul of poor animals being taken to slaughter for human consumption exemplifies the peace he sought for all beings.

Saint Margaret of Cortona

c. 1250 - 1297 CE
February 22

After the death of her husband, Saint Margaret raised her young children alone, then spent her life nursing the sick in a hospital she helped build.

Saint Margaret was born into a poor farming family near Tuscany. She had the misfortune to have lost her mother when she was only seven years of age. Her father then married a woman who showed the classic lack of affection in a harsh stepmother. Her stepmother turned her out of the house when she was only eleven years of age. By the age of fourteen, Margaret eloped, taking refuge with a young nobleman. Being of different social classes, the couple was not permitted to marry, so she openly and faithfully lived with this man for nine years, bearing a son.

One day after the nobleman failed to come home, Margaret went out looking for him and found his murdered body in a pit. She attempted to return to her family's home as a penitent, but her stepmother refused to receive her. Having suffered so much herself, Margaret had become able to recognize the needs of others, so she began to nurse and care for the sick among the poor of the village. Although she lived on alms herself, she gave away the better part of what she received to those in greater need of charity.[50]

Several other pious women joined her in her cottage. Together they nursed the sick back to health. Eventually, fame of her services to the needy spread and the city helped her create an entire hospital. She also formed an organization of women, Our Lady of Mercy, which supported the hospital. She searched out and supported the poor of the region. Throughout all of this outward success, Margaret remained simple and austere in her personal wants. She slept on the bare ground, spent the evenings in prayer and contemplation, and remained faithful to her vegetarian lifestyle, allowing herself only bread, raw herbs, and water as her sole sustenance.[51] She lived as a humble woman, never seeking personal gain, never harming animal or human, and always sharing love with those most in need of compassion.

Saint Clare of Rimini

c. 1265 - 1346 CE
February 10

Saint Clare was so dedicated to others that she once sold herself into slavery to free a man who was going to have his hands chopped off.

Saint Clare was an exceptionally dedicated, sacrificial woman. She had been born into a wealthy Italian family and was given in marriage at a young age, only to have her husband die shortly thereafter. Due to a civil war, Clare was sent into exile.

Upon her return, she witnessed her father and brothers perish on the scaffold. She was married a second time. But by this time, the suffering and human tragedy she had experienced had made an indelible mark on her soul.

She felt a calling to live a life of sacrifice, penance, and total devotion to others. She lived the simplest of lives, slept on a hard board, and consumed only vegetarian meals of bread and water. She took no spices and added oil only on Sundays. She spent her nights in prayer and in close communion with God, the effect of which gave her a sense of charity toward all humankind.[52]

She went to the bedside of one of her brothers who had been banished from the lands, and after nursing him to health, began to help the multitude of others within her community afflicted with illness during those troubled times.

Clare helped all in need during those tragic times of disease, famine, and starvation. Upon hearing that the Sisters of Poor Clare were without fuel, she carried a huge load of wood to them to help them maintain a source of warmth. Once, upon hearing that a man was going to have his hand chopped off, she even sold herself as a slave to obtain funds to redeem him from this fate.[53]

She was a woman who wanted little for herself, yet strove to sacrifice for the welfare of many. Her decision to live as a vegetarian and, thereby, inflict no harm upon any of God's creatures was but one facet of her self-sacrificing and dedicated soul.

Saint Frances of Rome

1384 - 1440 CE
March 9

During a devastating war, Saint Frances gave away all her jewels and unrelentingly aided those dying of starvation, disease, and plague.

Saint Frances was a gentle woman who had been born into a family of piety and of ample means in Rome. At the age of eleven, she asked permission to become a nun, but her request was refused. Instead, she was contracted into marriage at the age of thirteen. She entered into marriage and although she felt a deep relationship with her husband, she still felt a calling to help those less fortunate.

Coincidentally, Vannozza, the young wife of her husband's brother, was a woman of similar spiritual calling. The two women entered into a kinship that was to last throughout their lives. Both of these young women shared a longing for a life of religious dedication and prayer. They began to work together, dressing plainly, visiting the poor of Rome, and ministering to the needy. Fortunately, their husbands were devoted to both of them and raised no objections to their charities and austerities.

Frances raised her children herself until civil war broke out. People were dying in the streets from starvation, disease, and plague. Vannozza and Frances worked unrelentingly in their efforts to help those suffering. They sold their own jewels and went door to door begging for food or money for the poor. In the midst of war, pillage, poverty, and famine, two of her own children died. So weakened by the stress of the entire situation, Frances fell ill to plague herself, but was able to survive.

Frances now felt even closer to God. She had long ago resolved to subsist on foods causing no harm to other creatures — merely dry bread with occasional vegetables. Her husband, whose love and reverence for her only increased with age, released her from the obligations of marriage and she was able to carry out a project of organizing a society of women who would offer themselves to God and serve the poor. The society was first known as the Oblates of Mary.

After numerous years of dedication and sacrifice for the welfare of all, stating that the angel of God beckoned her, Frances died.[54] Her life was one of pure devotion to all people and all beings. She lived a humble self-sacrificing life in the truest image of one sharing God's mercy with all.

Saint James de la March

1386 - 1476 CE
November 28

Saint James grieved at the plight of the poor forced to pawn all they owned just to survive another day. He organized charitable pawn shops where they might borrow money and not lose all they owned.

Saint James was born to poor parents in Ancona, Italy but was later sent to Perugia to be educated. He joined the Franciscan Order and sought to live a religious life of sacrifice for others, as well as for God. He performed difficult and self-sacrificing chores, slept but a few hours every night so that he could spend his days helping others, and resolved to consume a vegetarian diet devoid of animal flesh.

James was dedicated in his conviction to devote his entire life to holy sacrifice, and tried to educate others whom he observed to be dishonest, or on paths to selfish goals.[55] He was known for his integrity and principle, and for the fact that he would not bend to the wants of others if he did not feel such actions were consistent with justice and truth.

James spent his work days fostering the development of charitable pawnshops, so that the poor might be able to borrow money at reasonable rates, rather than at high rates that made them lose all they possessed. He spent his free time preaching throughout the countryside. He was offered the position of papal legate to Hungary, as well as a similar position in Milan. He refused both of these positions, however, so that he might continue toiling as a simple preacher. His preaching was based upon the Bible, although he added references to works of many theologians and moralists, as well as to Dante's *Divine Comedy* (which he knew by heart).[56] He was a man of scholarship, principle, and kindness, whose dietary principles of non-violence were an example of his commitment and concern for the welfare of all others.

Saint Michael of Giedroyc

Died c. 1485 CE
May 4

Though born with physical deformities and serious health challenges, Saint Michael was given the power of prophecy. He used this to heal many.

Saint Michael was born severely and permanently handicapped physically. His parents were well-respected, holy people who resided in a castle in Lithuania.[57] His very frail constitution was due to numerous medical complications of his having been born a dwarf. In addition, an accident during his youth deprived him of the use of one of his legs.

During the era in which he lived, and because of his orientation toward piety, his parents felt that he would find solace in a religious life. They began to instill in him spiritually oriented education under the guidance of wise and holy individuals; however, his classes were often interrupted and quite sporadic due to his weak medical state.[58]

Ill as he was, Michael still longed for a life of even greater austerity. He lived in the most meager of surroundings, prayed late into the night, seldom spoke, and chose to live solely on vegetables and salt, never consuming meat. He sought to live in simplicity, never acquiring or demanding more than the minimal amount his body required. Others recognized that his life of humility, austerity and prayer seemed to empower him with gifts of religious insight and prophecies. Miracles had been attributed to his gentle presence.[59] His life as a spiritually dedicated man and peace-oriented vegetarian exemplified the character of this humble man who used all his fragile strength so that he might share God's grace with others.

Saint Mariana
of Quito

1618 - 1645 CE
May 26

When the people of her land suffered a terrible earthquake followed by an epidemic, Saint Mariana offered herself to God in exchange for the lives of her people.

Saint Mariana was born to a family considered of noble Spanish stock in Quito, Ecuador.[60] Both her parents died when she was very young, but her loving and concerned older sister raised her. Even as a child, Mariana showed signs of piety. She guided other children on how to pray the rosary, prayed stations of the cross, and attempted to convert others within the community. She eventually decided to devote her life to prayer, contemplation, and simplicity. With time, she gravitated to the most austere of lives imbued with the faith that she was sacrificing herself for the sake of others.

She slept but briefly every night, spending the rest of her time in prayer.

She lived without personal possessions, owned no unnecessary clothing, and subsisted on a diet devoid of flesh foods, consuming only bread and water. When a terrible earthquake hit Quito in 1645, it caused much initial devastation and was soon followed by an epidemic. Hearing of the needs of those afflicted within her country and seeing the widespread suffering Mariana felt deeply moved.

So she offered herself to God, so that He might take her life in exchange for stopping the suffering and sparing the lives of others. Immediately the quakes stopped; but Mariana was seized with maladies that led to her rapid demise. She was twenty-six years old at the time and the entire city mourned her death and considered her their savior.[61] Mariana lived in austerity and as a vegetarian in her sincere belief that a life devoid of personal excesses, yet filled with sacrifices for others, was a life lived in the image of God.

Saint John de Britto

1647-1693 CE
February 4

Saint John was called upon to help the poorest of India during a terrible plague. He helped many survive this devastating catastrophe.

Saint John was born into a well-respected family in Portugal. His father died when he was only four years of age and his mother thought it best to transfer his upbringing over to the care of Jesuit priests. These holy men educated John until he was nine years of age, then sent him to live in the court of the future heir to the throne of Portugal. John remained prayerful and pious throughout his years there, even though he was often subjected to the ridicule of his fellow pages for his religious orientation. The ridicule he endured only served to intensify his religious convictions. Once, his fellow workers beat him so cruelly that he was on the brink of death. It was after his mother invoked the name of his idol, Saint Francis Xavier, that he began to heal from these wounds. He survived and decided to enter the seminary, eventually being ordained a Jesuit priest.[62]

John's ministry led him as a missionary to Goa and Madurai[63] in the south of India, following in the footsteps of Saint Francis Xavier. He met many intelligent and holy individuals while there, and resolved to conduct his life in the manner of the holy men of India. He distinguished himself by following an ascetic life, renouncing pleasures of this world, wearing simple garb and sandals, and consuming a totally vegetarian diet, merely one of rice and vegetables. As the holy men of the Hindu tradition believed animal life was too sacred to be used for the purpose of food, so, too, did John revere the life of each animal.

He and the other missionaries suffered excessive hardships, yet they were able to continue working for the poor and helped many survive the plague. After fourteen years in India, John set sail and returned to Portugal with his fellow priests. In Portugal, the whole city came to greet him, as news of John's sanctity and heroism had reached their shores.

He remained in Europe for several years, but longed to return to the people of India. He was able to return to India for the last three years of his life, dedicating himself to helping the poor and sharing God's wisdom and mercy with them.[64] He maintained his vegetarian values throughout his life, believing that all beings are manifestation of God's love.

Chapter 11

Saints Known for Animal Mercy

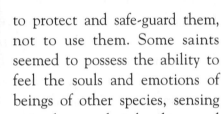

As stated by Andrew Linzey, "to love animals is not sentimentality...but true spirituality."[1] Within the ancient writings and legends describing Christian saints of the early Church are several biographies concerning saints who seemed to relate to animals almost mystically. These saints often risked their lives for the sake of animals, and animals often did the same. Some are sensitive tales, in which saints sacrificed their possessions, status, and safety to help weaker creatures; others are stories in which saints felt deep emotional communion with one, some, or all living creatures. All, however, believed that God gave humans dominion over animals to protect and safe-guard them, not to use them. Some saints seemed to possess the ability to feel the souls and emotions of beings of other species, sensing that the animals were their brothers, and perceiving the image of God in all His creatures.

Some saints felt that as God had formed all creatures, it was God alone, who had the wisdom and the right to take life from an animal. Throughout all these messages runs a strong theme of mercy. The messages embody the concept that those wishing to live in God's image and wishing to share His mercy must live in a state of unconditional compassion toward all creatures. The following saints exemplify such values.

Saint Callistratus

Died c. 304 CE
September 26

Some cruel sailors tied up
Saint Callistratus in a sack
and threw him overboard.
Dolphins recognized his
gentle nature and freed him,
carrying him back to safety.

Saint Callistratus was a native of
Chalcedon in Greece.[2] He journeyed to
enlist as a soldier at Byzantium[3] near the
Bosphorus Strait.[4] Although he was
serving in the military, he began to feel
overcome with spiritual thoughts of how
one might avoid conflict through the
attainment of mutual understanding. He
recognized that in war, no side truly won,
yet each side suffered tragic losses. As his
beliefs in non-violence evolved, he also
developed a strong conviction that
humans should not harm weaker creatures.

Some of the soldiers accused him of
being a Christian. He could not hide his
beliefs. So he confessed that he had
become a Christian and that it was his goal
to spread peace and love, rather than per-
petuate violence. Because of his
admission, he was beaten and
placed in a sack that was then
sewn up and flung overboard
into the waters of the Bosphorus.

Forty-nine soldiers attest to
the fact that they saw the sack
burst opened when it hit the
water and that Callistratus was able to
climb out of the sack. After he climbed out
of the sack, two dolphins carried him on
their backs safely to shore.[5]

Although there are no explicit passages
stating that Saint Callistratus consistently
sustained himself on a diet free of animal
flesh, many statements, concerning his
commitment to avoid infliction of harm
upon any being, seem to imply that he was
a vegetarian, particularly after the dolphins
saved his life. The story of the dolphins'
concern for him, and his mutual sense of
appreciation toward them, has survived as
a two thousand year old bridge filling the
gap in misunderstanding that humans
have had for centuries about these gentle
creatures.

Saint Marianus

Died c. 473 CE
April 20

Saint Marianus seemed to possess a spiritual bond with animals, both tamed and wild. Creatures of the forest would come up to him and birds would eat out of his hands.

Not much is known of the early life of Saint Marianus. The only information available begins when he was still a young man, seeking refuge in a monastery in Auxerre.[6] Warring forces had occupied his homeland; and, he was forced to flee. He wanted to become a member of the religious community. After remaining with this community, and after exhibiting much piety and obedience, he was admitted to the clergy. The abbot, however, wished to test his commitment. So he gave him the lowest possible job, that of cowman and shepherd.

Although such a position was not his initial choice, Marianus accepted it with reverence and humility. Then over time, others noticed that the animals seemed to behave differently when Marianus was around. When under his care, the animals thrived in health and excelled in growth. They increased greatly in numbers and were remarkably obedient to him. Others also noticed that he seemed to possess a spiritual bond with the animals—and out of this bond grew mutual respect and caring between the quiet priest and the animals.

With time, all animals seemed to undergo an almost mystical conversion when with him. Birds flocked to eat from his hands. After hearing his words, bears and wolves would leave the pastures and not harm the herd. Once, a wild boar fled from a group of hunters, who were trying to take its life, and sought refuge with Marianus, who hid the frightened animal, saving its life.[7] Marianus would never harm or take the life of any bird or animal; rather, he protected all, feeling their cries of pain when they were in danger. His was a sense of love and spiritual communion with all creatures.

Saint Brendon of Clonfert

c. 487-575 CE
May 16

Saint Brendon understood the language, actions, and needs of other creatures. Legend has it that his friendship with a bird saved the lives of all on board his ship.

Saint Brendon was a monk of Irish heritage, with a following among a large number of people of Ireland, Wales, and Scotland. A famous legend, as related in a seafaring tale, *The Navigation of Saint Brendon*, tells of his sea voyage with a group of Irish monks in search of an island of promise in the Atlantic Ocean. The story tells of various adventures, all of which coincided with feasts of the liturgical year, and all of which were followed by a narrative in which a bird predicted all events. The bird possessed the ability to interpret the spiritual and religious meaning of events that occurred on the stormy and tumultuous voyage.

For example, in the legend, the bird recounts that, "On the journey four seasons have been determined for you: that is, the day of the Lord's Supper is to be celebrated with a holy man, Easter [will be celebrated] on the island..."[8] and likewise Pentecost and Christmas on other islands. In the story, the bird also foretold that at the end of the seventh year the monks would reach the land they were seeking, would remain there forty days, and would then be brought back to their homeland.

In the tale, birds joined in psalms with the monks, as well as in spiritual prayer. All faced encounters with icebergs, volcanoes, and whales on their fateful voyage as a team. We shall never know if all, or only portions, of the legend are true. Irish monks were known to have traveled to Iceland, yet the details of their journeys were not always documented. The important message within the legend is that man and beast may achieve a mutually beneficial outcome if they unite to face life's challenges and uncertainties as brothers. Saint Brendon bonded with all the animals as brothers and protected them from all adversity. The mystical component of this tale, that birds and humans are one in their ability to act as trusting concerned beings, has survived for centuries as a message fostering respect and concern for all God's creatures.

Saint Kieran

Fifth Century
March 5

Saint Kieran lived along-side the forest animals, considering all as brothers. This bond taught him that it was not humankind's nature to eat the flesh of other beings.

Saint Kieran lived the first thirty years of his life in Ireland as a man devoted to holiness and integrity, without ever having been baptized. Upon hearing of the Christian faith, he set out on a journey to Rome so that he might learn more about it. After studying Christian principles and values, he was finally baptized. After baptism, he was sent back to Ireland to serve as a priest, and as word of his holiness spread, he was eventually ordained as bishop.

Although he was climbing up within the hierarchy of the Church, his heart felt drawn to live a solitary life of simplicity and austerity. So he left to live as a hermit —building himself a small cell within a cave. This tiny cell eventually became the nucleus from which an entire monastery grew. According to legend, found amidst the writings called *Saint Kieran's Lives*, his first disciples were Brother Boar, Brother Badger, Brother Fox, Brother Wolf, and Brother Deer.

When a wild boar initially met Saint Kieran, he recognized the sincerity within the holy man's face as embodying that of a man at peace with all creation. So he tore brush and branches to help Kieran build his monastery. The boar brought other animals that knew the forest well; and, all used their skills to help the lone monk. When Brother Fox began to chew the monk's shoes, the other animals brought him to his master for penance. The Saint said to him, 'Wherefore, brother didst thou do this ill deed, which it becomes not monks to do? Behold, our water is sweet and free to us, and food is here for us alike to share. And if thou hadst a longing, as is thy nature, to eat flesh, Almighty God would have made it for thee from the roots of these trees, if we had asked Him.'[9]

Saint Kieran lived his entire life as a vegetarian because of his compassion for all beings. He believed that God supplied all the foods needed by the energy of the sun and the bounty of the soil. Although this story contains a mystical component, the heart of its meaning rests in the fact that Saint Kieran would harm no living being, as his heart possessed compassion for all.[10]

Saint Stephen of Mar Saba

c. 710 - 784 CE
March 31

Saint Stephen valued all life. Extending compassion to all creatures, he fed birds from his hands and picked up worms from the road so no harm would befall them.

Saint Stephen began his life as a man deeply rooted in spirituality. When only ten years of age, his uncle, Saint John Damascene, brought him to live with him in a remote semi-hermitic desert monastery in Palestine. It was quite rare for a child, then termed 'a man without a beard' to be permitted within monastery life. So a special dispensation must have been arranged for him.

As Stephen grew, he became known as a man who dispensed his wisdom generously to all seeking knowledge. When he reached twenty-five years of age, however, his uncle died. He requested permission to perform eight years of service to the community, and once having received permission, proceeded to do so.

By the age of thirty-seven, he embarked upon a life of complete solitude for fifteen years, venturing out only three times so that he might journey to the Dead Sea in observance of Lent. After those times, he returned to his simple contemplative life in the desert and took on disciples to teach. He possessed infinite compassion for his fellow man and a seemingly Godly gift of being able to help others in difficulty, whether such difficulties were physical or spiritual. He cured sickness of the body, as well as sickness of the soul, and his mere presence often seemed to have been an instrument of healing.[11]

His compassion extended to all creatures, as he fed starlings, ravens, doves, and gazelles with his own hand. He never hurt or took the life of any being. Birds alighted on his shoulders and would accept his offerings of food. He was particularly concerned about the black worms on the ground of the hermitage, painstakingly collecting them to put them in a safe place so no harm would befall them. Saint Stephen pleaded with others, "Do you not realize that if a person acts without compassion toward irrational nature, he will do the same toward his neighbor?"[12]

Saint biographer, Leontius, wrote that as Saint Stephen aged, "Whatever help, spiritual or material he was asked to give, he gave. He possessed nothing and lacked nothing. In total poverty, he possessed all things."[13] So ended the kindly, contemplative, and non-violent life of this gentle sage who could not consume, harm, or take the life of any being.

Saint Anselm

Archbishop of Canterbury
c. 1033-1109 CE
April 21

As archbishop, Saint Anselm fostered humanitarian and altruistic causes. He beseeched hunters not to harm weaker beings, even saving a small hare.

Saint Anselm was a man born of noble Italian parentage. He had been a dedicated student and even from youth seemed to possess a calling for monastic life. He was devastated when his mother died. So he ran away over the mountains toward France to remove himself from his father's harshness. Although he eventually became heir to his father's fortune, he gave all away to the poor and became a monk.

With time, it became obvious that Anselm's strengths resided within the wisdom he expressed in his teachings. At the monastery, an older man questioned Anselm if he thought it right to constrain students who were incorrigible. Saint Anselm, understanding the need for people to learn and grow in freedom of thought replied, "If you planted a tree in your garden and tied it up on all sides, so that it could not stretch forth its branches, what sort of tree would it turn out when, after some years you gave it room to spread?"[14]

The principles he used to guide his life were those of the Rules of Saint Benedict. He felt one must live without greed, anger, hostility, and hate. Eventually, he became a successful Abbot and spiritual guide, writing eleven major treatises.[15]

Legend has it that one day after Saint Anselm had been made archbishop young men came riding past with their dogs chasing a hare. Anselm reigned in his horse and forbid the dogs to hurt the hare. The dogs surrounded the hare, began to lick it in friendship, and did it no harm. When the soldiers crowded around in triumph concerning their catch, Anselm burst into tears. The men began to laugh at the saint, yet he gently advised them, "For the poor unhappy creature there is nothing to laugh at or be glad; its mortal foes are about it, and it flies to us for life."[16] With that, the hunters rode on. Saint Anselm was a man who could not bear to see any creature lose its life for food, sport, or any other reason. The compassion he felt for the poor innocent hare has remained a legacy and an example of his conviction that love and concern should be extended to all creatures.

Saint Martin de Porres

1575-1639 CE
November 3

Saint Martin saw the image of God in all creatures. He tried to help others feel compassion towards mice and rats stating that the only reason they acted as they did was because they were ill fed.

Saint Martin was the first individual of mixed ethnicity to have been recognized by the Church for his heroic acts of Christian virtue. Born in Peru, Martin's father was of Spanish heritage and his mother had been a freed black slave from Panama. When Martin was baptized, his father publicly refused to acknowledge him and, effectively, subjected him to being defined as illegitimate.

Fortunately, Martin's mother was a well-respected practitioner of herbal medicine and was able to share with Martin a solid foundation in medical knowledge. Even as a youth, Martin seemed to possess extraordinary powers of healing. When one of the priests was being prepared to have his leg amputated because of ulcers, Martin beseeched the surgeon to stop, as he knew he would be able to heal the priest's ulcers without the need for amputation.

Martin applied his herbs, and in a few days, the priest's leg was completely healed.

Martin shared his compassion with the entire community. He healed the sick of the city, established an orphanage, set up a home for abandoned newborns, distributed alms to the poor, and cared for slaves who were brought from Africa to Peru. His love extended to all animals; and, he became known as the Saint Francis of the Americas. There are many accounts of his devotion to animals, and his mystical communion with their thoughts and feelings. He could not bear the thought of any action that caused harm to animals, and he would not use any animal as food, beast of burden, or for profit.

Saint Martin saw God in all beings, and his concern for weaker creatures extended even to rodents. He excused the actions of mice and rats stating that they were forced to behave as scavengers because they were ill fed.[17] His ability to sense the presence of God in all beings crossed every boundary of race, species, size, and form and he sought to protect all beings out of his deep empathy and love.

Chapter 12

Martyr Saints

Saints who were honored as martyrs do not constitute a large percentage of those Christian saints who were vegetarian. This was not because martyrs lacked humanitarian concerns; but rather their energies and goals were oriented in vastly different directions. Martyrs were those men and women who sacrificed their possessions, wealth, health, and finally their lives to ensure the survival of Christianity. Martyrs were canonized during those early years of Christianity when individuals were forced either to renounce their faith or to sacrifice their lives. Their actions often replicated the sacrifice of Jesus and they often died similar tragic deaths.

As the word martyr actually means primary witness, the apostles were the original martyrs. Little has been written and therefore little is known concerning the diets of either the initial apostles or the later martyred saints. During the formative years of Christianity, many followers lost their lives to martyrdom either by the sword or by being thrown to wild beasts. It was only after Christianity had attained the status of a unified faith that the Church recognized the profound message that pacific saints had upon the direction Christianity would take. Only after martyrs had sacrificed themselves for the faith could pacific individuals even practice Christianity and be considered as choices for canonization.

Reverend Alban Butler summarized the values of the martyr saints as follows:

"In the lives of the Saints we see the happiness rooted in virtue, which, by repeated fervent exercise, is formed into strong and lasting exercise of temperance, meekness, humility, charity and holy zeal. Such a virtue is never warped by selfish beliefs, or is inconsistent with itself; it vanquishes all enemies, discovers their snares, triumphs over their assaults, and is faithful to the end."[1]

Saint Procopius

Died c. 303 CE
July 8

Saint Procopius was a man of
peace and of dedication to
Jesus. He accepted death
(beheading) by the governor
of Caesaria rather than sacrifice to pagan gods.

Saint Procopius was said to have been the first of the martyrs of Palestine. He was a man who devoted his life to prayer and holiness, and who had come to the assistance of many in need. He filled his days with meditation of the divine word. He was able to cast out evil spells by laying his hands upon people afflicted with diseases. Although he might have used these gifts for his own purposes, his only goal was to share his abilities with others. In his quest to live mercifully, he chose to live on a diet devoid of animal flesh. Although he was a small, thin man, he consumed only bread and water, and ate only every two to three days. He was a man filled with goodness and peace, yet he regarded himself as the least of men.

One day, he went with some of his companions to Caesaria[2] and had scarcely passed the city gates when he was caught by soldiers and brought in front of the governor. Although he was urged by the judge to sacrifice to pagan gods, he refused saying there is but one God, the creator and the author of all things.[3] On July seventh, in the year 303, the authorities beheaded this humble cleric.[4] Procopius was a man who would harm no other being, and who sacrificed his life to preserve the name of Jesus Christ.

Saint Boniface of Tarsus

c. 307 CE
May 14

Saint Boniface sacrificed his own life to ransom other Christians from execution. He suffered the same fate himself for having done so.

Saint Boniface was the chief steward of a beautiful and wealthy, young woman in Rome. Although he had been her lover and lived a wild life, he was also known to have been compassionate and kind. He often helped travelers and always gave to the poor whatever they were lacking. Over time, his mistress, Aglae, began to feel concern for the followers of Christianity in the East who were being tortured for their faith. Boniface saved some money. With her blessings, he ventured forth to ransom and save those he could from execution.[5]

Once committed to this mission, Boniface became a changed man. He spent many hours in prayer, tears, and penitence, resolving never again to consume the flesh of other beings. When he reached his destination, he went directly to the governor, only to witness the cruel torture and execution of no less than twenty people. Boniface cried out to those being executed: "Great is the God of the Christians, great is the God of the holy martyrs. Servants of God, pray for me that I may join you in fighting against the devil." The governor was insulted by such words being said in his presence and asked Boniface in great wrath who he was. Boniface replied that he was a Christian, and that as such, he feared nothing the governor could do.[6]

The following day the governor called for him and had him beheaded. Aglae, upon receiving information of the affair, thanked God for Boniface's victory over death. She built a monument, and then a chapel over his remains. Boniface was led to a life of compassion and concern for others. It was his conversion to a life of sacrifice for the welfare of others that led him to die as a martyr in the name of Jesus.

Saint Serenus

Died c. 327 CE
February 23

Saint Serenus sought nothing more than the life of a humble gardener. When it was discovered that he was a follower of Jesus, he did not deny this, preferring execution rather than worship other gods.

Saint Serenus was born into a well established Greek family. When quite young, however, he left his family's estate choosing to live an ascetic life in simplicity and in prayerful service to God. He traveled to Hungary where he purchased a small garden and began to cultivate it with his own hands. He sought a life of gentle deeds and of simple wants. He manifested these goals in both his lack of desire for possessions and his vegetarian dietary choices. He existed merely on the fruits and vegetables his tiny garden produced, and resolved that never would he consume the flesh of animals.

One evening, a woman asked his permission to walk through his garden. Because Serenus noted that the light was dimming, he told the woman that it was improper for her to be out alone in the evening. He thought it best she not enter the garden. The woman felt rebuffed by his answers. She wrote to her husband that the aged gardener had insulted her.

Serenus, just a quiet and humble gardener, was taken to the governor to answer charges that he insulted the woman. Upon recognizing Serenus' gentle mannerism, the authorities readily recognized he was innocent. The governor, however, also recognized that he might have been a Christian. Serenus admitted this was true and professed his faith as a follower of Christ. He was ordered to sacrifice to the pagan gods. Upon his refusal to reject his own faith, he was carried off and beheaded.[7]

Throughout the gentle monk's entire life, he lived by Jesus' principles of brotherly love and compassion toward all. He lived grounded in Christian values and showed kindness toward all beings, human or non-human. His humble gentleness was exemplified by his wish to spare animals from suffering, to take or use no more of this earth than he needed, and to die rather than deny his belief in the teachings of Jesus.

Chapter 13

Legacy of the Vegetarian Christian Saints

Those vegetarian Christian saints whose lives are narrated within these pages are but a small sample of the many Christians who have lived spiritually motivated lives of non-violence and vegetarianism. It is of interest that such a large number of them lived as meditative and contemplative hermits, monks, and ascetics—lifestyles one generally considers as exemplifying Eastern sages. It is of even greater interest that many felt instinctive mystical and spiritual unions with all creatures and all creation, and saw God in all beings

Many of these saints held beliefs that contemplation and meditation elevated their souls to higher levels of consciousness and helped them attain increased levels of spiritual awareness. Some felt that their following lives of simplicity and asceticism had been necessary stages in drawing their minds from worldly thoughts to spiritual

ones. A good number of these saints attained what those of Eastern faiths term realization. Having attained realization, they recognized that all creation was a manifestation of God and all creation was worthy of respect, compassion, non-violence, and love.

Although many of the values of these saints may not initially appear to be what one generally considers traditional to the Church, at least during their time, they must have been – as these individuals were canonized!

When one commonly thinks of individuals who have lived in total non-violence toward all beings, one usually envisions aged ascetic sages of Eastern faith meditating under banyan trees. Now, with the information shared within these pages, one can envision spiritually wise, peaceful, and enlightened individuals specifically of Christian faith.

Many of these vegetarian saints held life-long commitments of non-violence toward all humans, all animals, and all creation. Many protected all from harms' way, even their enemies. Others protected the land, water, and vegetation, and lived with reverence toward them. They lived without waste, were content with simplicity, avoided inflicting any harm upon nature, and emptied their minds of the desire to possess or destroy any and all that God had created.

The depth and breadth of their peace with all creation often included never harming anyone, anything, or any being through action, word, or thought. Some prayed that the slightest harm never befall any being, even those beings that humans might never have the ability to communicate with or relate to. Their lives epitomized God's wish for mercy and peace for all. Although the term ecology had not been coined at the time most of these saints lived, many seemed to possess instinctive insight concerning the need to respect the environment.

The lives of these vegetarian saints spanned many centuries and involved a variety of cultures. They included saints who lived as desert hermits, monks, ascetics, mystics, contemplative sages, sacrificial martyrs, patron saints, doctors of the church, and even as a pope. In trying to piece together the messages one can learn by reading their lives, two important questions exist. "What inspired these holy individuals to live without consumption of animal flesh?" and "Why did the later saint historians believe that their flesh-free diets were facts even worthy enough to mention?"

One can only hypothesize that, somehow, each saint was spiritually guided. Some were guided to lives of non-violence, while others to lives of personal sacrifice. Some were blessed with the ability to feel love for the God in all beings. Understanding why historians even noted that these saints lived on flesh-free diets is more complicated. We must look into the lives of the historians themselves to gain insight. Most of the initial saint biographers were of the clergy and they, too, must have held reverence for the value of all life. Many seemed to have been emotionally touched when they wrote of the saints' passions, particularly as they detailed the saints' acts of sacrifice, compassion, and mystical relationship with the essence of God in all.

The saints who lived as vegetarians ranged from most obscure to the most world renowned individuals, and their messages are both sensitive and profound.

Some of these saints lived in quiet seclusion spending years in prayerful contemplation[1] while others, such as Saint Catherine of Siena and Saint Jean-Marie Vianney ministered to thousands.[2] Each and every story possesses such meaning that, as a unit, they amassed a profound message leading to the advancement of universal non-violence and peace.

An understanding of the patterns of sanctity of these saints has added insight into their motivations. Many perceived God's presence in all creation: the small and the large, the powerful and the weak, the beautiful and the detestable. They recognized that a life lived protecting all beings, was a life lived sharing God's mercy with all His creation.

One must extend sincere appreciation to the Church for having preserved the life stories of these holy individuals through the tradition of canonization. It has been through such recordings that each of us can benefit from learning of the passions, motivations, and values of these holy sages. It is reassuring to know that Church leaders conferred their highest honor upon such humble and unassuming men and women of peace. The messages of these saints have the potential to disseminate values of peace and mercy not just to the faithful of the Christian community, but to the entirety of creation.

The German philosopher Fredrich Wilhelm Nietzsche (1844-1900) has stated that

> Deeper minds of all ages have had pity for animals…

And concerning the legacy left by the saints, Nietzsche stated that

> Nature needs the Saint…[for]…in him [and her] the ego has melted away, and the suffering of his life is, practically, no longer felt as an individual, but as the spring of the deepest sympathy and intimacy with all living creatures."[3]

May each of us grow in wisdom and grace through the legacies left by the sacrificing, compassionate, mystical, and peace loving vegetarian Christian saints.

Vegetarian Saints by Saint Days

JANUARY		FEBRUARY	
Saint Fulgentius of Ruspe	January 1	Saint Anskar	February 3
Saint Basil the Great	January 2	Saint Aventine of Troyes	February 4
Saint Genevieve	January 2	Saint Gilbert of Sempringham	February 4
Saint Macarius the Younger		Saint John de Britto	February 4
(of Alexandria)	January 2	Saint Amandus	February 6
Saint William of Bourges	January 10	Saint Luke the Younger	February 7
Saint Palaemon	January 11	Saint Stephen of Grandmont	February 8
Saint Theodosius the Cenobiarch	January 11	Saint Clare of Rimini	February 10
Saint Kertigan of Glasgow	January 13	Saint William of Malavalle	February 10
Saint Maurus of Glanfeuil	January 15	Saint Jonas the Gardener	February 11
Saint Paul the Hermit	January 15	Saint Fintan of Clonenagh	February 17
Saint Henry of Coquet	January 16	Saint Silvin	February 17
Saint Anthony of Egypt	January 17	Saint Benedict of Aniane	February 21
Saint Julian Sabas	January 17	Saint Margaret of Cortona	February 22
Saint Macarius the Elder		Saint Dositheus	February 23
(of Egypt)	January 19	Saint Peter Damian	February 23
Saint Wulfstan	January 19	Saint Serenus, a Gardener	February 23
Saint Apollo	January 25	Saint Porphyry of Gaza	February 26
Saint Paula	January 25	Saint Lupicinus	February 28
Saint Publius	January 25	Saint Romanus of Condat	February 28
Saint Alberic	January 26		
Saint Stephen Harding	January 26		
Saint Angela Merici	January 27		
Saint Aphraates	January 29		
Saint Sulpicius Severus	January 29		

MARCH

Saint David	March 1
Saint Winwaloe	March 3
Saint Kieran	March 5
Saint Gerasimus	March 5
Saint Stephen of Obazine	March 8
Saint Frances of Rome	March 9
Saint Paul Aurelian	March 12
Saint Euphrasia	March 13
Saint Abraham Kidunaja	March 16
Saint Gregory of Makar	March 16
Saint Benedict	March 21
Saint John of Capistrano	March 27
Saint John of Egypt	March 27
Saint Gundelinis	March 28
Saint Stephen of Mar Saba	March 31

APRIL

Saint Francis of Paola	April 2
Saint Mary of Egypt	April 2
Saint Richard of Wyche	April 3
Saint Aybert	April 7
Saint Guthlac	April 12
Saint Elphege	April 19
Saint Agnes of Montepulciano	April 20
Saint Marianus	April 20
Saint Anselm	April 21
Saint Theodore of Sykeon	April 22
Saint Catherine of Siena	April 29
Saint Robert of Molesme	April 29

MAY

Saint Michael of Giedroyc	May 4
Saint Pachomius	May 9
Saint John the Silent	May 13
Saint Boniface of Tarsus	May 14
Saint Brendon of Clonfert	May 16
Saint Simon Stock	May 16
Saint Felix of Cantalice	May 18
Saint Ivo Helory	May 19
Saint Peter Celestine	May 19
Saint Godric	May 21
Saint Hospitius	May 21
Saint Humility of Florence	May 22
Saint Rita of Cascia	May 22
Saint Yvo of Chartres	May 23
Saint Mary Magdalen of Pazzi	May 25
Saint Mariana of Quito	May 26
Saint Philip Neri	May 26

JUNE

Saint Herculanus of Piegaro	June 2
Saint Kevin	June 3
Saint Liphardus	June 3
Saint Urbicius	June 3
Saint Dorotheus the Theban	June 5
Saint John Francis Regis	June 16
Saint Ephraem	June 18
Saint Mary Onigines	June 25
Saint Maxentius	June 26
Saint Theobald of Provins	June 30

JULY

Saint Monegundis	July 2
Saint Ulrich	July 4
Saint Procopius	July 8
Saint Antony of the Caves of Kiev	July 10
Saint Theodosius Pechersky	July 10
Saint James of Nisibis	July 11
Saint Olympias	July 25
Saint Lupus of Troyes	July 29

AUGUST

Saint Jean-Marie Vianney	August 4
Saint Molua	August 4
Saint Albert of Trapani	August 7
Saint Dominic	August 8
Saint Clare of Assisi	August 11
Saint Bernard	August 20
Saint Philip Benizi	August 22
Saint Fantinus	August 30
Saint Jerome	August 30

SEPTEMBER

Saint Giles	September 1
Saint Laurence Justinian	September 5
Saint Nicholas of Tolentino	September 10
Saint Amatus	September 13
Saint Albert of Jerusalem	September 14
Saint Robert Bellarmine	September 17
Saint Joseph of Cupertino	September 18
Saint Callistratus	September 26
Saint Lioba	September 28

OCTOBER

Saint Bavo	October 1
Saint Ammon	October 4
Saint Francis of Assisi	October 4
Saint Thais	October 8
Saint Bruno	October 11
Saint Dominic Loricatus	October 14
Saint Euthymius the Younger	October 15
Saint Hedwig	October 17
Saint Peter of Alcantara	October 19
Saint Hilarion	October 21
Saint Malchus	October 21

Saint Senoch	October 24
Saint Coleman of Kilmacduagh	October 29

NOVEMBER

Saint Marcian	November 2
Saint Martin de Porres	November 3
Saint Joannicus	November 4
Saint Leonard Noblac	November 6
Saint Theodore the Studite	November 11
Saint Laurence O'Toole	November 14
Saint Elizabeth of Hungary	November 17
Saint Leonard of Porto-Maurizio	November 26
Saint James de la March	November 28

DECEMBER

Saint Francis Xavier	December 3
Saint Asella	December 6
Saint Sabas	December 8
Saint Paul of Latros	December 15
Saint John of Matha	December 17
Saint John of Kanti	December 23

Appendix 2

Vegetarian Saints in Alphabetical Order

1. Saint Abraham Kidunaja — March 16
2. Saint Agnes of Montepulciano — April 20
3. Saint Alberic — January 26
4. Saint Albert of Jerusalem — September 14
5. Saint Albert of Trapani — August 7
6. Saint Amandus — February 6
7. Saint Amatus — September 13
8. Saint Ammon — October 4
9. Saint Angela Merici — January 27
10. Saint Anselm — April 21
11. Saint Anskar — February 3
12. Saint Anthony of Egypt — January 17
13. Saint Antony of the Caves of Kiev — July 10
14. Saint Aphraates — January 29
15. Saint Apollo — January 25
16. Saint Asella — December 6
17. Saint Aybert — April 7
18. Saint Aventine of Troyes — February 4
19. Saint Basil the Great — January 2
20. Saint Bavo — October 1
21. Saint Benedict — March 21
22. Saint Benedict of Aniane — February 21
23. Saint Bernard — August 20
24. Saint Boniface of Tarsus — May 14
25. Saint Brendon of Clonfert — May 16
26. Saint Bruno — October 11
27. Saint Callistratus — September 26
28. Saint Catherine of Siena — April 29
29. Saint Clare of Rimini — February 10
30. Saint Clare of Assisi — August 11
31. Saint Coleman of Kilmacduagh — October 29
32. Saint David – Patron Saint of Wales — March 1
33. Saint Dominic — August 8
34. Saint Dominic Loricatus — October 14
35. Saint Dorotheus the Theban — June 5
36. Saint Dositheus — February 23
37. Saint Elizabeth of Hungary — November 17
38. Saint Elphege — April 19
39. Saint Ephraem — June 18
40. Saint Euphrasia — March 13
41. Saint Euthymius the Younger — October 15
42. Saint Fantinus — August 30
43. Saint Felix of Cantalice — May 18
44. Saint Fintan of Clonenagh — February 17
45. Saint Francis of Assisi — October 4
46. Saint Francis of Paola — April 2
47. Saint Frances of Rome — March 9
48. Saint Francis Xavier — December 3
49. Saint Fulgentius of Ruspe — January 1
50. Saint Genevieve — January 2
51. Saint Gerasimus — March 5
52. Saint Gilbert of Sempringham — February 4
53. Saint Giles — September 1
54. Saint Godric — May 21
55. Saint Gregory of Makar — March 16
56. Saint Gundelinis — March 28
57. Saint Guthlac — April 12

57.	Saint Guthlac	April 12
58.	Saint Hedwig	October 17
59.	Saint Henry of Coquet	January 16
60.	Saint Herculanus of Piegaro	June 2
61.	Saint Hilarion	October 21
62.	Saint Hospitius	May 21
63.	Saint Humility of Florence	May 22
64.	Saint Ivo Helory	May 19
65.	Saint James de la March	November 28
66.	Saint James of Nisibis	July 11
67.	Saint Jean-Marie Vianney	August 4
68.	Saint Jerome	August 30
69.	Saint Joannicus	November 4
70.	Saint John de Britto	February 4
71.	Saint John of Kanti	December 23
72.	Saint John of Capistrano	March 27
73.	Saint John of Egypt	March 27
74.	Saint John Francis Regis	June 16
75.	Saint John of Matha	December 17
76.	Saint John the Silent	May 13
77.	Saint Jonas the Gardener	February 11
78.	Saint Joseph of Cupertino	September 18
79.	Saint Julian Sabas	January 17
80.	Saint Kertigan of Glasgow	January 13
81.	Saint Kevin	June 3
82.	Saint Kieran	March 5
83.	Saint Laurence Justinian	September 5
84.	Saint Laurence O'Toole	November 14
85.	Saint Leonard Noblac	November 6
86.	Saint Leonard of Porto-Maurizio	November 26
87.	Saint Lioba	September 28
88.	Saint Liphardus	June 3
89.	Saint Luke the Younger	February 7
90.	Saint Lupicinus	February 28
91.	Saint Lupus of Troyes	July 29
92.	Saint Macarius of Alexandria (the Younger)	January 2
93.	Saint Macarius the Elder (of Egypt)	January 19
94.	Saint Malchus	October 21
95.	Saint Margaret of Cortona	February 22
96.	Saint Marcian	November 2

97.	Saint Mariana of Quito	May 26
98.	Saint Marianus	April 20
99.	Saint Mary of Egypt	April 2
100.	Saint Mary Magdalen of Pazzi	May 25
101.	Saint Mary Onigines	June 25
102.	Saint Martin de Porres	November 3
103.	Saint Maurus of Glanfeuil	January 15
104.	Saint Maxentius	June 26
105.	Saint Michael of Giedroyc	May 4
106.	Saint Molua	August 4
107.	Saint Monegundis	July 2
108.	Saint Nicholas of Tolentino	September 10
109.	Saint Olympias	July 25
110.	Saint Pachomius	May 9
111.	Saint Palaemon	January 11
112.	Saint Paul Aurelian	March 12
113.	Saint Paul the Hermit	January 15
114.	Saint Paul of Latros	December 15
115.	Saint Paula	January 25
116.	Saint Peter of Alcantara	October 19
117.	Saint Peter Celestine	May 19
118.	Saint Peter Damian	February 23
119.	Saint Philip Benizi	August 22
120.	Saint Philip Neri	May 26
121.	Saint Porphyry of Gaza	February 26
122.	Saint Procopius	July 8
123.	Saint Publius	January 25
124.	Saint Richard of Wyche	April 3
125.	Saint Rita of Cascia	May 22
126.	Saint Robert Bellarmine	September 17
127.	Saint Robert of Molesme	April 29
128.	Saint Romanus of Condat	February 28
129.	Saint Sabas	December 8
130.	Saint Senoch	October 24
131.	Saint Serenus the Gardener	February 23
132.	Saint Silvin	February 17
133.	Saint Simon Stock	May 16
134.	Saint Stephen of Grandmont	February 8
135.	Saint Stephen Harding	January 26
136.	Saint Stephen of Mar Saba	March 31

137.	Saint Stephen of Obazine	March 8
138.	Saint Sulpicius Severus	January 29
139.	Saint Thais	October 8
140.	Saint Theobald of Provins	June 30
141.	Saint Theodore the Studite	November 11
142.	Saint Theodore of Sykeon	April 22
143.	Saint Theodosius the Cenobiarch	January 11
144.	Saint Theodosius Pechersky	July 10
145.	Saint Ulrich	July 4
146.	Saint Urbicius	June 3
147.	Saint William of Bourges	January 10
148.	Saint William of Malavalle	February 10
149.	Saint Winwaloe	March 3
150.	Saint Wulfstan	January 19
151.	Saint Yvo of Chartres	May 23

Appendix 3
End Notes

Introduction and Chapter One—
Evolution of Vegetarian Values

1. Mervyn G Herdinge, and Hulda Crooks, "Non-Flesh Dietaries," *Journal of American Dietetic Association*, Vol. 43. (1963) 545-549.

2. James C Whorton, "Historical development of vegetarianism," *American Journal of Clinical Nutrition*. 59 (supplement), (1994), 1103-9S.

3. Donald C. Johanson, "Face to Face with Lucy's Family" *National Geographic Magazine*, Vol 189, no.3, March 1996 (Washington, D.C.: National Geographic Society), 114-117.

4. Michael Pitts and Mark Roberts, *Fairweather Eden* (New York, New York: Fromm International, 2000), 12.

5. Michael Pitts and Mark Roberts, *Fairweather Eden* (New York, New York: Fromm International, 2000), 310.

6. L.R. Binford, *In Pursuit of the Past: Decoding the Archaeological Record* (London, England: Thames & Hudson).

7. Pitts, 155.

8. Marc Bekoff, Ed. *Encyclopedia of Animal Rights and Animal Welfare* (Westport, Connecticut: Greenwood Press, 1998), 38.

9. Roberta Kalechofsky, *Vegetarian Judaism: A Guide for Everyone* (Marblehead, Massachusetts: Micah Publications, 1998), 21.

10. Mervyn G. Hardinge and Hulda Crooks, "Non-Flesh Dietaries," *Journal of American Dietetic Association, volume* 43, Dec 1963, 545-549.

11. Zondervan, publ., *Comparative Study Bible,*

"New International" (Grand Rapids Michigan: Zondervan Publishing, 1999), 1767.

12. Stephen M. Wylen, *The Jews in the Time of Jesus* (Mahwah, New Jersey: Paulist Press, 1996), 133.

13. William Whiston, translator. *Josephus, the Complete* (Nashville, Tennessee: Thomas Nelson Press, 1998), 415, reprinted from William Whiston's 1737 English translation of *The Works of Josephus*.

14. Kerry S. Walters and Lisa Portmess, ed. *Religious Vegetarianism, from Hesiod to the Dalai Lama* (Albany, New York: State University of New York Press, 2000), 94 quoting Rabbi Samuel Dressler, *The Jewish Dietary Laws: Their Meaning for Our Time* (The Rabbinical Assembly of America, 1982).

15. Whiston, 572-573.

16. Kerry S. Walters and Lisa Portmess, ed. *Ethical Vegetarianism, from Pythagoras to Peter Singer* (Albany, New York: State University of New York Press, 1999), 14 referencing Iambichus, *On the Pythagorean Life*, c. 250-325: Diogenes Laertius, *Life of Pythagoras*, third century BCE; Ovid, *15th of Ovid's Metamorphosis*, c. 43 BCE to 18 CE.

17. Ryan Berry, *Famous Vegetarians* (New York, New York: Pythagorean Publishers, 1996), 3.

18. Daniel Dombrowski, *The Philosophy of Vegetarianism* (Amherst, Massachusetts: University of Massachusetts Press, 1984) 36-37.

19. Kerry S. Walters and Lisa Portmess, ed. *Ethical*

Vegetarianism, from Pythagoras to Peter Singer (Albany, New York: State University of New York Press, 1999), 16-17 quoting book 15 of Ovid's (c. 43 BCE – 18 CE) *Metamorphosis.*

20. Herdinge, 426.
21. Walters, ibid, 27-28, excerpted from *On the Eating of Flesh*, Plutarch, c.56-129.
22. Daniel A. Dombrowski, *The Philosophy of Vegetarianism* (Amherst, Massachusetts: University of Massachusetts Press, 1984), 2.
23. James C. Whorton, "Historical development of vegetarianism," *American Journal of Clinical Nutrition* 1994; 59(supplement): 1103S- 9S.
24. Wylen, 139.
25. Bekoff, 66.
26. Bekoff, 66-67.
27. Kerry S. Walters, and Lisa Portmess, ed. *Religious Vegetarianism, from Hesiod to the Dalai Lama* (Albany, New York: State University of New York Press, 2000), 123.
28. Rudolph Arbesmann, Emily Joseph Daly, and Edwin A. Quain, transl. *Fathers of the Church, Terullian Apologetical Works*, (Washington, D.C.: Catholic University of America Press, 1950), vii.
29. Arbesmann, 3.
30. Colin Spencer, *The Heretic's Feast: A History of Vegetarianism* (Hanover, New Hampshire: University of New England Press, 1995), 118-119.
31. Herdinge, 546.
32. Simon P. Wood, transl. *The Fathers of the Church, Clement of Alexandria* (New York, New York: Fathers of the Church, Inc. 1954), vi-xiv.
33. Wood, 108.
34. Spencer, 120.
35. Upton Sinclair Ewing, *The Prophet of the Dead Sea Scrolls*, 3rd ed. (Joshua tree, California: Tree of Life Publications, 1994), 148.
36. Victor Parachin, 365 *Good Reasons to be a Vegetarian* (Garden City Park, New York: Avery Publishing, 1998), 76.
37. Ryan Berry, *Foods for the Gods* (New York, New York: Pythagorean Publishers, 1998), 213.
38. Herdinge, 546.
39. Ryan Berry, *Foods for the Gods* (New York, New York: Pythagorean Publishers, 1998), 271.
40. Ibid, 272.
41. Ibid, 272.
42. Ministerial Association of General Conference of Seventh-day Adventists, *Seventh-day Adventists Believe* (Hagerstown, Maryland: Review and Herald Publishing, 1988), 224.

Chapter 2—The Meaning of Sainthood

1. Theodore Maynard, *Saints for our Times* (New York, New York: Appleton-Century-Crofts, 1951), vii.
2. Herbert Thurston and Donald Attwater, *Butler's Lives of the Saints*, volume IV (New York, New York: P.J. Kennedy & Sons, 1956), 667.
3. Woodward, 7.
4. Paul Burns, ed. *Butler's Lives of the Saints: New Full Edition, January* (Collegeville, Minnesota: The Liturgical Press, 1995), xii.
5. Burns, Jan xii.
6. Maynard, vii.
7. Macken, 15-16.
8. Ibid, 17.
9. Burns, Jan, xiii.
10. Ibid, Jan, xiv.
11. Macken, A.
12. Woodward, 65.
13. Burns, Jan, xv.
14. Thomas F. Macken, *Canonization of Saints* (New York, N Y: Benziger Brothers, 1909 Vol. Jan), p. A.
15. Woodward, 67.
16. Ibid, 68.
17. Ibid, 69.
18. Ibid, 70.

19. Ibid, 71.
20. Ibid, 71.
21. Macken, 34-35.
22. Ibid, 38.
23. Ibid, 115.
24. Ibid, 135-139.
25. Woodward, 66.
26. Ibid, 75-76.
27. Burns, Jan, xvii.
28. Woodward, 168-169.
29. Ibid, 55.
30. Macken, 1.
31. Paul Molinari, *Saints: Their Place in the Church* (New York, New York: Sheed and Ward, 1965), 15.
32. Woodward, 9.
33. Ibid, 17.
34. Ibid, 5.
35. Ibid, 7.
36. Woodward, 402-403. Testimony of Carmelite Sisters in process of beatification and canonization of Edith Stein reported in Schwabisches Tageblatt (Tubingen), August 11, 1987.
37. Paul Molinari, *Saints: Their Place in the Church* (New York, New York: Sheed and Ward, 1965), 14.

Chapter 3:
Eastern Monastic & Hermitic Saints

1. Thomas Merton, *The Wisdom of the Desert* (New York, New York: New Directions Book, 1960), 3-6.
2. Ibid, 3.
3. Ibid, 5.
4. Ibid, 10-14.
5. Rene Fulop-Miller, *The Saints that Moved the World* (Salem, New Hampshire: Ayer Company Publishing, 1991), 20-21.
6. Paul Burns, *Butler's Lives of the Saints, New Full Edition, January Volume* (Collegeville, Minnesota: The Liturgical Press, 1998), 122-126.
7. Fulop-Miller, *The Saints that Moved the World,* 24.
8. The Arabian Desert lies in eastern Egypt between the Mediterranean Sea in the north, the Red Sea and the Gulf of Suez on the east, the Nubian Desert on the south, and the Nile River on the west.
9. Charles Warren Currier, *History of Religious Orders* (New York, New York: Murphy & McCarthy, 1896), 66.
10. Paul Burns, *Butler's Lives of the Saints,* (New Full Edition, January Volume, 1998), 125.
11. Thomas Merton, *The Wisdom of the Desert* (New York, New York: New Directions, 1960), 3.
12. Thomas Merton, *The Wisdom of the Desert,* 29.
13. Burns, *Butler's Lives of the Saints,* January, 125.
14. Ibid, 124.
15. Fulop-Miller, 68.
16. The Gaza region was located on the coast of the Mediterranean Sea. It was southwest of Jerusalem and on a road linking Egypt with central Palestine.
17. The delineation of the region termed Palestine has varied greatly over ancient times. The Roman emperor, Constantine the Great, legalized Christianity there in 313 CE.
18. Peter Doyle, *Butler's Lives of the Saints,* October Volume (Collegeville, Minnesota: Liturgical Press, 1996), 146.
19. S. Baring-Gould. *The Lives of the Saints,* October (Edinburgh, Scotland: John Grant Publishers, 1929), 509.
20. Herbert Thurston, *Butler's Lives of the Saints,* Volume III (New York, New York: P.J. Kennedy & Sons, 1956), 163.
21. Alban Butler, *Lives of The Fathers, Martyrs and other Principal Saints.* Volume IV (Great Falls, Montana: St. Bonaventure Publications, republished 1997), 102.
22. Peter Doyle, *Butler's Lives of the Saints,* October Volume (Collegeville, Minnesota: Liturgical Press, 1996), 146.

23. All of these nations border the Mediterranean Sea. Cyprus is the third largest island in the Mediterranean and is located west of Syria and south of Turkey.

24. Alban Butler, *Lives of The Fathers, Martyrs and other Principal Saints*. Volume IV (Great Falls, Montana: St. Bonaventure Publications, republished 1997), 102.

25. Peter Doyle, *Butler's Lives of the Saints*, October Volume (Collegeville, Minnesota: Liturgical Press, 1996), 147.

26. S. Baring Gould, *The Lives of the Saints*, January (Edinburgh, Scotland: John Grant Publishers, 1929), 221- 222.

27. Paul Burns, *Butler's Lives of the Saints*, January (Collegeville, Minnesota: Liturgical Press, 1995), 133-134.

28. Herbert Thurston and Nora Lesson, *The Lives of the Saints, originally compiled by Rev. Alban Butler*, vol. I. January (New York, New York: P.J. Kennedy & Sons, 1932), 187.

29. S. Baring-Gould, *The Lives of the Saints*. First Volume (Edinburgh, Scotland: John Grant Publishers, 1929), 149-150.

31. Herbert Thurston and Nora Lesson, *The Lives of the Saints, originally compiled by Rev. Alban Butler*, vol. V. May (New York, New York: P.J. Kennedy & Sons, 1932), 111 – 113.

32. David Hugh Farmer, *Butler's Lives of the Saints*, May (Collegeville, Minnesota: Liturgical Press, 1996), 47-48.

33. Herbert Thurston, *The Lives of the Saints, originally compiled by Rev. Alban Butler*, vol. I (New York, New York: P.J. Kennedy & Sons, 1926), 182-185.

34. Paul Burns, *Butler's Lives of the Saints, New Full Edition, January Volume* (Collegeville, Minnesota: The Liturgical Press, 1998), 104-105.

35. S. Baring-Gould, *The Lives of the Saints*, January (Edinburgh, Scotland: John Grant Publishers, 1929), 217-218.

36. S. Baring-Gould, *The Lives of the Saints*, November (Edinburgh, Scotland: John Grant Publishers, 1929), 54.

37. Herbert Thurston, and Donald Attwater, *The Lives of the Saints, originally compiled by Rev. Alban Butler*, vol. XI. November (New York, New York: P.J. Kennedy & Sons, 1938), 21.

38. Sarah Fawcett Thomas, *Butler's Lives of the Saints*, November Volume (Collegeville, Minnesota: Liturgical Press, 2000), 13.

39. Sarah Fawcett Thomas, *Butler's Lives of the Saints*, November Volume (Collegeville, Minnesota: Liturgical Press, 2000), 13.

40. Herbert Thurston and Nora Lesson, *The Lives of the Saints, originally compiled by Rev. Alban Butler*, vol. I. January (New York, New York: P.J. Kennedy & Sons, 1932), 20.

41. S. Baring Gould, *The Lives of the Saints*, January (Edinburgh, Scotland: John Grant Publishers, 1929), 31.

42. Herbert Thurston, *Butler's Lives of the Saints*, Volume I (New York, New York: P.J. Kennedy & Sons, 1956), 20.

43. S. Baring Gould, *The Lives of the Saints*, January (Edinburgh, Scotland: John Grant Publishers, 1929), 33.

44. Paul Burns, *Butler's Lives of the Saints* (Collegeville, Minnesota: Liturgical Press, 1995), 19-20.

45. Edessa was an ancient city in Mesopotamia. Now the city of Sanliurfa in southeast Turkey stands on this site.

46. Mesopotamia is a Greek word for "between two rivers." This was one of the earliest centers of urban civilizations and presently includes Iraq, eastern Syria, and southeast Turkey.

47. Herbert Thurston, *Butler's Lives of the Saints*, volume II (New York, New York: P.J. Kennedy & Sons, 1956), 45.

48. Antioch is a city in southern Turkey near the Mediterranean Sea on the west and Syria on the east.

49. Arians were an early sect of Christians who did not believe in the full divinity of Jesus Christ.

50. Herbert Thurston, *Butler's Lives of the Saints*, volume II (New York, New York: P.J. Kennedy & Sons, 1956), 46.

51. Mesopotamia means the lands between two rivers, essentially present day Iraq.

52. The Ecumenical Councils were a series of meetings initially held 325 C.E. and convened by Constantine the Great, emperor of Rome. Their goal was to resolve debates related to the nature of Jesus Christ.

53. Nicea was a region in what would not be considered Turkey, at the site of the city Iznik.

54. Peter Doyle, *Butler's Lives of the Saints*, July (Collegeville, Minnesota: Liturgical Press, 2000), 115.

55. Athanasius was a Christian theologian born in Egypt who at the council of Nicea defined the Son of God and God to be of the same essence.

56. Alban Butler, *Lives of The Fathers, Martyrs and other Principal Saints*. Volumes III (Great Falls, Montana: St. Bonaventure Publications, republished 1997), 31-34.

57. Nisibis was a region in what would presently be considered Syria.

58. Alban Butler, *Lives of the Fathers, Martyres and other Principal Saints*. Volume III (Great Falls, Montana: St. Bonaventure Publications, republished 1997), 33-37.

59. Peter Doyle, *Butler's Lives of the Saints*, October (Collegeville, Minnesota: Liturgical Press, 1996), 27.

60. Herbert Thurston, *Butler's Lives of the Saints*, volume III (New York, New York: P.J. Kennedy & Sons, 1956), 32 – 33.

61. Mesopotamia in this instance may have referred to the lands of southern Turkey, as well as to Iraq or Syria.

62. Persia referred to the region presently known as Iran.

63. S. Baring-Gould, *The Lives of the Saints*, October (Edinburgh, Scotland: John Grant Publishers, 1929), 273-475.

64. Ibid, 475.

65. Antioch was a city in southern Turkey.

66. David Hugh Farmer, *Butler's Lives of the Saints*, January (Collegeville, Minnesota: Liturgical Press, 1995), 126.

67. S. Baring-Gould, *The Lives of the Saints*. First Volume (Edinburgh, Scotland: John Grant Publishers, 1929), 372-274.

68. Herbert Thurston, *Butler's Lives of the Saints*, volume 1 (New York, New York: P.J. Kennedy & Sons, 1956), 691-692.

69. Herbert Thurston, and Nora Leeson, *The Lives of the Saints, originally compiled by Rev. Alban Butler*, vol. III. March (New York, New York: P.J. Kennedy & Sons, 1932), 416-417.

70. Theodosius was the last emperor to rule a united Roman empire. He was a strong champion of Orthodox Christianity.

71. Herbert Thurston, and Nora Lesson, *The Lives of the Saints*, originally compiled by Rev Alban Butler, vol. III. March. New York, New York: P.J. Kennedy & Sons, 1932. 418.

72. Alexandria was a large seaport city in northern Egypt founded in 322 BCE by Alexander the Great. It is on the Nile River Delta.

73. Herbert Thurston and Donald Attwater, *The Lives of the Saints, originally compiled by Rev. Alban Butler*, vol. X October (New York, New York: P.J. Kennedy & Sons, 1936), 99 – 100.

74. S. Baring-Gould, *The Lives of the Saints*, October (Edinburgh, Scotland: John Grant Publishers, 1929), 167 – 169.

75. S. Baring Gould, *The Lives of the Saints*. First Volume (Edinburgh, Scotland: John Grant Publishers, 1929), 263.

76. Alban Butler, *The Lives of the Fathers, Martyrs, and other Principal Saints*, vol. I (Great Falls, Montana: Republished by St. Bonaventure, 1997), 325-326.

77. Macedonia represented the region later known as the former Yugoslav Republic. It represented the lands in southeastern Europe that were north of Greece.

78. Alban Butler, *The Lives of the Fathers, Martyrs, and other Principal Saints*, vol. I (Great Falls, Montana: Republished by St. Bonaventure, 1997), 259 –260.

79. Herbert Thurston and Nora Lesson, *The Lives of the Saints, originally compiled by Rev. Alban Butler*, vol. II. February (New York, New York: P.J. Kennedy & Sons, 1932), 359 –363.

80. Although both were located in Palestine, there were separate bishops for the inland city of Jerusalem and the costal region of Gaza.

81. Paul Burns, *Butler's Lives of the Saints*, February (Collegeville, Minnesota: Liturgical press, 1998), 252-253.

82. S. Baring Gould, *The Lives of the Saints*. Second Volume (Edinburgh, Scotland: John Grant Publishers, 1929), 66.

83. Cappadocia was an ancient country in eastern Asia Minor extending from the Black Sea on the east to the Taurus Mountains of Turkey.

84. S. Baring- Gould, *The Lives of the Saints*. First Volume (Edinburgh, Scotland: John Grant Publishers, 1929), 151 – 157.

85. Herbert Thurston and Nora Lesson, *The Lives of the Saints, originally compiled by Rev. Alban Butler*, vol. I. January (New York, New York: P.J. Kennedy & Sons, 1932), 139 – 143.

86. Anastasius was a Byzantine (the eastern region of the Roman empire) emperor living in Constantinople. Constantinople represents present day Istanbul, the capitol of Turkey.

87. Alban Butler, *The Lives of the Fathers, Martyrs, and other Principal Saints*, vol. I (Great Falls, Montana: Republished by St. Bonaventure, 1997), 39 – 42.

88. Caesarea was an ancient seaport city in Palestine located south of Joppa (present day Tel Aviv).

89. Herbert Thurston, *Butler's Lives of the Saints*, volume III (New York, New York: P.J. Kennedy & Sons, 1956), 494.

90. Kathleen Jones, *Butler's Lives of the Saints. New Full Edition, December Volume* (Collegeville, Minnesota: The Liturgical Press, 2000), 49.

91. S. Baring-Gould, *The Lives of the Saints*. Volume Four (Edinburgh, Scotland: John Grant Publishers, 1929), 56.

92. Kathleen Jones, *Butler's Lives of the Saints. New Full Edition, December Volume* (Collegeville, Minnesota: The Liturgical Press, 2000), 50.

93. An ancient city on the northern coast of Africa near Tunis, Tunisia.

94. The Romans referred to invading Germans from the north as Barbarians.

95. The Arians, a group of Christians who denied the full divinity of Christ, were very powerful particularly during the fourth century.

96. Alban Butler, *The Lives of the Fathers, Martyrs, and other principal Saints*, Vol. I (Great Falls, Montana: reprinted by St. Bonaventure Publications, 1997), 4-9.

97. Ibid, 8.

98. Paul Burns, *Butler's Lives of the Saints*, January (Collegeville, Minnesota: Liturgical Press, 1995), 6-7.

99. Asia Minor represents the region presently know as Turkey.

100. Jericho is a city in Palestine on the West Bank of the Jordan River.

101. Herbert Thurston and Nora Lesson, *The Lives of the Saints, originally compiled by Rev. Alban Butler*, vol. III. March (New York, New York: P.J. Kennedy & Sons, 1932), 60-61.

102. Teresa Rodriguez, Butler's Lives of the Saints, March (Collegeville, Minnesota: Liturgical Press, 1999), 44-45.

103. The lands east of the Jordan River contained deserts, deep canyons, and scant vegetation.

104. S. Baring-Gould, *The Lives of the Saints*, April (Edinburgh, Scotland: John Grant Publishers, 1929), 15-21.

105. Herbert Thurston, *Butler's Lives of the Saints*, volume II (New York, New York: P.J. Kennedy & Sons, 1956), 14-15.

106. Jacobus de Voragine, *The Golden Legend, Readings on the Saints* (Princeton, New Jersey: Princeton University Press, 1993), 227-228.

107. Peter Doyle, Butler's Lives of the Saints (Collegeville, Minnesota: Liturgical Press, 1996), 102-103.

108. S. Baring-Gould, *The Lives of the Saints*, March (Edinburgh, Scotland: John Grant Publishers, 1929), 275 – 278.

109. Herbert Thurston and Nora Lesson, *The Lives of the Saints, originally compiled by Rev. Alban Butler*, vol. III. March (New York, New York: P.J. Kennedy & Sons, 1932), 275– 278.

110. Ibid, 277-278.

111. Armenia is a small mountainous nation in western Asia within the cluster of nations between the Black Sea and the Caspian Sea.

112. Herbert Thurston, *Butler's Lives of the Saints*, volume II (New York, New York: P.J. Kennedy & Sons, 1956), 161-163.

113. S. Baring-Gould, *The Lives of the Saints*, April (Edinburgh, Scotland: John Grant Publishers, 1929), 259.

114. Tiberius was a region conquered by the Roman Emperor Tiberius that became part of the Roman Empire.

115. Emperor Constantine was a Byzantine Emperor, the Byzantine region having been the eastern part of the Roman Empire.

116. Herbert Thurston, *Butler's Lives of the Saints*, Volume II (New York, New York: P.J. Kennedy & Sons, 1956), 146 –147.

117. Peter Doyle, Paul Burns, Butler's Lives of the Saints, April (Collegeville, Minnesota: Liturgical Press, 1999), 159 –160.

Chapter 4: Western Monastic & Hermitic Saints

1. Herbert Thurston and Donald Attwater *The Lives of the Saints, originally compiled by Rev Alban Butler*, vol. XI. November (New York, New York: P.J. Kennedy & Sons, 1933), 69.

2. Gaul was an ancient designation for that part of Western Europe substantially identical with France.

3. Arles was a city in southern Gaul (France).

4. Alban Butler, *Lives of The Fathers, Martyrs and other Principal Saints*. Volume III (Great Falls, Montana: St. Bonaventure Publications, republished 1997), 91-93.

5. Troyes was a city in Northeastern France on the Seine River.

6. Attila the Hun was a fierce warrior leader of a group of nomadic Asian people who populated the region from the Caspian Sea all the way eastward to the Danube River.

7. Alban Butler, *Lives of the Fathers, Martyrs, and other Principal Saints*, Volume III (Great Falls, Montana: St. Bonaventure Publications, republished 1997), 93.

8. Peter Doyle, *Butler's Lives of the Saints*, July (Collegeville, Minnesota: Liturgical Press, 2000), 238-239.

9. Herbert Thurston, *The Lives of the Saints, originally compiled by Rev. Alban Butler*, Vol. II February (New York, New York: P.J. Kennedy & Sons, 1930), 438.

10. Paul Burns, Butler's Lives of the saints, February (Collegeville, Minnesota: Liturgical Press, 1998), 264.

11. Herbert Thurston, *The Lives of the Saints, originally compiled by Rev. Alban Butler*, Vol. II February (New York, New York: P.J. Kennedy & Sons, 1930), 438.

12. Herbert Thurston and Nora Lesson, *The Lives of the Saints, originally compiled by Rev. Alban Butler*, Vol. III. March (New York, New York: P.J. Kennedy & Sons, 1932), 435.

13. Teresa Rodrigues, *Butler's Lives of the Saints* (Collegeville, Minnesota: Liturgical Press, 1999), 269-270.

14. Herbert Thurston and Nora Lesson, *The Lives of the Saints, originally compiled by Rev. Alban Butler*, Vol. III. March (New York, New York: P.J. Kennedy & Sons, 1932), 435.

15. Kathleen Jones, *Butler's Lives of the Saints*, June (Collegeville, Minnesota: Liturgical press, 1997), 28.

16. Herbert Thurston and Nora Lesson, *The Lives of the Saints, originally compiled by Rev. Alban Butler*, Vol. VI June (New York, New York: P.J. Kennedy & Sons, 1937), 34-35.

17. Herbert Thurston, *Butler's Lives of the Saints*, volume II (New York, New York: P.J. Kennedy & Sons, 1956), 463.

18. Meung-sur-Loire was a region in Central France south of Paris.

19. Herbert Thurston, *Butler's Lives of the Saints*, Volume I (New York, New York: P.J. Kennedy & Sons, 1956), 234-235.

20. Paul Burns, *Butler's Lives of the Saints*, January (Collegeville, Minnesota: Liturgical Press, 1995), 107.

21. Loire River is the longest river in France running from northwest to southeast.

22. Herbert Thurston, *Butler's Lives of the Saints*, volume II (New York, New York: P.J. Kennedy & Sons, 1956), 463.

23. Kathleen Jones, *Butler's Lives of the Saints*, June (Collegeville, Minnesota: Liturgical Press, 1997), 28.

24. Tours is a city in west Central France.

25. Herbert Thurston and Donald Attwater, *The Lives of the Saints, originally compiled by Rev. Alban Butler*, vol. X October (New York, New York: P.J. Kennedy & Sons, 1936), 324.

26. Villefranche in a region in Southeastern France on the Mediterranean Sea, quite close to Monaco and the western border of Italy.

27. Herbert Thurston, *Butler's Lives of the Saints*, volume II (New York, New York: P.J. Kennedy & Sons, 1956), 260.

28. The term Prince of Wales refers to the leader of both Great Britain and northern Ireland.

29. Alban Butler, *The Lives of the Fathers, Martyrs, and other Principal Saints*, vol. I (Great Falls, Montana: Republished by St. Bonaventure, 1997), 275-276.

30. Teresa Rodrigues, Butler's Lives of the Saints, March (Collegeville, Minnesota: Liturgical Press, 1999), 23–24.

31. The Picts were ancient inhabitants of central and northern Scotland and Northern Ireland.

32. Scotland had its own king until the crowns of Scotland and England merged into one monarchy.

33. S. Baring Gould, *The Lives of the Saints*, January (Edinburgh, Scotland: John Grant Publishers, 1929), 187-193.

34. Glasgow is a city in Western Scotland.

35. Baring Gould, *The Lives of the Saints*, January (Edinburgh, Scotland: John Grant Publishers, 1929), 190.

36. Herbert Thurston and Donald Attwater, *The Lives of the Saints, originally compiled by Rev. Alban Butler*, Vol. I, January (New York, New York: P.J. Kennedy & Sons, 1932), 162-164.

37. David Hugh Farmer, *Butler's Lives of the Saints*, January (Collegeville, Minnesota: Liturgical Press, 1995), 92-93.

38. S. Baring-Gould, *The Lives of the Saints*, February (Edinburgh, Scotland: John Grant Publishers, 1929), 324-325.

39. Paul Burns, *Butler's Lives of the Saints* (Collegeville, Minnesota: Liturgical Press, 1998), 171.

40. Limerick is a city in Southwestern Ireland.

41. Herbert Thurston, *Butler's Lives of the Saints*, volume II (New York, New York: P.J. Kennedy & Sons, 1956), 264-265.

42. John Cummings, *Butler's Lives of the Saints*, August (Collegeville, Minnesota: Liturgical Press, 1998), 33-34.

43. S. Baring-Gould, *The Lives of the Saints*, September (Edinburgh, Scotland: John Grant Publishers, 1929), 192 – 194.

44. S. Baring-Gould, *The Lives of the Saints*, September (Edinburgh, Scotland: John Grant Publishers, 1929), 192 – 194.

45. S. Baring-Gould, *The Lives of the Saints*, April (Edinburgh, Scotland: John Grant Publishers, 1929), 163-173.

46. Herbert Thurston, *Butler's Lives of the Saints*, volume II (New York, New York: P.J. Kennedy & Sons, 1956), 72-73.

47. Herbert Thurston and Nora Leeson. *The Lives of the Saints, originally compiled by Rev. Alban Butler*, vol. IV. April (New York, New York: P.J. Kennedy & Sons, 1933), 136-138.

48. Mount Olympus is a mountain in Northern Greece with an elevation of 9,570 feet.

49. Sarah Fawcett Thomas, *Butler's Lives of the Saints*, November (Collegeville, Minnesota: Liturgical Press, 2000), 34-35.

50. S. Baring-Gould, *The Lives of the Saints*, November (Edinburgh, Scotland: John Grant Publishers, 1929), 109-111.

51. Sarah Fawcett Thomas, *Butler's Lives of the Saints*, November (Collegeville, Minnesota: Liturgical Press, 2000), 87- 90.

52. Herbert Thurston and Donald Attwater, *The Lives of the Saints, originally compiled by Rev. Alban Butler*, vol. IX. September (New York, New York: P.J. Kennedy & Sons, 1934), 348-351.

53. Sarah Fawcett Thomas, *Butler's Lives of the Saints*, September (Collegeville, Minnesota: Liturgical Press, 2000), 263-265.

54. Galatia is an ancient site in the plateau region of Central Turkey.

55. S. Baring-Gould. *The Lives of the Saints*, April (Edinburgh, Scotland: John Grant Publishers, 1929), 378- 381.

56. Herbert Thurston, *Butler's Lives of the Saints*, volume IV (New York, New York: P.J. Kennedy & Sons, 1956), 122-123.

57. Herbert Thurston and Donald Attwater, *The Lives of the Saints, originally compiled by Rev. Alban Butler*, vol. X. October (New York,

New York: P.J. Kennedy & Sons, 1936), 215-217.

58. Aegina is an island off the coast of Central Greece near Athens.

59. Herbert Thurston and Nora Lesson, *The Lives of the Saints, originally compiled by Rev. Alban Butler*, vol. II. February (New York, New York: P.J. Kennedy & Sons, 1932), 107 – 108.

60. Paul Burns, *Butler's Lives of the Saints*, February (Collegeville, Minnesota: Liturgical Press, 1998), 69-70.

61. Asia Minor refers to what is presently considered Turkey.

62. Mount Latros possibly refers to the mountain range in Eastern Turkey, close to the borders of Armenia and Iran.

63. Herbert Thurston, *Butler's Lives of the Saints*, volume IV (New York, New York: P.J. Kennedy & Sons, 1956), 565 – 566.

64. Ibid, 566.

65. Constantine Porphyrogenitus was a Byzantine emperor, 913 - 959 CE, also known as Constantine VII. He encouraged his people to convert to Christianity.

66. Kathleen Jones. *Butler's Lives of the Saints*, December (Collegeville, Minnesota: Liturgical Press, 2000), 133 – 134.

67. Kiev is a city in Central Ukraine, east of Hungary and west of Russia.

68. Peter Doyle, *Butler's Lives of the Saints. New Full Edition*, May (Collegeville, Minnesota: The Liturgical Press, 2000), 73.

69. Byzantine monasticism refers to the Christian monastic movement evolving in the western part of the Roman empire.

70. Peter Doyle, *Butler's Lives of the Saints. New Full Edition*, May (Collegeville, Minnesota: The Liturgical Press, 2000), 73.

71. Herbert Thurston, *Butler's Lives of the Saints*, volume III (New York, New York: P.J. Kennedy & Sons, 1956), 65.

72. Herbert Thurston, *Butler's Lives of the Saints*, volume III (New York, New York: P.J. Kennedy & Sons, 1956), 66.

73. Peter Doyle, *Butler's Lives of the Saints. New Full Edition*, May (Collegeville, Minnesota: The Liturgical Press, 2000), 73.

74. Calabria is a region in the southern 'toe' of Italy.

75. Peloponnesus is a region in Southern Greece.

76. Herbert Thurston, *Butler's Lives of the Saints*, volume III (New York, New York: P.J. Kennedy & Sons, 1956), 448.

77. Warwickshire is a region in Central England.

78. Herbert Thurston and Nora Lesson, *The Lives of the Saints, originally compiled by Rev. Alban Butler*, vol. I January (New York, New York: P.J. Kennedy & Sons, 1932), 236-237.

79. Bristol is a city in Central England.

80. The Vikings were a people of Danish, Swedish, and Norwegian origin who raided and settled in large parts of Europe beginning 800 CE.

81. Paul Burns, *Butler's Lives of the Saints*, January (Collegeville, Minnesota: Liturgical Press, 1995), 131 – 133.

82. Armenia during those times was a region, which now belongs to Turkey, Iran, and Armenia.

83. Herbert Thurston, *Butler's Lives of the Saints*, volume II (New York, New York: P.J. Kennedy & Sons, 1956), 608.

84. Winchester is a city located in Southern England.

85. Herbert Thurston, *Butler's Lives of the Saints*, volume II (New York, New York: P.J. Kennedy & Sons, 1956), 608.

86. Herbert Thurston, *Butler's Lives of the Saints*, volume II (New York, New York: P.J. Kennedy & Sons, 1956), 678.

87. Luxembourg is a small country in Western Europe bounded by Belgium and Germany.

88. Kathleen Jones, *Butler's Lives of the Saints. New Full Edition, June Volume* (Collegeville, Minnesota: The Liturgical Press, 1997), 245 – 246.

89. Alban Butler, *The Lives of the Fathers, Martyrs, and other Principal Saints*, vol. I (Great Falls, Montana: Republished by St. Bonaventure, 1997), 199 –201.

90. S. Baring-Gould, *The Lives of the Saints*, February (Edinburgh, Scotland: John Grant Publishers, 1929), 224 – 226.

91. Herbert Thurston, *Butler's Lives of the Saints, originally compiled by Rev. Alban Butler*, vol. II February (New York, New York: P.J. Kennedy & Sons, 1933), 125 – 128.

92. Northumberland is a county in the extreme Northeastern part of England.

93. Herbert Thurston and Nora Lesson, *Butler's Lives of the Saints, originally compiled by Rev. Alban Butler*, vol. I (New York, New York: P.J. Kennedy & Sons, 1932), 205.

94. Paul Burns, *Butler's Lives of the Saints*, January (Collegeville, Minnesota, Liturgical Press 1995), 116-117.

95. Paul Burns, *Butler's Lives of the Saints*, February (Collegeville, Minnesota, Liturgical Press 1998), 101 – 102.

96. Tuscany is a region in Central Italy.

97. Siena is a city in Tuscany (central Italy).

98. Herbert Thurston, *Butler's Lives of the Saints*, volume I (New York, New York: P.J. Kennedy & Sons, 1956), 295.

99. S. Baring-Gould, *The Lives of the Saints*, February (Edinburgh, Scotland: John Grant Publishers, 1929), 255 –256.

100. Durham is a county in Northeastern England.

101. Herbert Thurston, *Butler's Lives of the Saints*, volume II (New York, New York: P.J. Kennedy & Sons, 1956), 258-259.

102. Saint John the Baptist walked along the western border of the Jordan River, south of Nazareth.

103. S. Baring-Gould, *The Lives of the Saints*. First Volume (Edinburgh, Scotland: John Grant Publishers, 1929), 322-331.

104. David Hugh Farmer, *Butler's Lives of the Saints*, May (Collegeville, Minnesota: Liturgical Press, 1996), 112-113.

105. Teresa Rodrigues, Butler's Lives of the Saints, October (Collegeville, Minnesota: Liturgical Press, 1999), 77 – 78.

106. Herbert Thurston, *Butler's Lives of the Saints*, volume I (New York, New York: P.J. Kennedy & Sons, 1956), 527 –528.

107. Alban Butler, *The Lives of the Fathers, Martyres and other Principal Saints*, Vol. I (Great Falls, Montana: Reprinted by St. Bonaventure, 1997), 36 – 39.

108. Bourges is a city in Central France.

109. Paul Burns, *Butler's Lives of the Saints*, January (Collegeville, Minnesota: Liturgical Press, 1995), 70 – 71.

110. Herbert Thurston, *Butler's Lives of the Saints*, volume I (New York, New York: P.J. Kennedy & Sons, 1956), 65 – 66.

111. Herbert Thurston, *Butler's Lives of the Saints*, volume II (New York, New York: P.J. Kennedy & Sons, 1956), 368.

112. David Hugh Farmer, *Butler's Lives of the Saints*, May (Collegeville, Minnesota: Liturgical Press, 1996), 117-118.

113. Kent is a region in Southeastern England.

114. Mount Carmel is a short mountain range in Northwest Palestine (Israel).

115. Alban Butler, *The Lives of the Fathers, Martyrs, and other Principal Saints*, vol. II (Great Falls, Montana: Republished by St. Bonaventure, 1997), 167 – 169.

116. David Hugh Farmer, *Butler's Lives of the Saints*, May (Collegeville, Minnesota: Liturgical Press, 1996), 89 –90.

117. Herbert Thurston, *Butler's Lives of the Saints*, volume II (New York, New York: P.J. Kennedy & Sons, 1956), 211 – 213.

118. Tuscany is a region in Northern Italy.

119. Herbert Thurston and Nora Lesson, *The Lives of the Saints, originally compiled by Rev. Alban Butler*, vol. IV April (New York, New York: P.J. Kennedy & Sons, 1933), 235-236.

120. Alban Butler, *The Lives of the Fathers, Martyrs and other Principal Saints*, Vol. III (Great Falls, Montana: Reprinted by St. Bonaventure, 1997), 323 – 330.

121. Umbria is a region in Central Italy.

122. Herbert Thurston, *Butler's Lives of the Saints*, volume II (New York, New York: P.J. Kennedy & Sons, 1956), 444.

123. Lucca is a city in Tuscany in northern Italy.

124. The Florentines were citizens of Florence, a city Southeast of Lucca.

125. Kathleen Jones, *Butler's Lives of the Saints*, June (Collegeville, Minnesota: Liturgical Press, 1997), 20-1.

Chapter 5: Mystic Saints

1. Paul M. Allen and Joan deRis Allen, *Francis of Assisi's Canticles of the Creation* (New York, New York, Continuum, 1996), 142.

2. Alban Butler, *Lives of The Fathers, Martyrs and other Principal Saints* (Volume III. Great Falls, Montana: St. Bonaventure Publications, republished 1997), 459.

3. Assisi is a city in central Italy.

4. Peter Doyle, *Butler's Lives of the Saints*. New Full Edition, October Volume (Collegeville, Minnesota: The Liturgical Press, 1999), 17.

5. Herbert Thurston, and Donald Attwater, *The Lives of the Saints, originally compiled by Rev. Alban Butler*, vol. XI. October (New York, New York: P.J. Kennedy & Sons, 1936), 39-41.

6. S. Baring-Gould, *The Lives of the Saints*, October (Edinburgh, Scotland: John Grant Publishers, 1929), 87.

7. Herbert Thurston, *Butler's Lives of the Saints*, Volume IX (New York, New York: P.J. Kennedy & Sons, 1956), 25-26.

8. S. Baring-Gould, *The Lives of the Saints*, October (Edinburgh, Scotland: John Grant Publishers, 1929), 94.

9. Christian Feldman, *God's Gentle Rebels, Great Saints of Christianity* (New York, New York: Crossroads Publishing, 1995), 19.10. St. Bonaventure, "Major and Minor Life of

St. Francis" *English Omnibus of Sources for the Life of Saint Francis* (Chicago, Illinois: Franciscan Herald Press, 1973), 663.

11. Thomas of Celano, "The First Life of St. Francis, Part I" *English Omnibus of Sources for the Life of Saint Francis* (Chicago, Illinois: Franciscan Herald Press, 1973), 272.

12. Marion A. Habig, ed. *St. Francis of Assisi: Writings and Early Biographies* (Chicago, Illinois: Franciscan Herald Press, 1973), 31-34.

13. Habig, 43.

14. Christian Feldman, *God's Gentle Rebels, Great Saints of Christianity* (New York, New York: Crossroads Publishing, 1995), 24.

15. Father Cuthbert, *The Romanticism of St. Francis* (London, England: Longmans, Green and Co., 1924), 50.

16. Thomas of Celano, "The First Life of St. Francis, Part I", *English Omnibus of Sources for the Life of St. Francis* (Chicago, Illinois: Franciscan Herald Press, 1973), 279-294.

17. Father Cuthbert, *The Romanticism of Francis* (New York, New York: Longmans, Green and Co., 1924), 44-45.

18. Cuthbert, 49.

19. Cuthbert, 49-52.

20. Stigmata are wounds on a person's body resembling the wounds suffered by Jesus Christ in the crucifixion.

21. Herbert Thurston, and Donald Attwater, *The Lives of the Saints, originally compiled by Rev. Alban Butler*, vol. X. October (New York, New York: P.J. Kennedy & Sons, 1936), 49-51.

22. Herbert Thurston and Donald Attwater. *The Lives of the Saints, originally compiled by Rev. Alban Butler*, Vol. VIII. August (New York, New York: P.J. Kennedy & Sons, 1933), 142-147.

23. John Cummings, *Butler's Lives of the Saints. New Full Edition, August Volume* (Collegeville, Minnesota: The Liturgical Press, 2000), 86.

24. Cummings, 88.

25. Troyes is a city in northeastern France.

26. S. Baring-Gould, *The Lives of the Saints. First Volume* (Edinburgh, Scotland: John Grant Publishers, 1929), 84-85.

27. David Hugh Farmer, *Butler's Lives of the Saints* (Collegeville, Minnesota: Liturgical Press, 1996), 98-99.

28. Herbert Thurston and Nora Leeson, *The Lives of the Saints, originally compiled by Rev. Alban Butler*, Vol. V. May (New York, New York: P.J. Kennedy & Sons, 1933), 230-233.

29. Alban Butler, *Lives of The Fathers, Martyrs and other Principal Saints*. Volume I (Great Falls, Montana: St. Bonaventure Publications, republished 1997), 379-380.

30. Sarah Fawcett Thomas, *Butler's Lives of the Saints*, September (Collegeville, Minnesota: Liturgical Press, 2000), 175-178.

Chapter 6: Founders of Monastic Orders

1. Ministry of Information and Broadcasting, Government of India, *The Collected Works of Mahatma Gandhi*, Volume 48, 2nd Revised Edition (Ahmedabad, India: Navajivan Trust, 2000), 318.

2. M.K. Gandhi *The Words of Gandhi*, Second Edition selected by Richard Attenborough, (New York, New York: Newmarket Press, 2000), 5.

1. Herbert Thurston, *Butler's Lives of the Saints*, volume I (New York, New York: P.J. Kennedy & Sons, 1956), 650-651.

2. Adalbert de Vogue, *The Life of Saint Benedict, commentary on Gregory the Great's writings* (Petersham, Massachusetts: St. Bede's Publications, 1982), 11.

3. S. Baring-Gould. *The Lives of the Saints*, July (Edinburgh, Scotland: John Grant Publishers, 1929), 394- 395.

4. Ibid, 396-397.

5. Leonard J. Doyle, *Saint Benedict's Rule for Monasteries* (Collegeville, Minnesota: Liturgical Press, 1948), 175.

6. Peter Doyle, *Butler's Lives of the Saints. New Full Edition, July Volume* (Collegeville, Minnesota: The Liturgical Press, 2000), 78.

7. Leonard J. Doyle, *Saint Benedict's Rule for Monasteries* (Collegeville, Minnesota: Liturgical Press, 1948), 162.

8. Alban Butler, The Lives of The Fathers, Martyrs and Saints, Vol. IV (Great Falls, Montana: Saint Bonaventure, 1997 – republished from London: Virtue & Co.), 2-8.

9. S. Baring-Gould, *The Lives of the Saints*. Third Volume (Edinburgh, Scotland: John Grant Publishers, 1929), 141-151.

10. The desert of Chartreuse is in a valley near Grenoble, in the south of France.

11. Herbert Thurston, *Butler's Lives of the Saints*, volume IV (New York, New York: P.J. Kennedy & Sons, 1956), 40-44.

12. Ibid, 42.

13. Alban Butler, The Lives of The Fathers, Martyrs and Saints, Vol. IV (Great Falls, Montana: Saint Bonaventure, 1997 –republished from London: Virtue & Co.), 4.

14. Peter Doyle, *Butler's Lives of the Saints. New Full Edition, October Volume* (Collegeville, Minnesota: The Liturgical Press, 1996), 36-38.

15. Alban Butler, The Lives of The Fathers, Martyrs and Saints, Vol. IV (Great Falls, Montana: Saint Bonaventure, 1997 – republished from London: Virtue & Co.), 6-7.

16. Herbert Thurston, *Butler's Lives of the Saints*, volume I (New York, New York: P.J. Kennedy & Sons, 1956), 321.

17. Paul Burns, *Butler's Lives of the Saints*, January (Collegeville, Minnesota: Liturgical Press, 1995), 191-194.

18. Champagne is a region of northeast France.

19. Molesme is a site in France near Citeaux where the Cistercian monks built their abbey.

20. Alban Butler, The Lives of The Fathers, Martyrs and Saints, Vol. II (Great Falls, Montana: Saint Bonaventure, 1997 –republished from London: Virtue & Co.), 60-61.

21. Dorsetshire is a county in southern England on the English Channel.

22. Herbert Thurston and Nora Leeson, *The Lives of the Saints, originally compiled by Rev. Alban Butler*, vol. IV, April (New York, New York: P.J. Kennedy & Sons, 1933), 200-203.

23. Ibid, 202.

24. Paul Burns, *Butler's Lives of the Saints*, January (Collegeville, Minnesota: Liturgical Press, 1995), 191-194.

25. Lincolnshire is a county in northeastern England.

26. Herbert Thurston and Nora Leeson, *The Lives of the Saints, originally compiled by Rev. Alban Butler*, vol. II, February (New York, New York: P.J. Kennedy & Sons, 1932),73-74.

27. Thomas Becket was a chancellor of England who became the bishop of Canterbury, and eventually a Roman Catholic saint.

28. Paul Burns, *Butler's Lives of the Saints* (Collegeville, Minnesota: Liturgical Press, 1998), 41-43.

29. Old Castile was a historic region in the heart of Spain where the Christians fought the Moors.

30. Herbert Thurston and Donald Attwater. *The Lives of the Saints, originally compiled by Rev. Alban Butler*, Vol. VIII. August (New York, New York: P.J. Kennedy & Sons, 1933), 43-45.

31. Ibid, 48.

32. John Cummings, *Butler's Lives of the Saints. New Full Edition, August Volume* (Collegeville, Minnesota: The Liturgical Press, 2000), 55-64.

33. Provence is a region in southeastern France.

34. Herbert Thurston, *Butler's Lives of the Saints*, volume IV (New York, New York: P.J. Kennedy & Sons, 1956), 115-117.

35. During the Crusades many Christians became prisoners of war.

36. Herbert Thurston, *Butler's Lives of the Saints*, volume IV (New York, New York: P.J. Kennedy & Sons, 1956), 117.

37. Kathleen Jones, *Butler's Lives of the Saints*, December (Collegeville, Maryland: Liturgical Press, 2000), 148-149.

38. Parma is a region in Northern Italy.

39. Sarah Fawcett Thomas, *Butler's Lives of the*

Saints, September (Collegeville, Minnesota: Liturgical Press, 2000), 121-122.

40. Mount Carmel is the mountain range in northwestern Palestine (Israel).

41. Herbert Thurston and Donald Attwater. *The Lives of the Saints, originally compiled by Rev. Alban Butler*, vol. IX, September (New York, New York: P.J. Kennedy & Sons, 1934), 318-319.

42. Lombardy is a region in Northern Italy.

43. David Hugh Farmer, *Butler's Lives of the Saints*, January (Collegeville, Minnesota: Liturgical Press, 1995), 197-200.

44. Herbert Thurston and Nora Lesson, *The Lives of the Saints, originally compiled by Rev. Alban Butler*, Vol. X. May (New York, New York: P.J. Kennedy & Sons, 1936), 370-372.

45. Ibid, 370-372.

Chapter 7: Patron Saints

1. Herbert Thurston and Nora Lesson, *The Lives of the Saints, originally compiled by Rev. Alban Butler*, vol. XI. November (New York, New York: P.J. Kennedy & Sons, 1932), 316-319.

2. S. Baring Gould, *The Lives of the Saints*, January (Edinburgh, Scotland: John Grant Publishers, 1929), 384-388.

3. Paul Burns, *Butler's Lives of the Saints*, January (Collegeville, Minnesota: Liturgical Press, 1995), 189-190.

4. Herbert Thurston, *The Lives of the Saints, originally compiled by Rev. Alban Butler*, vol. I (New York, New York: P.J. Kennedy & Sons, 1926), 52-56.

5. Alban Butler, *Lives of The Fathers, Martyrs and other Principal Saints*. Volume I (Great Falls, Montana: St. Bonaventure Publications, republished 1997) 14-17.

6. Childeric was king of the Franks, a group of German tribes who invaded France.

7. Paul Burns, *Butler's Lives of the Saints, New Full Edition, January Volume* (Collegeville, Minnesota: The Liturgical Press, 1998), 28-30.

8. Thurston, *Butler's Lives of the Saints*, volume I (New York, New York: P.J. Kennedy & Sons, 1956), 1.

9. Herbert Thurston and Donald Attwater, *The Lives of the Saints*, Vol. VIII, August (New York, New York: P.J. Kennedy & Sons, 1933), 2.

10. Teresa Rodriguez, *Butler's Lives of the Saints*, March (Collegeville, Minnesota: Liturgical Press, 1999), 1-2.

11. Herbert Thurston, *Butler's Lives of the Saints*, volume IV (New York, New York: P.J. Kennedy & Sons, 1956), 273.

12. Herbert Thurston and Donald Attwater, *The Lives of the Saints, originally compiled by Rev. Alban Butler*, vol. XI. November (New York, New York: P.J. Kennedy & Sons, 1933), 68-69.

13. Sarah Fawcett Thomas, *Butler's Lives of the Saints*, November, (Collegeville, Minnesota: Liturgical Press 2000), 45-46.

14. Kathleen Jones, *Butler's Lives of the Saints*, June (Collegeville, Minnesota: Liturgical Press, 1997), 28-29.

15. Herbert Thurston and Nora Lesson, *The Lives of the Saints*, Vol. VI, June (New York, New York: P.J. Kennedy & Sons, 1933), 463-464.

16. Herbert Thurston, *Butler's Lives of the Saints*, Vol. II (New York, New York: P.J. Kennedy & Sons, 1956), 35-37.

17. Helen Waddell, *Beasts and Saints* (Grand Rapids, Michigan: William B. Eerdmann's Publishing, 1996) 119-122.

18. Kathleen Jones, *Butler's Lives of the Saints*, June (Collegeville, Minnesota: Liturgical Press, 1997), 29.

19. Amiens is a city in Northern France.

20. Hamburg is a city in north central Germany.

21. Herbert Thurston, *Butler's Lives of the Saints*, volume I (New York, New York: P.J. Kennedy & Sons, 1956), 243-244.

22. Paul Burns, *Butler's Lives of the Saints*, February (Collegeville, Minnesota: Liturgical Press, 1998), 35-37.

23. Peter Doyle, *Butler's Lives of the Saints*, July

(Collegeville, Minnesota: Liturgical Press, 1996), 29 – 30.

24. Alban Butler, *Lives of The Fathers, Martyrs and other Principal Saints*. Volume III (Great Falls, Montana: St. Bonaventure Publications, republished 1997), 6 – 9.

25. Augsburg is a city in south central Germany in the Bavarian Mountains.

26. Alban Butler, *Lives of the Fathers, Martyrs, and other Principal Saints*, Volume III (Great Falls, Montana: St. Bonaventure Publications, republished 1997), 8.

27. Chartres is a region in north central France.

28. Herbert Thurston, *Butler's Lives of the Saints*, volume II (New York, New York: P.J. Kennedy & Sons, 1956), 284 –285.

29. Herbert Thurston and Donald Attwater, *The Lives of the Saints, originally compiled by Rev. Alban Butler*, vol. XI. November (New York, New York: P.J. Kennedy & Sons, 1933), 175-179.

30. Glendalough is a mountainous region of Ireland.

31. Herbert Thurston and Donald Attwater, *The Lives of the Saints, originally compiled by Rev. Alban Butler*, vol. XI. November (New York, New York: P.J. Kennedy & Sons, 1933), 176.

32. Sarah Fawcett Thomas, *Butler's Lives of the Saints* (Collegeville, Minnesota: Liturgical Press, 2000), 112-114.

33. Alban Butler, *Lives of The Fathers, Martyrs and other Principal Saints*. Volume IV. (Great Falls, Montana: St. Bonaventure Publications, republished 1997) 206-209.

34. S. Baring Gould, *The Lives of the Saints*, October (Edinburgh, Scotland: John Grant Publishers, 1929), 456-464.

35. Ibid, 460.

36. Peter Doyle, *Butler's Lives of the Saints*, October (Collegeville, Minnesota: Liturgical Press, 1996), 105.

37. Flanders is a region in northern Europe, now embracing part of Belgium, Netherlands, and Northern France.

38. Kathleen Jones, *Butler's Lives of the Saints*, June (Collegeville, Minnesota: Liturgical Press, 1997), 178-179.

39. Alban Butler, *Lives of The Fathers, Martyrs and other Principal Saints*. Volume II (Great Falls, Montana: St. Bonaventure Publications, republished 1997) p. 386-387.

40. Thuringia was a historic region in central Germany.

41. Sarah Fawcett Thomas, *Butler's Lives of the Saints*, November (Collegeville, Minnesota: Liturgical Press, 2000), 145.

42. Alban Butler, *The Lives of the Fathers, Martyrs and other Principal Saints*, Vol. I V (Great Falls, Montana: Reprinted by St. Bonaventure, 1997), 231-238.

43. Brittany is a historic region of France bordering the English Channel.

44. David Hugh Farmer, *Butler's Lives of the Saints*, May (Collegeville, Minnesota: Liturgical Press, 1996), 104-105.

45. Herbert Thurston and Nora Lesson, *The Lives of the Saints*, Vol. V, May (New York, New York: P.J. Kennedy & Sons, 1936), 242-243.

46. Herbert Thurston, *Butler's Lives of the Saints*, volume II (New York, New York: P.J. Kennedy & Sons, 1956), 351-352.

47. John Cumming, *Butler's Lives of the Saints*, August (Collegeville, Minnesota: Liturgical Press, 1998), 220-221.

48. Herbert Thurston, *Butler's Lives of the Saints*, volume III (New York, New York: P.J. Kennedy & Sons, 1956), 385 – 387.

49. Herbert Thurston and Donald Attwater, *The Lives of the Saints, originally compiled by Rev. Alban Butler*, vol. VII. August (New York, New York: P.J. Kennedy & Sons, 1933), 86-87.

50. John Cummings, *Butler's Lives of the Saints*, August (Collegeville, Minnesota: Liturgical Press, 1998), 50.

51. Fermo is a region in central Italy.

52. S. Baring Gould, *The Lives of the Saints*, September (Edinburgh, Scotland: John Grant Publishers, 1929), 160-165.

53. Sarah Fawcett Thomas, Butler's Lives of the Saints, September (Collegeville, Minnesota: Liturgical Press), 92-94.

54. Herbert Thurston, *Butler's Lives of the Saints*, volume III (New York, New York: P.J. Kennedy & Sons, 1956), 524-526.

55. Ibid, 526.

56. Ibid, 526.

57. Herbert Thurston and Nora Lesson, *The Lives of the Saints, originally compiled by Rev. Alban Butler*, vol. V May (New York, New York: P.J. Kennedy & Sons, 1933), 273 – 275.

58. David Hugh Farmer, Butler's Lives of the Saints, May (Collegeville, Minnesota: Liturgical Press), 118 – 119.

59. Herbert Thurston, *Butler's Lives of the Saints*, volume V (New York, New York: P.J. Kennedy & Sons, 1956), 273 – 275.

60. Calabria is a region in southern Italy.

61. Thurston, Herbert. *Butler's Lives of the Saints*, volume II (New York, New York: P.J. Kennedy & Sons, 1956), 10-12.

62. S. Baring-Gould. *The Lives of the Saints*, April (Edinburgh, Scotland: John Grant Publishers, 1929), 25.

63. Ibid, 11.

64. Constantinople refers to present day Istanbul. This region was conquered by the Turks and became Turkey, an Islamic nation.

65. Herbert Thurston, and Nora Leeson, *The Lives of the Saints, originally compiled by Rev. Alban Butler*, vol. IV. April (New York, New York: P.J. Kennedy & Sons, 1933), 13-17.

66. Ibid, 16.

67. Peter Doyle, *Butler's Lives of the Saints*. New Full Edition, April Volume (Collegeville, Minnesota: The Liturgical Press, 1999), 11-12.

68. Capistrano is a region on the west coast of Italy.

69. Perugia is a city in central Italy.

70. Emperor Frederick III was the emperor of Rome who sought the pope's assistance.

71. Belgrade was the capital city of Serbia and Montenegro (formerly the Republic of Yugoslavia).

72. Hunyady was a well-respected Hungarian military leader.

73. Herbert Thurston, *Butler's Lives of the Saints*, volume I (New York, New York: P.J. Kennedy & Sons, 1956), 421-423.

74. Kathleen Jones, *Butler's Lives of the Saints*, December (Collegeville, Minnesota: Liturgical Press, 2000), 174.

75. Herbert Thurston and Donald Attwater, *The Lives of the Saints, originally compiled by Rev. Alban Butler*, vol. X. October (New York, New York: P.J. Kennedy & Sons, 1936), 272-273.

76. Herbert Thurston, *Butler's Lives of the Saints*, volume IV (New York, New York: P.J. Kennedy & Sons, 1956), 144-148.

77. Peter Doyle, Butler's Lives of the Saints, October (Collegeville, Minnesota: Liturgical press, 1996), 135 – 137.

78. Ibid, 137.

79. S. Baring-Gould, *The Lives of the Saints*. Fourth Volume (Edinburgh, Scotland: John Grant Publishers, 1929), 603-610.

80. Goa is a city on the southwest coast of India. The inhabitants are of mixed Portuguese and Indian descent and Portugal ruled the region from 1505 until it gained sovereignty in 1974.

81. Herbert Thurston, and Donald Attwater. *The Lives of the Saints, originally compiled by Rev. Alba Butler*, vol. XI. November (New York, New York: P.J. Kennedy & Sons, 1938), 36-37.

82. Kathleen Jones, *Butler's Lives of the Saints. New Full Edition, December Volume* (Collegeville, Minnesota: The Liturgical Press, 2000), 27.

83. Ceylon is presently known as Sri Lanka. It is an island republic in the Indian Ocean off the southeast tip of India.

84. Malay Peninsula is a strip of land in the Indian Ocean extending down from Thailand to Indonesia.

85. Herbert Thurston and Nora Lesson, *The Lives of the Saints, originally compiled by Rev. Alban Butler*, vol. V May (New York, New York: P.J. Kennedy & Sons, 1936), 310-315.

86. Herbert Thurston, *Butler's Lives of the Saints*, volume II (New York, New York: P.J. Kennedy & Sons, 1956), 395-399.

87. David Hugh Farmer, *Butler's Lives of the Saints*, May (Collegeville, Minnesota: Liturgical Press,1996), 144-147.

88. The Medicis were an Italian banking and political family that ruled Florence for almost three hundred years.

89. Herbert Thurston, *Butler's Lives of the Saints*, volume II (New York, New York: P.J. Kennedy & Sons, 1956), 416- 418.

90. Alban Butler *Lives of The Fathers, Martyrs and other Principal Saints*. Volume II (Great Falls, Montana: St. Bonaventure Publications, republished 1997) p. 206-211.

91. Alban Butler, *Lives of The Fathers, Martyrs and other Principal Saints*. Volume II (Great Falls, Montana: St. Bonaventure Publications, republished 1997), 342-354.

92. Maurizio is a region in Southern Italy.

93. S. Baring-Gould, *The Lives of the Saints*. Volume IV (Edinburgh, Scotland: John Grant Publishers, 1929), 549-561.

94. Ibid, 558-560.

95. Lyon is a city in east central France.

96. Joseph Vianney, *Saint John Vianney: Cure D'Ars, Patron of Parish Priests* (London, England: Burn Oats & Washbourne, 1929), 2-3.

97. Herbert Thurston, *Butler's Lives of the Saints*, volume III (New York, New York: P.J. Kennedy & Sons, 1956), 103-106.

98. Christian Feldman, *God's Gentle Rebels, Great Saints of Christianity* (New York, New York: Crossroads Publishing, 1995), 138.

99. John Cummings, *Butler's Lives of the Saints. New Full Edition, August Volume* (Collegeville, Minnesota: The Liturgical Press, 2000), 28-32.

100. Ibid, 138-139.

101. Herbert Thurston, and Donald Attwater, *The Lives of the Saints, originally compiled by Rev. Alban Butler*, Vol. VIII. August (New York, New York: P.J. Kennedy & Sons, 1933), 103-112.

102. R.H.J. Steuart, *Diversity in Holiness* (New York, New York: Sheed & Ward, 1936), 188.

Chapter 8: Doctors of the Church

1. David Hugh Farmer, Butler's Lives of the Saints, January (Collegeville, Maryland: Liturgical Press, 1995), 13-16.

2. Alban Butler, *Lives of The Fathers, Martyrs and other Principal Saints*. Volumes I (Great Falls, Montana: St. Bonaventure Publications, republished 1997), 327-339.

3. Ibid, 332-333.

4. Cappadocia was an ancient country in Asia Minor that is now considered Turkey.

5. David Hugh Farmer, Butler's Lives of the Saints, January (Collegeville, Maryland: Liturgical Press, 1995), 16.

6. Antioch is in southern Turkey and this region is quite arid.

7. Sarah Fawcett Thomas, *Butler's Lives of the Saints*, September Volume (Collegeville, Minnesota: Liturgical Press, 2000), 274-275.

8. Ibid, 277-278.

9. Herbert Thurston, *Butler's Lives of the Saints*, volume III (New York, New York: P.J. Kennedy & Sons, 1956), 684-692.

10. Herbert Thurston, *Butler's Lives of the Saints*, volume II (New York, New York: P.J. Kennedy & Sons, 1956), 226-231.

11. Ibid, 230.

12. S. Baring-Gould, *The Lives of the Saints*. Second Volume (Edinburgh, Scotland: John Grant Publishers, 1929), 386 – 392.

13. Herbert Thurston, *Butler's Lives of the Saints*, volume I (New York, New York: P.J. Kennedy & Sons, 1956), 312 – 316.

14. Paul Burns, *Butler's Lives of the Saints*, February (Collegeville, Minnesota: Liturgical press, 1998), 208-211.

15. Clairvaux is a town in France.

16. Herbert Thurston, *Butler's Lives of the Saints*, volume III (New York, New York: P.J. Kennedy & Sons, 1956), 193-194.

17. The Crusades were a series of wars, from 1096 through the 13th century, during which the Western Christians sought to recapture the Holy Lands from the Moslems.

18. John Cumming, *Butler's Lives of the Saints. New Full Edition, August Volume* (Collegeville, Minnesota: The Liturgical Press, 2000), 196-197.

19. Cummings, 197.

20. Siena is a city in central Italy.

21. Suzanne Noffke, *Catherine of Siena, Vision Through a Distant Eye* (Collegeville, Minnesota: The Liturgical Press, 1996), 1-2.

22. Peter Doyle, *Butler's Lives of the Saints. New Full Edition, April Volume* (Collegeville, Minnesota: The Liturgical Press, 1999), 206-215.

23. Ibid, 207.

24. Herbert Thurston, *Butler's Lives of the Saints*, volume II (New York, New York: P.J. Kennedy & Sons, 1956), 338.

25. Aubrey Richardson, *The Mystic Bride*, (London, England: T. Werner Laurie, 1907), 145.

27. Christian Feldman, *God's Gentle Rebels, Great Saints of Christianity* (New York, New York: Crossroads Publishing, 1995), 36.

26. Peter Doyle, *Butler's Lives of the Saints. New Full Edition, April Volume* (Collegeville, Minnesota: The Liturgical Press, 1999), 214-215.

28. Sarah Fawcett Thomas, *Butler's Lives of the Saints*, September (Collegeville, Minnesota: Liturgical Press, 2000), 155 – 158.

29. Herbert Thurston, *Butler's Lives of the Saints*, volume II May (New York, New York: P.J. Kennedy & Sons, 1956), 292 – 296.

30. Ibid, 295.

Chapter 9: The Vegetarian Pope

1. Herbert Thurston, *Butler's Lives of the Saints*, volume II (New York, New York: P.J. Kennedy & Sons, 1956), 234-237.

2. Herbert Thurston and Nora Leeson, *The Lives of the Saints, originally compiled by Rev. Alban Butler*, Vol. V. May (New York, New York: P.J. Kennedy & Sons, 1936), 234-237.

3. David Hugh Farmer, *Butler's Lives of the Saints. New Full Edition, May Volume* (Collegeville, Minnesota: The Liturgical Press, 1998), 102-104.

Chapter 10: Vegetarian Ascetic Saints

1. Thomas Merton, *The Wisdom of the Desert* (New York, New York: New Directions Books, 1960), 16-17.

2. Victor-Antoine d'Avila-Latourrette, *From a Monastery Kitchen* (Liguori, Missouri: Triumph Books, 1989), 9.

3. Alban Butler, *Lives of The Fathers, Martyrs and other Principal Saints*. Volume IV (Great Falls, Montana: St. Bonaventure Publications, republished 1997), 350-352.

4. Peter Doyle, *Butler's Lives of the Saints*, July (Collegeville, Minnesota: Liturgical Press, 2000), 200-201.

5. Tributaries of the Euphrates River originate in Turkey and flow through Syria and Iraq.

6. Paul Burns, *Butler's Lives of the Saints*, January (Collegeville, Minnesota, Liturgical Press, 1995), 182.

7. Herbert Thurston, *Butler's Lives of the Saints*, volume I (New York, New York: P.J. Kennedy & Sons, 1956), 182.

8. The Bedouins are nomadic tribes of Arabs who inhabit areas of the Middle East and Northern Africa.

9. Herbert Thurston, *Butler's Lives of the Saints*, volume IV (New York, New York: P.J. Kennedy & Sons, 1956), 168-169.

10. S. Baring-Gould, *The Lives of the Saints*. Fourth Volume (Edinburgh, Scotland: John Grant Publishers, 1929), 68.

11. Alban Butler, *Lives of The Fathers, Martyrs and other Principal Saints*. Volume I (Great Falls, Montana: St. Bonaventure Publications, republished 1997), 151-154.

12. Tours is a city in west central France.

13. Herbert Thurston and Nora Lesson, *The Lives of the Saints, originally compiled by Rev. Alban Butler*, vol. I January (New York, New York: P.J. Kennedy & Sons, 1936), 375-377.

14. Lyon is a region in east central France.

15. Herbert Thurston, *Butler's Lives of the Saints*, volume II (New York, New York: P.J. Kennedy & Sons, 1956), 349-350.

16. Chartres is a city in north central France.

17. Peter Doyle, *Butler's Lives of the Saints*, July (Collegeville, Minnesota: Liturgical Press, 2000), 13.

18. Herbert Thurston, *Butler's Lives of the Saints*, volume III (New York, New York: P.J. Kennedy & Sons, 1956), 8.

19. Herbert Thurston, *Butler's Lives of the Saints*, volume I (New York, New York: P.J. Kennedy & Sons, 1956), 574 – 575.

20. Theresa Rodriguez, Butler's Lives of the Saints, March (Collegeville, Minnesota: Liturgical Press, 1999), 122-123.

21. Herbert Thurston, *Butler's Lives of the Saints*, volume IV (New York, New York: P.J. Kennedy & Sons, 1956), 218.

22. Peter Doyle, *Butler's Lives of the Saints. New Full Edition, October Volume* (Collegeville, Minnesota: The Liturgical Press, 1996), 200-201.

23. Brabant represents two of the provinces in Belgium.

24. Flanders represents the entirety of the region presently considered Belgium.

25. Herbert Thurston, *Butler's Lives of the Saints*, volume IV (New York, New York: P.J. Kennedy & Sons, 1956), 5.

26. Herbert Thurston, and Donald Attwater. The Lives of the Saints, originally compiled by Rev. Alban *Butler*, vol. X. October (New York, New York: P.J. Kennedy & Sons, 1936), 9.

27. S. Baring Gould, *The Lives of the Saints*. Fourth Volume (Edinburgh, Scotland: John Grant Publishers, 1929),

28. Herbert Thurston, The Lives of the Saints, originally compiled by Rev. Alban *Butler*, Vol. II February (New York, New York: P.J.

29. Paul Burns, *Butler's Lives of the Saints*, February (Collegeville, Minnesota: Liturgical press, 1998), 64-66.

30. Marseilles is a city in southern France.

31. Herbert Thurston and Nora Lesson, *The Lives of the Saints, originally compiled by Rev. Alban Butler*, vol. IX. September (New York, New York: P.J. Kennedy & Sons, 1934),1-4.

32. S. Baring-Gould, *The Lives of the Saints*. First Volume (Edinburgh, Scotland: John Grant Publishers, 1929), 8-10.

33. Ibid, 5-7.

34. Herbert Thurston, *Butler's Lives of the Saints*, volume I (New York, New York: P.J. Kennedy & Sons, 1956), 358.

35. Toulouse is a city in southern France.

36. Paul Burns, *Butler's Lives of the Saints*, February (Collegeville, Minnesota: Liturgical Press, 1998), 173.

37. The cupbearer was entrusted to taste the king's wine prior to his drinking it to ensure it had not been poisoned.

38. Charlemagne was king of the Franks (France).

39. Herbert Thurston. *The Lives of the Saints, originally compiled by Rev. Alban Butler*, vol. II. February (New York, New York: P.J. Kennedy & Sons, 1930), 172-173.

40. S. Baring-Gould, *The Lives of the Saints*. First Volume (Edinburgh, Scotland: John Grant Publishers, 1929), 284.

41. Paul Burns, Butler's Lives of the Saints, February (Collegeville, Minnesota: Liturgical Press, 1998), 124-126.

42. Herbert Thurston. *The Lives of the Saints, originally compiled by Rev. Alban Butler*, vol. II. February (New York, New York: P.J. Kennedy & Sons, 1930), 174.

43. Tournai is a city in southwest Belgium.

44. Herbert Thurston and Nora Leeson. *The Lives of the Saints, originally compiled by Rev. Alban Butler*, vol. IV. April (New York, New York: P.J. Kennedy & Sons, 1933), 85.

45. Herbert Thurston, *Butler's Lives of the Saints*, volume II (New York, New York: P.J. Kennedy & Sons, 1956), 86.

46. Umbria is a city in central Italy.

47. Herbert Thurston, *Butler's Lives of the Saints*, volume IV (New York, New York: P.J. Kennedy & Sons, 1956), 110-111.

48. Peter Doyle, *Butler's Lives of the Saints*, April (Collegeville, Minnesota: Liturgical Press, 1999), 17 – 18.

49. Herbert Thurston, *Butler's Lives of the Saints*, volume II (New York, New York: P.J. Kennedy & Sons, 1956), 22 – 24.

50. Paul Burns, *Butler's Lives of the Saints*, February (Collegeville, Minnesota: Liturgical Press, 1998), 224-226.

51. Herbert Thurston and Nora Lesson. *The Lives of the Saints, originally compiled by Rev. Alban Butler*, vol. II. February (New York, New York: P.J. Kennedy & Sons, 1932), 307-11.

52. S. Baring Gould, *The Lives of the Saints*. First Volume (Edinburgh, Scotland: John Grant Publishers, 1929), 256-257.

53. Paul Burns, Butler's Lives of the Saints, February (Collegeville, Minnesota: Liturgical Press, 1998), 103-104.

54. Herbert Thurston, *Butler's Lives of the Saints*, volume I (New York, New York: P.J. Kennedy & Sons, 1956), 529-533.

55. S. Baring-Gould, *The Lives of the Saints*. Fourth Volume (Edinburgh, Scotland: John Grant Publishers, 1929), 587-588.

56. Sarah Fawcett Thomas, *Butler's Lives of the Saints*, November (Collegeville, Minnesota: Liturgical Press, 2000), 222-223.

57. Lithuania is a republic in northeastern Europe.

58. Herbert Thurston, *Butler's Lives of the Saints*, volume II (New York, New York: P.J. Kennedy & Sons, 1956), 233.

59. David Hugh Farmer, *Butler's Lives of the Saints*, May (Collegeville, Minnesota: Liturgical Press, 1996), 26.

60. Quito is the capital city in northern Ecuador high in the Andes Mountains.

61. Herbert Thurston, *Butler's Lives of the Saints*, volume II (New York, New York: P.J. Kennedy & Sons, 1956), 401.

62. S. Baring-Gould, *The Lives of the Saints*, February (Edinburgh, Scotland: John Grant Publishers, 1929), 112-115.

63. Goa was a Portuguese-Indian region on the southwest coast of India, and Madurai is further inland and south, also in southern India.

64. Paul Burns, *Butler's Lives of the Saints*, February (Collegeville, Minnesota: Liturgical Press, 1998), 50-51.

Chapter 11: Saints known for Animal Mercy

1. Andrew Linzey, *Christianity and Animal Rights* (London, England: Holy Trinity Church, 1987), 45.

2. S. Baring-Gould, *The Lives of the Saints*, September (Edinburgh, Scotland: John Grant Publishers, 1929), 25.

3. Byzantium was later called Constantinople.

4. The Bosphorus Strait is a narrow waterway connecting the Black Sea and the Sea of Marmara. It delineated Asian Turkey from European Turkey.

5. S. Baring-Gould, *The Lives of the Saints*, September (Edinburgh, Scotland: John Grant Publishers, 1929), 25.

6. Auxerre is a city in France, southeast of Paris.

7. Herbert Thurston and Nora Lesson *The Lives of the Saints, originally compiled by Rev. Alban Butler*, vol. IV. April (New York, New York: P.J. Kennedy & Sons, 1933), 238.

8. David Hugh Farmer, *Butler's Lives of the Saints. New Full Edition*, May (Collegeville, Minnesota: The Liturgical Press, 1998), 87-88.

9. Helen Waddell, *Beasts and Saints* (Grand Rapids, Michigan: William B. Eerdmans Publishing, 1996), 91-95.

10. Teresa Rodriguez, Butler's *Lives of the Saints*, March Volume (Collegeville, Minnesota: Liturgical Press, 1999), 46-47.

11. Teresa Rodriguez, *Butler's Lives of the Saints*, March (Collegeville, Minnesota: Liturgical Press, 1999), 285.

12. Ibid, 287.

13. Ibid, 287.

14. S. Baring-Gould, *The Lives of the Saints*, April (Edinburgh, Scotland: John Grant Publishers, 1929), 266.

15. Peter Doyle, *Butler's Lives of the Saints*. New Full Edition, April Volume, (Collegeville, Minnesota: The Liturgical Press, 1999), 152.

16. S. Baring-Gould, *The Lives of the Saints*, April (Edinburgh, Scotland: John Grant Publishers, 1929), 269.

17. Sarah Fawcett Thomas, *Butler's Lives of the Saints*, November Volume (Collegeville, Minnesota: Liturgical Press, 2000), 22-23.

Chapter 12: Martyr Saints

1. Alban Butler, *Lives of The Fathers, Martyrs and other Principal Saints*. Volume III (Great Falls, Montana: St. Bonaventure Publications, republished 1997), 230-231.

2. Caesarea, the costal city on the western border of Palestine was under Roman rule.

3. Herbert Thurston, *Butler's Lives of the Saints*, volume III (New York, New York: P.J. Kennedy & Sons, 1956), 39 – 40.

4. Peter Doyle, *Butler's Lives of the Saints*, July (Collegeville, Minnesota: Liturgical Press, 2000), 55.

5. David Hugh Farmer, *Butler's Lives of the Saints: New Full Edition*, May (Collegeville, Minnesota: The Liturgical Press, 1995), 76-77.

6. Alban Butler, *Lives of The Fathers, Martyrs and other Principal Saints*. Volumes II (Great Falls, Montana: St. Bonaventure Publications, republished 1997), 153-155.

7. Alban Butler, *The Lives of the Fathers, Martyrs and other Principal Saints*, Vol. I (Great Falls, Montana: Reprinted by St. Bonaventure, 1997), 236-237.

Chapter 13: Legacies of the Vegetarian Saints

1. S. Baring-Gould, *The Lives of the Saints*. Fourth Volume (Edinburgh, Scotland: John Grant Publishers, 1929), 68.

2. Ibid, 138-139.

3. Paul Clark and Andrew Lindsey, eds. *Political Theory and Animal Rights* (London, England: Pluto Press, 1990), 148-152.

Glossary

Aegina: An island off the coast of central Greece near Athens.

Alexandria: A large seaport city in Northern Egypt founded in 322 BCE by Alexander the Great. It is on the Nile River Delta.

Amiens: A city in Northern France.

Anastasius was a Byzantine (the eastern region of the Roman empire) emperor living in Constantinople. Constantinople represents present-day Istanbul, the capital of Turkey.

Antioch: A city in southern Turkey near the Mediterranean Sea to its west and Syria to its east.

Arabian Desert: Lies in eastern Egypt between the Mediterranean Sea on the north, the Red Sea and the Gulf of Suez on the east, the Nubian Desert on the south, and the Nile River on the west.

Arians: An early sect of Christians who did not believe in the full divinity of Jesus Christ.

Arles: A city in Southern Gaul (France).

Armenia: During ancient times this referred to the region between the Black Sea and the Caspian Sea. It is now located partly within Turkey, Iran, and Armenia.

Asia Minor: Refers to what is presently considered Turkey.

Assisi: A city in Central Italy.

Athanasius: A Christian theologian born in Egypt who at the council of Nicea defined the Son of God and God to be of the same essence.

Attila the Hun: A fierce leader of a group of nomadic Asian people who populated the region from the Caspian Sea all the way eastward to the Danube River.

Augsburg: A city in south central Germany in the Bavarian Mountains.

Barbarians: The term the Romans used when referring to invading Germans from the north.

Becket, Thomas: Chancellor of England who became the bishop of Canterbury, and eventually a Roman Catholic saint.

Belgrade: The capital city of Serbia and Montenegro (formerly the Republic of Yugoslavia).

Bourges: A city in central France.

Bristol: A city in central England.

Brittany: A historic region of France bordering the English Channel.

Byzantine monasticism: The Christian monastic movement that evolved in the eastern part of the Roman Empire.

Calabria: A region in the southern 'toe' of Italy.

Capistrano: A region on the west coast of Italy.

Cappadocia: An ancient country in eastern Asia Minor extending from the Black Sea on the east to the Taurus Mountains of Turkey.

Caesarea: An ancient seaport city in Palestine located south of Joppa (present day Tel Aviv).

Ceylon: Region presently known as Sri Lanka. It is an island republic in the Indian Ocean off the southeast tip of India.

Chartreuse: A desert in a valley near Grenoble, in the south of France.

Childeric: King of the Franks, a group of German tribes who invaded France.

Clairvaux: A town in France.

Constantine Porphyrogenitus: A Byzantine emperor, 913–959 CE, also known as Constantine VII who encouraged his people to convert to Christianity.

Constantinople: Refers to present day Istanbul. This region was conquered by the Turks and became Turkey, an Islamic nation.

Crusades: A series of wars, from 1096 through the 13th century, during which the Western Christians sought to recapture the Holy Lands from the Moslems.

Cyprus: The third largest island in the Mediterranean. It is located west of Syria and south of Turkey.

Dorsetshire: A county in southern England on the English Channel.

Durham: A region in Northeastern England.

Ecumenical Councils: A series of meetings initially held 325 C.E. and convened by Constantine the Great, emperor of Rome. Their goal was to resolve debates related to the nature of Jesus Christ.

Edessa: An ancient city in Mesopotamia. Now the city of Sanliurfa in southeast Turkey stands on this site.

Fermo: A region in central Italy.

Flanders: A region in northern Europe, now embracing parts of Belgium, Netherlands, and Northern France.

Florentines: Term for the citizens of Florence, a city southeast of Lucca.

Frederick III: Emperor of Rome who sought the pope's assistance.

Galatia: Term for an ancient region in the plateau region of central Turkey.

Gaul: An ancient designation for that part of Western Europe substantially identical with France.

Gaza Region: Located on the coast of the Mediterranean Sea. It was southwest of Jerusalem and on a road linking Egypt with central Palestine.

Glasgow: A city in Western Scotland.

Glendalough: A mountainous region of Ireland.

Goa: A city on the southwest coast of India. Some of the inhabitants are of mixed Portuguese and Indian descent. Portugal ruled the region from 1505 until it gained sovereignty.

Hamburg: A city in north central Germany.

Hunyady: A well-respected Hungarian military leader.

Jericho: A city in Palestine on the West Bank of the Jordan River.

Kent: A region in Southeastern England.

Kiev: A city in central Ukraine, east of Hungary and west of Russia.

King of Scotland: Scotland had its own king until the crowns of Scotland and England merged into one monarchy.

Limerick: A city in Southwest Ireland.

Lincolnshire: A county in Northeast England.

Loire River: The longest river in France running from northwest to southeast.

Lombardy: A region in Northern Italy.

Lucca: A city in Tuscany in Northern Italy.

Luxembourg: A small country in Western Europe bounded by Belgium and Germany.

Lyon: A city in east central France.

Macedonia: The region later known as the former Yugoslav Republic. It represented the lands in Southeastern Europe that were north of Greece.

Magyars: An ethnic group of Hungary.

Malay Peninsula: A strip of land in the Indian Ocean extending down from Thailand to Indonesia.

Maurizio: A region in Southern Italy.

Medicis: An Italian banking and political family that ruled Florence for almost three hundred years.

Mesopotamia: A Greek word for lands "between two rivers." This was one of the earliest centers of urban civilizations and presently includes Iraq, Eastern Syria, and Southeast Turkey.

Meung-sur-Loire: A region in central France south of Paris.

Molesme: A site in France near Citeaux where the Cistercian monks built their abbey.

Mount Carmel: A short mountain range in Northwest Palestine (Israel).

Mount Latros: The mountain range in Eastern Turkey, close to the borders of Armenia and Iran.

Mount Olympus: A mountain in Northern Greece with an elevation of 9,570 feet.

Nicea: A region in what is now considered Turkey, at the city Iznik.

Nisibis: A region in what would presently be considered Syria.

Northumberland: A region within North Eastern England.

Old Castile: A historic region in the heart of Spain where the Christians fought the Moors.

Palestine: The delineation of the region has varied greatly over ancient times. It presently refers to Israel. The Roman emperor, Constantine the Great, legalized Christianity there in 313 CE.

Parma: A region in Northern Italy.

Peloponnesus: A region in Southern Greece.

Perugia: A city in central Italy.

Persia: The region presently known as Iran.

Picts: Name of the ancient inhabitants of Central and Northern Scotland and Northern Ireland.

Prince of Wales: Term used to refer to the prince of both Great Britain and Northern Ireland.

Provence: A region in Southeastern France.

Saint John the Baptist: Land upon which he walked were those of the Western border of the Jordan River, south of Nazareth.

Siena: A city in Tuscany in central Italy.

Stigmata: Wounds on a person's body resembling the wounds suffered by Jesus Christ in the crucifixion.

Theodosius: The last emperor to rule a united Roman empire. He was a strong champion of Orthodox Christianity.

Thuringia: A historic region in central Germany.

Tiberius: The region conquered by the Roman Emperor Tiberius that became part of the Roman Empire.

Tours: A city in west central France.

Tuscany: A region in central Italy.

Troyes: A city in Northeastern France on the Seine River.

Umbria: A region in central Italy.

Villefranche: A region in South-eastern France on the Mediterranean Sea, quite close to Monaco and the western border of Italy.

Vikings: People of Danish, Swedish, and Norwegian origin who raided and settled in large parts of Europe beginning 800 CE.

Warwickshire: A region in Central England.

Winchester: A city located in Southern England.

Bibliography

Adams, Carol. *Ecofeminism and the Sacred.*
New York, New York: Continuum, 1993.

Adams, Carol. *The Sexual Politics of Meat:*
A Feminist-Vegetarian Critical Theory.
New York, New York: Continuum, 1990.

Alchin, A.M. *The World is a Wedding: Explorations*
in Christian Spirituality. London, England: Darton,
Longman and Todd, 1978.

Allen, Paul M. and Joan de Ris Allen, *Francis of*
Assisi's Canticles of the Creation. New York,
New York, Continuum, 1996.

Arbesmann, Rudolph, Emily Joseph Daly, and
Edwin A. Quain, transl. *Fathers of the Church,*
Terullian Apologetical Works. Washington, D.C.:
Catholic University of America Press, 1950.

Attwater, Donald. *The Golden book of Eastern*
Saints. Milwaukee, Wisconsin: Bruce, 1938.

Ballentine, Rudolph. *Transition to Vegetarianism.*
Honesdale, Pennsylvania: Himalayan
International Institute of Yoga Science and
Philosophy, 1987.

Baring-Gould, S. *Lives of the Saints.* Edinburgh,
Scotland: John Grant, 1914.

Baring-Gould, S. *The Lives of the Saints.*
Four Volumes. Edinburgh, Scotland: John Grant
Publishers, 1929.

Barnes, Michael Horace. *An Ecology of the Spirit:*
Religious Reflection and Environmental Conscious-
ness. Langham, Maryland: University Press of
America : College Theology Society, 1994.

Bazell, Diane M. "Strife among the Table Fellows:
Conflicting Attitudes of Early and Midevil
Christians toward the Eating of Meat." *Journal of*
the American Academy of Religion. 65 (Spring
1997), p. 73-99.

Beckett, Wendy. *Sister Wendy's Book of Saints.*
London, England: Dorling Kindersley, 1998.

Bekoff, Marc. Ed. *Encyclopedia of Animal Rights*
and Animal Welfare. Westport, Connecticut:
Greenwood Press, 1998.

Berry, Ryan. *Famous Vegetarians.* New York,
New York: Pythagorean Publishers, 1996.

Berry, Ryan. *Food for the Gods.* New York,
New York: Pythagorean Publishers, 1998.

Berry, Thomas, CP. *Befriending the Earth:*
A Theology of Reconciliation between Humans and
the Earth. Mystic Connecticut: Twenty-third
Publications, 1991.

Binford, L.R. *In Pursuit of the Past: Decoding the*
Archaeological Record. London, England: Thames
& Hudson, 1967.

Boccaccini, Gabriele. *Beyond the Essene Hypothesis*. Grand Rapids, Michigan: William B. Eerdmans Publishing, 1998.

Bonaventure, St. "Major and Minor Life of St. Francis". *English Omnibus of Sources for the Life of St. Francis*. Chicago, Illinois: Franciscan Herald Press, 1973.

Bradley, Ian. *God is Green. Ecology for Christians*. New York, New York: Doubleday, 1990.

Broderick, James. *A procession of Saints*. New York, New York: Longmans, Green & Co., 1949.

Bulfinch Press, editors, and Alban Butler. *One Hundred Saints, Their Lives and Likenesses drawn from Butler's Lives of the Saints and other great works of Western Art*. New York, New York: Little, Brown and Company, 1993.

Burns, Paul. *Butler's Lives of the Saints. New Full Edition, January Volume*. Collegeville, Minnesota: The Liturgical Press, 1998.

Burns, Paul. *Butler's Lives of the Saints. New Full Edition, February Volume*. Collegeville, Minnesota: The Liturgical Press, 1998.

Butler, Alban. *Lives of The Fathers, Martyrs and other Principal Saints*. Volumes I–IV. Great Falls, Montana: St. Bonaventure Publications, republished 1997.

Carmody, Denise Lardner, and John Tully Carmody. *Christianity, an Introduction 3rd Edition*. Belmont, California: Wadsworth Publishing, 1995.

Celano, Thomas. "The First Life of St. Francis, Part I", *English Omnibus of Sources for the Life of St. Francis*. Chicago, Illinois: Franciscan Herald Press, 1973.

Clark, Paul and Andrew Lindsey, eds. *Political Theory and Animal Rights*. London, England: Pluto Press, 1990.

Cluny, Roland. *Holiness in Action*. New York, New York: Hawthorn Books, 1963.

Cohn-Sherbok, editor. *Using the Bible Today*. London, England: Bellow Publications, 1991.

Collins, Adrien. *Thoughts out of Season*. Edinburgh: T.N. Foulis, 1909.

Conlon, James. *Earth Story, Sacred Story*. Mystic, Connecticut: Twenty-third Publications, 1994.

Costello, Hilary, and Eoin de Bhaldraithe, translators. *The Life of Saint Benedict*. Petersham, Massachusetts: St. Bede's Publications, 1982.

Cottrell Free, Ann, ed. *Animals, Nature and Albert Schweitzer*. Washington, D.C.: Flying Fox Press, 1996.

Couillet, Jacques. *What is a Saint?* New York, New York: Hawthorn Books, 1958.

Creusen, Joseph. *Religious Men and Women in the Code, 4th rev*. Milwaukee, Wisconsin: Bruce Publishing, 1940.

Cumming, John. *Butler's Lives of the Saints. New Full Edition, August Volume*. Collegeville, Minnesota: The Liturgical Press, 2000.

Cunningham, Lawrence. *The Catholic heritage: martyrs, ascetics, pilgrims, warriors, mystics, theologians, artists, humanists, activists, outsiders, and saints*. New York, New York: Crossroads, 1983.

Currier, Charles Warren. *History of Religious Orders*. New York, New York: Murphy & McCarthy, 1894.

Cuthbert, Father. *The Romanticism of Francis*. New York, New York: Longmans, Green and Co., 1924.

D'Arcy, Mary Ryan. *The Saints of Ireland*. St. Paul, Minnesota: Irish American Cultural Institute, 1974.

Das, G.N. *The Maxims of Kabir*. New Delhi, India: Abhinav Publications, 1999.

d'Avila-Latourrette, Victor-Antoine. *From a Monastery Kitchen*. Liguori, Missouri: Triumph Books, 1989.

Dawber, TR, and WB Kannel, "An epidemiologic study of heart disease: the Framingham study", *Nutrition. Rev*; 16 (1). Jan 1958.

de Mello, Anthony. *Anthony de Mello, Writings*. Maryknoll, New York: Orbis Books, 1999.

de Mello, Anthony. *Sadhana, A Way to God*. New York, New York: Doubleday, 1978.

de Robeck, Nesta. *The Life of St. Francis of Assisi*. Assisi, Italy: Casa Editrice Francescana, 2000.

de Nicholas, Antonio T ed. *St. John of the Cross, Alchemist of the Soul*. York Beach, Maine: Samuel Weiser, 1996.

de Voragine, Jacobus. *The Golden Legend: Readings on the Saints*. Princeton, New Jersey: Princeton University Press, 1993.

Dikshitar, Ramachandra V.R. *Tirukkural of Tiruvalluvar*. Madras, India: Adyar Library and Research Centre, 1994, reprinted in 2000.

Dombrowski, Daniel A. *The Philosophy of Vegetarianism*, Amherst, Massachusetts: University of Massachusetts Press, 1984.

Doyle, Peter. *Butler's Lives of the Saints. New Full Edition, April Volume*. Collegeville, Minnesota: The Liturgical Press, 1999.

Doyle, Peter. *Butler's Lives of the Saints. New Full Edition, July Volume*. Collegeville, Minnesota: The Liturgical Press, 2000.

Doyle, Peter. *Butler's Lives of the Saints. New Full Edition, October Volume*. Collegeville, Minnesota: The Liturgical Press, 1996.

Ducket, Eleanor Shipley. *The Wandering Saints*. London, England: Collins, 1959.

Dundas, Paul. *The Jains*, Second Edition. New York, New York: Routledge. 1992

Edwards, Denis ed. *Earth Revealing, Earth Healing*. Collegeville Press, Liturgical Press, 2001.

Eisnitz, Gail A. *Slaughterhouse*. Amherst, New York: Prometheus Books, 1997.

Elliot, R, and A. Gare, eds. *Environmental Philosophy*. St. Lucia: University of Queensland Press, 1983. p. 201-230.

Ewing, Upton Clary *The Prophet of the Dead Sea Scrolls, 3rd ed.* Joshua tree, California: Tree of Life Publications, 1994.

Farmer, David Hugh ed. *Butler's Lives of the Saints: New Full Edition.* Collegeville, Minnesota: The Liturgical Press, 1995.

Feldman, Christian. *God's Gentle Rebels: Great Stories of Christian Saints.* New York, New York: Crossroads Publishing, 1995.

Fulop-Miller, Rene. *The Saints that Moved the World.* Salem, New Hampshire: Ayer Company, Publishers, Inc. 1991.

Gandhi, M.K. *The Moral Basis of Vegetarianism,* Ahmedabad, India: Navajivan India, 1959, reprinted in 1999.

Gandhi, M.K. *The Selected Works of Mahatma Gandhi,* Volume 5, The Voice of Truth. Amedabad, India: Navajivan Publishing, 1968.

Gandhi, M. K. *The Words of Gandhi,* selected by Richard Attenborough. New York, New York: New Market Press, 2000.

Gottlieb, Roger. *The Sacred Earth: Religion, Nature, Environment.* New York, New York: Routledge, 1996.

Habig, Marion A, editor. *St. Francis of Assisi: Writings and Early Biographies.* Chicago, Illinois: Franciscan Herald Press, 1973.

Haight, Roger. *Jesus as Symbol of God.* Maryknoll, New York: Orbis Books, 2000.

Hardinge, Mervyn G, and Hulda Crooks, "Non-Flesh Dietaries," *Journal of American Dietetic Association,* vol. 43, Dec 1963.

Hoyt, John A. *Animals in Peril.* Garden City Park, New York: Avery Publishing, 1994.

Hyland, JR. *The Slaughter of Terrified Beasts: A Biblical Basis for the Humane Treatment of Animals.* Sarasota, Florida: Victoria Ministries, 1988.

Johanson, Donald C. "Face to Face with Lucy's Family" *National Geographic Magazine,* Washington, D.C.: National Geographic Society. Vol. 189, no.3, March 1996.

Johnson-South, Ted. *Saints.* Binghamton, New York. Medieval & Renaissance Texts and Studies, 1996.

Jones, Kathleen. *Butler's Lives of the Saints. New Full Edition, June Volume.* Collegeville, Minnesota: The Liturgical Press, 1997.

Jones, Kathleen. *Butler's Lives of the Saints. New Full Edition, December Volume.* Collegeville, Minnesota: The Liturgical Press, 2000.

Jones, Kathleen. *Women Saints: Lives of Faith and Courage.* Maryknoll, New York: Orbis Books, 1999.

Jung, Shannon. *We are at Home. A Spirituality of the Environment.* Mahwah, New York: Paulist Press, 1993.

Kalechofsky, Roberta. *Vegetarian Judaism: A Guide for Everyone.* Marblehead, Massachusetts: Micah Publications, 1998.

Kieckhefer, Richard. *Sainthood: Its manifestations in world religions*. Berkley, California: University of California Press, 1988.

Kingsbury, Jack Dean. *Matthew as Story, 2nd ed.* Philadelphia, Pennsylvania: Fortress Press, 1988.

Lakhotia, R.N., *All You Wanted to Know about Vegetarianism*, New Delhi, India, Sterling Publishers, 2002.

La Chance, Albert J, and John E. Carroll, ed. *Embracing Earth, Catholic Approaches to Ecology*. Maryknoll, New York: Orbis Books, 1994.

Leckie, Robert. *These are my Heroes: a study of the saints*. New York, New York: Random House, 1964.

Linzey, Andrew. Animal Rights: *A Christian Assessment of Man's treatment of Animals*. London, England: SCM Press, 1976.

Linzey, Andrew. "The Theological basis of animal rights." *Christian Century*. 108 / 09, 1991.

Linzey, Andrew. *Christianity and the Rights of Animals*. London, England: Holy Trinity Church, 1987.

Linzey, Andrew, and Dan Cohn-Sherbok. *Celebrating Animals in Judaism and Christianity*. London, England: Cassell, 1997.

Linzey, Andrew, and Tom Regan. *Animals and Christianity: A Book of Readings*. New York, New York: Crossroads, 1988.

Liturgical Arts Society. *The Eastern branches of the Catholic church: six studies on the Oriental rites*. New York, New York: Longmans, Green and co. 1938.

Macken, Thomas F. *The Canonization of Saints*. New York, New York: Benziger Brothers, 1909.

Macklin, June. "Two faces of sainthood: the pious and the popular." *Journal of Latin American Lore*. 14 (Sum 1988).

Magel, Charles R. *Animal Rights, Key to Informational Sources*. Jefferson, North Carolina: McFarland Publishing, 1989.

Mandonnet, Pierre. *St. Dominic and His Work*. Saint Louis, Missouri: Herder Book Co. 1944.

Maynard, Theodore. *Saints of Our Times*. New York, New York: Appleton, Century, Crofts, 1951.

McClellan, Michael W, and Otto FA. *Monasticism in Egypt: Images and Words of the Desert Fathers*. Cairo, Egypt: American University of Cairo Press, 1999.

McFague, Sallie. *The Body of God, an Ecological Theology*. Minneapolis, Minnesota: Augsburg Fortress Press, 1993.

McFague, Sallie. *Life Abundant*, Minneapolis, Minnesota: Augsburg Fortress Press, 2001.

Meitzen, Manfred. "Ethics and Hunting: a Christian Perspective." *Dialog*. 16. Winter 1977.

Merton, Thomas. *The Wisdom of the Desert*. New York, New York: New Directions Books, 1960.

Ministerial Association of General Conference of Seventh-day Adventists. *Seventh-day Adventists Believe*. Hagerstown, Maryland: Review and Herald Publishing, 1988.

Ministry of Information and Broadcasting, Government of India, *The Collected Works of Mahatma Gandhi*, Volume 48, 2nd Revised Edition. Ahmedabad, India: Navajivan Trust, 2000.

Molinari, Paul, S.J. *Saints: Their Place in the Church*. New York, New York: Sheed and Ward, 1965.

Monro, Margaret T. *A Book of Unlikely Saints*. London, England: Longmans, Green & Co. 1943.

Muller, Max F., ed. *The Laws of Manu: The Sacred Books of the East*. Volume XXV. New Delhi, India. First published 1886, First LPP Reprint, 1996.

Narayan, Shrivan. *The Selected Works of Mahatma Gandhi, The Voice of Truth*, Volume Five. Ahmedabad, India, Navajivan Publishing House, 1968.

Noble, Thomas. *Soldiers of Christ*. University Park, Pennsylvania: Pennsylvania State University Press, 1995.

Noffke, Suzanne. *Catherine of Siena: Vision Through a Distant Eye*. Collegeville, Minnesota: The Liturgical Press, 1996.

Nomura, Yushi. *Desert Wisdom*. Maryknoll, New York: Orbis Books, 1982.

Nouwen, Henri J. *Desert Wisdom- Sayings from the Desert Wisdom: Sayings of the Desert Fathers*. Maryknoll, New York: Orbis Press, 2001.

Parachin, Victor. *365 Good Reasons to be a Vegetarian*, Garden City Park, New York: Avery Publishing, 1998.

Phillips, Anthony. "Respect for Life in the Old Testament." *King's Theological Review*. 6.Aut 1983.

Pinches, Charles Robert, and Jay B. McDaniel. *Good News for Animals? Christian approaches to animal well-being*. Maryknoll, New York: Orbis Press, 1993.

Pitts, Michael, and Mark Roberts, *Fairweather Eden*. New York, New York: Fromm International, 2000.

Pope John Paul II. *Solicitudo Rei Socialis*. Homebush, NSW: St. Paul Publications, sec 34, 1998.

Preece, Rod, and Lorna Chamberlain. *Animal Welfare and Human Values*. Ontario, Canada: Wilfrid Laurier University Press, 1993.

Regan, Tom. *Animal Sacrifices*. Philadelphia, Pennsylvania: Temple University Press, 1986.

Regan, Tom. *The Case for Animal Rights*. Berkley, California: University of California Press, 1983.

Rice, Stanley. *Hindu Customs and their Origins*. New Delhi: India: Low Price Publications. First published 1037, reproduced 1993.

Richardson, Mrs. Aubrey. *The Mystic Bride: A Study of the Life-story of Catherine of Siena*. London, England: T. Werner Laurie, 1907.

Robbins, John. *Diet for a New America*. Tiburon, California: H.J. Kramer, 1987.

Roche, Aloysius. *The Splendor of the Saints*. London, England: Burns, Oates & Washbourne, 1936.

Rodrigues, Teresa. *Butler's Lives of the Saints, March Volume*. Collegeville, Minnesota: Liturgical Press, 1999.

Rollin, Bernards E. *Animal Rights and Human Morality*. Buffalo, New York: Prometheus Books, 1981.

Rowlands, Mark. *Animal Rights, A Philosophical Defense*. New York, New York: Palgrave, 1998.

Sapontzis, S.F. *Morals, Reason, and Animal*. Philadelphia, Pennsylvania: Temple University Press, 1987.

Shaw, Teresa. *The Burden of the Flesh: Fasting and Sexuality in early Christianity*. Minneapolis, Minnesota: Fortress Press, 1988.

Shepard, Paul. *Traces of an Omnivore*. Washington, DC: Island Press, 1996.

Simons, F.J. *Eat Not This Flesh: Food Avoidances from Prehistory to the Present*, 2nd ed. Madison, University of Wisconsin Press, 1994.

Singer, Peter. *Animal Liberation*. New York, New York: Avon Books, 1990.

Singer, Peter. *Practical Ethics-Second Edition*. Cambridge, United Kingdom: Cambridge University Press, 1993.

Singer, Peter. *Writings on an Ethical Life*. New York, New York: Harper Collins, 2000.

Spencer, Colin. *The Heretic's Feast: a History of Vegetarianism*. Hanover, New Hampshire: University Press of New England, 1995.

Steuart, RHJ. *Diversity in Holiness*. New York, New York: Sheed & Ward, 1936.

Swami Sivananda. *All About Hinduism*. Tehri-Garhwal, U.P., Himalayas, India: Divine Life Society. 1997.

Terullian. *Disciplinary, moral, and ascetical works*, New York, New York: Fathers of the Church, 1959.

Thornton, John F. ed. *Desert Fathers*. New York, New York: Random House, 1998.

Thomas, Sarah Fawcett. *Butler's Lives of the Saints, September Volume*, Collegeville, Minnesota: Liturgical Press, 2000.

Thomas, Sarah Fawcett. *Butler's Lives of the Saints, November Volume*, Collegeville, Minnesota: Liturgical Press, 2000.

Thurston, Herbert. *The Lives of the Saints, originally compiled by Rev. Alban Butler*, vol. I. January. New York, New York: P.J. Kennedy & Sons, 1926.

Thurston, Herbert. *The Lives of the Saints, originally compiled by Rev. Alban Butler*, vol. II. February. New York, New York: P.J. Kennedy & Sons, 1930.

Thurston, Herbert, and Donald Attwater. *The Lives of the Saints, originally compiled by Rev. Alban Butler*, vol. VII. July. New York, New York: P.J. Kennedy & Sons, 1932.

Thurston, Herbert, and Donald Attwater. *The Lives of the Saints, originally compiled by Rev. Alban Butler*, vol. VIII. August. New York, New York: P.J. Kennedy & Sons, 1933.

Thurston, Herbert, and Donald Attwater. *The Lives of the Saints, originally compiled by Rev. Alban Butler*, vol. IX. September. New York, New York: P.J. Kennedy & Sons, 1934.

Thurston, Herbert, and Donald Attwater. *The Lives of the Saints, originally compiled by Rev. Alban Butler*, vol. X. October. New York, New York: P.J. Kennedy & Sons, 1936.

Thurston, Herbert, and Donald Attwater. *The Lives of the Saints, originally compiled by Rev. Alban Butler*, vol. XI. November. New York, New York: P.J. Kennedy & Sons, 1938.

Thurston, Herbert, and Donald Attwater. *The Lives of the Saints, originally compiled by Rev. Alban Butler*, vol. XII. December. New York, New York: P.J. Kennedy & Sons, 1938.

Thurston, Herbert, and Norah Leeson. *The Lives of the Saints, originally compiled by Rev. Alban Butler*, vol. III. March. New York, New York: P.J. Kennedy & Sons, 1932.

Thurston, Herbert, and Norah Leeson. *The Lives of the Saints, originally compiled by Rev. Alban Butler*, vol. IV. April. New York, New York: P.J. Kennedy & Sons, 1933.

Thurston, Herbert, and Norah Leeson. *The Lives of the Saints, originally compiled by Rev. Alban Butler*, vol. V. May. New York, New York: P.J. Kennedy & Sons, 1936.

Thurston, Herbert, and Norah Leeson. *The Lives of the Saints, originally compiled by Rev. Alban Butler*, vol. VI. June. New York, New York: P.J. Kennedy & Sons, 1937.

Thurston, Herbert S.J., and Donald Attwater, ed. *Butler's Lives of the Saints*. vol 1. New York, New York: P.J. Kennedy &Sons, 1956.

Ueshiba, Morihei. *The Art of Peace*. Boston, Massachusetts: Shambala Publications, 2002.

Vianney, Joseph. *Saint John Vianney*. London, England: Burns Oates & Washbourne, Ltd. 1929.

Vitz, Evelyn. *Images of Sainthood in Medieval Europe*. Ithaca, New York: Cornell University Press, 1991.

Waddell, Helen, translator. *Beasts and Saints*. Grand Rapids, Michigan: William B. Eerdmans Publishing Company, 1996.

Waddell, Helen. *The Desert Fathers*. New York, New York: Random House, 1998.

Walters, Kerry S, and Lisa Portmess, ed. *Ethical Vegetarians: from Pythagoras to Peter Singer*. Albany, New York: State University of New York Press, 1999.

Walters, Kerry S, and Lisa Portmess, ed. *Religious Vegetarianism : from Hesiod to the Dalai Lama*. Albany, New York: State University of New York Press, 2001.

Watkins, E.I. *Neglected Saints*. New York, New York: Sheed and Ward, 1955.

Whiston, William, transl. *Josephus, the Complete Works*. Nashville, Tennessee: Thomas Nelson Press, 1998.

Whorton James C. "Historical development of vegetarianism," *American Journal of Clinical Nutrition* 59 (supplement). 1994.

William Wilson, trans, *The Writings of Clement of Alexandria*, Hamilton & Co. 1867.

Williamson, Claude Charles H. *Great Catholics*. New York, New York: Macmillian Company, 1939.

Wood, Simon P. transl. *The Fathers of the Church, Clement of Alexandria*. New York, New York: Fathers of the Church, Inc. 1954.

Woodward, Kenneth L. *Making Saints: How the Catholic Church determines who becomes a saint, who doesn't and why*. New York, New York: Simon & Schuster, 1990.

Index of Saints

Saint Abraham Kidunaja, 56

Saint Agnes of Montepulciano, 97

Saint Alberic, 116

Saint Albert of Jerusalem, 124

Saint Albert of Trapani, 143

Saint Amandus, 185

Saint Amatus, 74

Saint Ammon, 37

Saint Angela Merici, 125

Saint Anselm ,205

Saint Anskar, 134

Saint Anthony of Egypt, 22

Saint Antony of the Caves of Kiev, 82

Saint Aphraates, 34

Saint Apollo, 39

Saint Asella, 178

Saint Aybert, 189

Saint Aventine of Troyes, 107

Saint Basil the Great, 159

Saint Bavo, 184

Saint Benedict, 112

Saint Benedict of Aniane, 188

Saint Bernard, 165

Saint Boniface of Tarsus, 209

Saint Brendon of Clonfert, 202

Saint Bruno, 114

Saint Callistratus, 200

Saint Catherine of Siena, 167

Saint Clare of Rimini, 193

Saint Clare of Assisi , 105

Saint Coleman of Kilmacduagh, 183

Saint David, 131

Saint Dominic, 121

Saint Dominic Loricatus, 190

Saint Dorotheus the Theban, 47

Saint Dositheus, 55

Saint Elizabeth of Hungary, 140

Saint Elphege, 87

Saint Ephraem, 163

Saint Euphrasia, 44

Saint Euthymius the Younger, 79

Saint Fantinus, 84

Saint Felix of Cantalice, 108

Saint Fintan of Clonenagh, 72

Saint Francis of Assisi, 102

Saint Francis of Paola, 146

Saint Frances of Rome, 194

Saint Francis Xavier, 151

Saint Fulgentius of Ruspe, 52

Saint Genevieve, 129

Saint Gerasimus, 53

Saint Gilbert of Sempringham, 120

Saint Giles, 186

Saint Godric, 92

Saint Gregory of Makar, 86

Saint Gundelinis, 64

Saint Guthlac, 75

Saint Hedwig, 138

Saint Henry of Coquet, 90

Saint Herculanus of Piegaro, 99

Saint Hilarion, 24

Saint Hospitius, 69

Saint Humility of Florence, 95

Saint Ivo Helory, 141

Saint James de la March, 195

Saint James of Nisibis, 35

Saint Jean-Marie Vianney, 156

Saint Jerome, 161

Saint Joannicus, 76
Saint John de Britto, 198
Saint John of Kanti, 149
Saint John of Capistrano, 148
Saint John of Egypt, 40
Saint John Francis Regis, 154
Saint John of Matha, 123
Saint John the Silent, 57
Saint Jonas the Gardener, 43
Saint Joseph of Cupertino, 109
Saint Julian Sabas, 38
Saint Kertigan of Glasgow, 71
Saint Kevin, 133
Saint Kieran, 203
Saint Laurence Justinian, 98
Saint Laurence O'Toole, 137
Saint Leonard Noblac, 132
Saint Leonard of Porto-Maurizio, 155
Saint Lioba, 78
Saint Liphardus, 65
Saint Luke the Younger, 80
Saint Lupicinus, 62
Saint Lupus of Troyes, 61
Saint Macarius of Alexandria (the Younger), 32
Saint Macarius the Elder (of Egypt), 26
Saint Malchus, 177
Saint Margaret of Cortona, 192
Saint Marcian, 30
Saint Mariana of Quito, 197
Saint Marianus, 201
Saint Mary of Egypt, 54
Saint Mary Magdalen of Pazzi, 153
Saint Mary Onigines, 139
Saint Martin de Porres, 206
Saint Maurus of Glanfeuil, 66
Saint Maxentius, 180
Saint Michael of Giedroyc, 196
Saint Molua, 73
Saint Monegundis, 181
Saint Nicholas of Tolentino, 144
Saint Olympias, 175
Saint Pachomius, 28

Saint Palaemon, 27
Saint Paul Aurelian, 182
Saint Paul the Hermit, 29
Saint Paul of Latros, 81
Saint Paula, 128
Saint Peter of Alcantara, 150
Saint Peter Celestine, 172
Saint Peter Damian, 164
Saint Philip Benizi, 142
Saint Philip Neri, 152
Saint Porphyry of Gaza, 45
Saint Procopius, 208
Saint Publius, 176
Saint Richard of Wyche, 191
Saint Rita of Cascia, 145
Saint Robert Bellarmine, 169
Saint Robert of Molesme, 117
Saint Romanus of Condat, 63
Saint Sabas, 50
Saint Senoch, 68
Saint Serenus the Gardener, 210
Saint Silvin, 187
Saint Simon Stock, 96
Saint Stephen of Grandmont, 89
Saint Stephen Harding, 118
Saint Stephen of Mar Saba, 204
Saint Stephen of Obazine, 93
Saint Sulpicius Severus, 179
Saint Thais, 42
Saint Theobald of Provins, 88
Saint Theodore the Studite, 77
Saint Theodore of Sykeon, 58
Saint Theodosius the Cenobiarch, 48
Saint Theodosius Pechersky, 83
Saint Ulrich, 135
Saint Urbicius, 67
Saint William of Bourges, 94
Saint William of Malavalle, 91
Saint Winwaloe, 70
Saint Wulfstan, 85
Saint Yvo of Chartres, 136

Notes

CPSIA information can be obtained
at www.ICGtesting.com
Printed in the USA
BVHW051600130820
586215BV00003B/55